People as Subject,
People as Object

New Directions in

Anthropological Writing

History, Poetics, Cultural Criticism

George E. Marcus, Rice University

James Clifford, University of California, Santa Cruz

Editors

People as Subject, People as Object
Selfhood and Peoplehood in Contemporary Israel

Virginia R. Domínguez

THE UNIVERSITY OF WISCONSIN PRESS

The University of Wisconsin Press
114 North Murray Street
Madison, Wisconsin 53715

3 Henrietta Street
London WC2E 8LU, England

Library of Congress Cataloging-in-Publication Data
Domínguez, Virginia R.
   People as subject, people as object : selfhood and peoplehood in
   contemporary Israel / Virginia R. Domínguez.
   254 pp.   cm.—(New directions in anthropological writing)
   Bibliography: pp. 207–230.
   Includes index.
   1. Israel—Ethnic relations.   2. Ethnicity—Israel.   3. National
characteristics, Israeli.   I. Title.   II. Series.
DS113.2.D65   1989
305.8′0095694—dc20   89-40254
ISBN 0-299-12320-0   CIP
ISBN 0-299-12324-3 (pbk.)

In memory of Eileen

Contents

Tables

Acknowledgments

THIS book is the product of long-term research I have conducted in and on Israel since the summer of 1980. I am most grateful to the various foundations that have funded various parts of that long-term study, and to the institutions that allowed me the time and the space to pursue it. The Trent Foundation funded two months of preliminary research in the summer of 1980. The U.S. Social Science Research Council, the Mellon Foundation, and the Duke University Research Council funded the period of intense fieldwork in Israel from May 1981 through August 1982. A Fulbright teaching award allowed me to spend another 14 months in Israel from June 1984 through August 1985, while teaching in the Department of Sociology and Social Anthropology at the Hebrew University. To all of them, my sincerest thanks.

In addition, I would like to thank the Jerusalem Institute for Israel Studies, the Department of Sociology and Social Anthropology at the Hebrew University, the Jerusalem Anthropology Circle, the Israel Anthropological Association, and the Jerusalem Semiotics Study Group for their hospitality and interest in my work. I'd like to thank Duke for giving me leaves when these wonderful opportunities arose. And I particularly want to thank my friends, acquaintances, colleagues, "informants," neighbors, students, research assistants, and even those I did not get along with so well in Israel for forcing me to examine questions and assumptions I had never before thought to question and always showing me greater and greater complexity. In the macropolitical climate in which Israel is an active participant, it is easy for an outsider to go for the "big picture" and miss the country's complexities.

Acknowledgments, as Eyal Ben-Ari (1987) has aptly pointed out, are a necessary and important part of any written text, though they always leave me frustrated. I always feel that if I thanked everyone I want to thank by name the acknowledgments would be as long as a chapter, and I would still commit unwanted sins of omission.

In the case of my work in and on Israel, the problem is compounded by the fact that my colleagues in Israel were among my targeted "informants," and many of my "informants" were also my colleagues. They have not just contributed "data" for this work; they have also read, heard, and/or critiqued drafts of papers or chapters in which I analyzed them along with aspects of Israeli society. The bibliography of this book would be quite thin were it not for their dedication to scholarship and their commitment to the continued, careful, and honest application of social science concepts and skills to the deciphering of life in Israel. I would especially like to thank those who took me into their homes and encouraged me to look into "their turf"—Victor Azarya, Eyal Ben-Ari, Joseph Ben-David (now deceased), Rina Ben-Shaoul, Meron and Shoshana Benvenisti, Yoram Bilu, Erik Cohen, Brenda Danet, Shmuel and Shulamit Eisenstadt, Shifra Epstein, Harvey and Judy Goldberg, Arye and Ayala Goren, Jeff Halper, Don and Leah Handelman, Chola Itzigsohn, Baruch Kimmerling, Gideon Kressel, Emanuel and Dalia Marx, Judah and Hagit Matras, Alan and Miki Rosenthal, Ilsa Schuster, Danielle Storper-Peretz, Rahel Wasserfall, Shalva and Michael Weil, Alex and Bracha Weingrod.

The problem is further compounded by the fact that I have made real friends in Israel, and that I struggled for years with the feeling of awkwardness on those occasions when I got my friends to play the role of "informants." They were usually very generous with their time and their patience, though I also know that it was often awkward for them, too— that it sometimes amused them to know that they were "playing informant," but that it also sometimes led them to wonder if our friendship rested on my needing them more than on my genuinely liking them.

Yet it is because of them—my *friends* in Israel—that I have felt compelled to write this book. They have invested time and energy in me; they have gotten to know me; they have loved me, put up with me, and taught me. They have also laughed and cried with me. To Irit, Emek, Rahel W., Danielle, Yael, Eyal, Edith, Heine, Ruth, Ilsa, Don, Chola, Daniella, Dani, Rachel S., Anat, Moshe, Dvorah, Rina, Rachel K., Renee and Uri—my love. To my students in Israel, most of whom I would gladly add to this list of Israelis I have loved and been loved by—Talma, Lida, Miriam T., Dani, Liat, Mikhail, Avner, Perla, Claudia, Miriam B., and Rachel—my hopes and my love. To Malka Porges, Shosh Halper, and Nevet Basker, my special thanks for the many hats they wore in their dealings with me —Malki as Hebrew tutor in Durham 1980–81, then as research assistant in Israel 1981–82, and throughout as patient and faithful friend; Shosh as research assistant, Israeli arts and literature teacher, political "soul mate," and friend since 1982; and Nevet as Hebrew tutor, car sitter, friend, and "family" since 1983.

At the research stage, Lea Petel, Bat-Zion Ziv, and Jeanine Harpaz provided much needed additional help typing, transcribing, and filing, as did Melissa Deane at the final stages of writing. In addition, I have been blessed with the generosity and criticism of Israelis and non-Israelis who had enough faith in me to agree to read various drafts of this book carefully, call my attention to areas to work on, sins of omission, and points to develop, or just urge me on. In this, I feel especially indebted to my colleagues Robert Paine, Lisa Gilad, Don Handelman, Benjamin Lee, Vincent Crapanzano, Judith Goldstein, George Marcus, William O'Barr, and Miriam Cooke, and to my former students Barbara Szudarek, Susan Hirsch, Yvonne Lassalle, and Steven Edbril. Special thanks go to Joanne Passaro—student, friend, and editorial assistant—who provided at least as much moral support at the end as she did bibliographic and editorial help. Finally, my thanks to the *Anthropology and Humanism Quarterly* for granting me permission to include sections of an article of mine, "Different and *Différance*," published summer 1989, in this book.

Above all, this book is the spiritual legacy of Eileen Basker, my beloved friend and colleague without whom I would never have had the courage or knowledge to see it through. Eileen was an anthropologist and a social critic, a housewife and a mother and a feminist, an atheist and a Jew, an Israeli and an American. In the nearly nine years since I first started going to Israel, no one played as central a role as Eileen in encouraging my efforts to understand Israel, being fascinated by what I as outsider would see in Israel, allowing me to tag along, and helping me sharpen my thoughts as they began to crystallize. Eileen was a fact of and in Israeli society; she was a guide to Israeli society, a critical insider and an eager, often frustrated, long-time outsider.

I thought of her as an "informant" when I first met her. I was in Israel at the time partly to study my fellow anthropologists and sociologists, and she was about to complete her doctorate in anthropology/sociology at the Hebrew University. That was spring of 1979. Since then and over the course of many years, she became both the ultimate "informant" and the farthest thing from it. She shared *her* Israel with me —her daily rituals, her frustrations, her memories of a more idealistic time, her growing alienation, the joys and struggles of motherhood, her acquaintances, friends, colleagues, and enemies. She did not see herself as an informant helping the anthropologist, but rather as a potential friend and an eager student, as someone with at least as much to learn from me as she had to teach me. In 1982, we began working on a paper we eventually coauthored in *Human Relations* (Basker and Dominguez 1984). Not insignificantly, it was entitled "Limits to Cultural Awareness: The Immigrant as Therapist." It critiqued psychiatric discounting of the relevance of the sociocultural background of the therapist to the worth or value of the therapeutic process. It examined mental health professionals who are themselves relatively new immigrants to Israel. We spent hours interviewing them, trying to find out to what extent they were aware of their lack of understanding of Israel, Israeli culture, and therefore, their clients/patients. We pushed them and pushed them on whether they thought they could really be useful given their limitations. And we asked ourselves why or how they might think so. I think it was a good analysis, but now in hindsight I also think Eileen and I were vicariously studying ourselves and our relationship with Israel—she as the veteran immigrant turned anthropologist, and I as an anthropologist turned quasi-immigrant. Between the two of us, we oscillated between being participant observers and being observing participants.

Eileen moved to Israel at the age of twenty-five in 1960 full of pioneering enthusiasm to help build the State of Israel. She saw in the young Israel a no-nonsense, down-to-earth attitude that fit her style much more than what she perceived she'd be getting into if she stayed in California. She saw a real opportunity to stand up and be counted. She believed Jews deserved an independent state of their own, and her year-long experience studying German history at the Frei Universität in Berlin her Junior Year in college only bolstered that conviction. She knew that Arabs in the Middle East were less than happy with the existence of the State of Israel, and that there were Arabs living within Israel. But for a number of years throughout the 1960s she seems to have compartmentalized those facts: she seemed to have approached being Jewish as having little to do with the existence of Arabs in general or Palestinians in particular.

Yet by the time she died she was not at all sure she was still a Zionist. Two of her daughters had served in the Israeli army. Eileen herself had devoted years to her own personal campaign to improve the Israeli medical establishment. Physically she had survived four wars in Israel. But something about her had changed and something, she felt, had changed for her about Israel.

It was the last war—the war in and on Lebanon—that I shared with her. She opposed it from the beginning. She was generous in her warm tolerance of my need to do something for Israel at the time. She accompanied me to give blood and arranged for me to be able to volunteer at a hospital treating wounded soldiers in Afula. But for her it was a bad dream turning itself into reality—the kind of experience that made her wonder if she had wasted twenty-five precious years of her adult life helping to shape a society many of whose values she came to believe she no longer held herself. Her alienation grew deeper and deeper the last few years of her life. Shortly before she died she went to Berlin to try to piece together the story of how and why she eventually moved to Israel. She was not comfortable with the idea, but she felt the need to explore it, nonetheless. She had become convinced that there was an intimate connection between her experience of postwar Germany when she was a college junior and her decision to move to Israel. She suspected that it wasn't even the history of anti-Semitism that had become so powerful a force in her decision to move to Israel, but rather her experience of the German assumption of German peoplehood. It was clear to her now that their Germanness had reinforced her Jewishness. But she suspected there was more—that perhaps Jewishness was not that different from the idea of German stock and Israel more like Germany than Israeli Jews could psychologically and politically swallow. In both cases, she sensed, the assumption of peoplehood was arguably not just central to the state but actually constitutive of it.

As she lay dying, she made it clear to friends, her siblings, and her daughters that she had no particular desire to be buried in Israel, especially since it would cost a fair amount of money to send her body to Israel for burial. And yet when I told her about possible cemeteries in the Triangle Area of North Carolina, she was dismayed that there did not seem to be any truly secular cemeteries. Most of the people buried in municipal ones came from Christian homes; there are crosses everywhere. When push came to shove, she opted for a small, new Jewish cemetery in the woods in Chapel Hill.

Eileen carried in her non-Jewish name a constant reminder of the Jewish Diaspora, of how it was, or could be, an argument for the existence of the State of Israel, and of how it was, or could be, an argument for alternative ways of being Jewish. Like her name, she was not always what she seemed and, as her name implied, she cared about being open to alternatives. Eileen had a knack for social criticism, but she was and always remained a Jew. Respecting her choices, though my gut could never quite understand it, is the spirit in which I have written this book. Eileen would not have written *this* book, but I think, I hope, she would have been pleased that *I* wrote it.

People as Subject,
People as Object

Introduction

CALL him Adam. He was a friend of a friend. He needed a ride not far from where I was going, and I had room in my little Fiat 127. We spoke Hebrew. He asked, seemingly rhetorically, if I was American. "Sort of," I replied. "I'm originally Cuban, but the U.S. has been home base for some time." "What are you doing *here*?" he then asked. "Are you Jewish?" "No," I said, answering the second question first. Then I added, "I'm an anthropologist. I came to do research." Adam immediately picked up on it. "Oh, on whom? the Beduin? the Yemenites?" "No," I replied, "on Israeli Jews more generally, the Ashkenazim as well as the Sephardim." He started squirming in his seat. If he had been the one driving, I was sure we would have braked suddenly. Looking at least as puzzled as he looked irritated, Adam turned to me and said, "But *we're* not primitive!"

I admit I was taken aback. I had been teaching introductory anthropology enough to know that many people not otherwise exposed to professional anthropology think that anthropology is the study of primitive peoples. What surprised me, perhaps naively, with Adam was that he would be so quick, so revealing, and so unguarded in his reaction. In one fell swoop, he commented on himself, anthropology, the Beduin and Yemenites, Jewishness, and social hierarchy. It was important to him that he was not primitive; it made sense to him that Jews would want to come to live in Israel; it did not make sense to him that a non-Jew might do so. He also considered himself educated. He was, after all, a medical student. He "knew" that both Jews and Arabs could be primitive. And although not particularly political, he believed that there were both Jews and Arabs who were not primitive. But if a non-Jewish anthropologist was in Israel doing research on a wide variety of Jews, including those of Central and

3

Eastern European origin, the Ashkenazim, could it possibly mean Israel was a primitive country? Or at least that—in yet another example of distortion and prejudice—non-Jews think all Jews are primitive?

I was uncomfortable with the exchange. I wasn't the anthropologist he thought I was, and I'd never thought of Israel as primitive. Suddenly I realized he had turned the tables around. I had given him the ride in part because I'd seen it as an opportunity to meet another Israeli and interview him informally. I had identified him as a member of a social category I was interested in, and wanted to elicit his version of what I took to be common themes in Israeli Jewish identity. Suddenly I was the one being labeled, the one under interrogation, the one feeling pressured to explain myself lest I (and my "people") be misunderstood.

The incident passed and I thought little about it until I tried to conceptualize this book. Then one day it just came back to me. The structure of that exchange, its content, my intentions and the ensuing role reversal, and my discomfort at the end all felt extremely familiar—as if the incident with Adam had taken place time and time again all these years of gathering "data" for this book, as if it were a metonym for the book itself.

This book was originally conceived as an exploration of "the problem of ethnicity" in Israel. But the longer I studied what I took to be ethnic phenomena, ethnic conflict, or ethnic references in Israel, the more I came to understand that "the problem of ethnicity" was a good starting point for my research but not necessarily its best end point. It was not so much that the subject matter changed but that, as the years went by, I probed more and more into what lies within and behind the discourse on ethnicity in Israel. The Jewish Diaspora, the rise of Zionism, and the Israeli notion of the Ingathering of the Exiles all had something to do with the perceived problem of ethnicity in Israel, but they, too, seemed to be products of something and not just explanations of "the problem." What made them possible?

Many of us seek in historical processes explanations for contemporary social problems but, in our zeal to present our cases in the best possible light, we often convince ourselves that the material we put together from a variety of written and oral sources represents historical *facts* sufficient to explain our contemporary social phenomena. But don't those "facts" themselves warrant explanation? What makes them factual? On what epistemological and social assumptions does their factuality rest?

As I probed further and further into the Israeli discourse on ethnicity, I began to wonder about the "object" I had set out to study. Whose construction was it? What did it have to do with the peoplehood of the Jews or with the existence, at least discursively, of something referred to as "Israeli society"?

Before going to Israel, I had done all of my work in the United States and the Caribbean. I had spent much of my scholarly life studying how and why people posit *difference,* rather than oneness. My concern had long been to show the unnatural nature of social categories people believe to be natural (e.g., races, ethnic groups), to show how these categories may change over time (despite the fact that "nature" has not changed), to show that these categories as we perceive them are far from universally posited, and to show that they are produced and reproduced within systems of power and inequality that they help to perpetuate. Somehow it never surprised me that people would want to differentiate themselves from others or to perceive themselves as different from those they regarded as beneath them in social status or economic position. I think I took the positing of difference as natural.

My original research proposal, submitted to the U.S. Social Science Research Council in the fall of 1980, drew its sources officially from the Israeli academic literature but obviously reflected my long-standing interests. In summarizing the objectives of the project, I wrote that I sought:

(1) to investigate the nature of folk theories of social identity and the relationship of these folk theories to how people classify themselves and others in practice;
(2) to determine the relationship of these folk theories to the social, economic, and political processes of social differentiation and stratification; and
(3) to investigate the extent to which the concept of ethnicity used by American and Israeli social scientists may itself be a folk theory of social differentiation more than an analytic tool with which to understand the processes of social differentiation in Israel.

I concentrated on how individuals classify themselves and others, how individuals explain their own patterns of classification, and how these variant assumptions about social identities shape and direct processes of group differentiation in Israel.

I drew explicit parallels between the United States and Israel. "Both," I wrote,

are societies of immigrants; both derive their mainstream ideologies from Europe; both espouse an ideology of equal opportunity (within Israeli *Jewish* society); and both have groups of people of certain regions of origin that are concentrated at the lower rungs of the socioeconomic scale and seem to have a particularly difficult time achieving upward mobility.

I saw individuals; I saw interest groups vying for power; I saw an unstable dynamic between stratification and group differentiation. I pictured asking individual Israelis about their views of Israeli society and expecting comments about the divisions and differences that *constitute* the society. I foresaw struggles over differentiation, not over collectivization. Never once did I even mention Judaism or Zionism, traditionalism or modernism, socialism, Revisionism, secularism, or nationalism.[1] They had just not seemed relevant to the focus on ethnicity.

CATEGORIES, FIGURES, AND DIFFERENCE

I had no problems finding language all over Israel that classified, separated, differentiated, and marked sectors of the population of Israel as identifiable sociocultural entities. The terms *Arabs* and *Jews, Sephardim* and *Ashkenazim, mizrachim* (Orientals), *Druze,* and *Beduin* are common in everyday conversations, along with further subdivisions and alternative terminology. A parallel and often very detailed system of classification appears in official government texts as well.

Writers almost always divide the population of Israel in presenting demographic, social, geographic, and economic statistics. They write of *population groups, country or region of origin groups, ethnic groups* (or the Hebrew term *edot*), or *religions* (or *religious communities*) freely. Far less frequently—except in sociological studies focusing on socioeconomic stratification—do we find the English or Hebrew words social *class, status* communities, or *ma'amadot* on Israeli statistical tables. Israel's annual statistical yearbook (whose title is officially translated as the *Statistical*

---

1. Many "isms" show up in Israelis' discussions of Israel and Israeli society. Some of these are more referentially specific than others. Revisionism is the political and social vision associated with Vladimir Jabotinsky in prestate Palestine and, in modified form, with Menachem Begin. It saw itself opposed to Labor Zionism and as an alternative to it. "Zionism" itself has had many forms and counterforms over the years (see Avineri 1981; Isaac 1976; Sachar 1982). They vary primarily according to their interpretation of the relevance of Judaism for the Jewish state and their incorporation of various socialist and/or capitalist strategies and goals in their vision of Jewish society in the Jewish state. Accordingly, there isn't one socialist movement, ideology, or party in Israel. There are, and have been, many. It is possible to be socialist *and* Zionist in Israel (Mapam, for example) just as much as socialist and non- or anti-Zionist (the Israeli Communist Party, for example). It is possible to be religious *and* Zionist in Israel (the National Religious Party, for example) just as much as religious and non- or anti-Zionist (Agudat Israel as an example of the former; Neturei Karta as an example of the latter). It is possible to be secular and traditional just as much as religious and modernist (cf. Avruch 1979; Bowes 1982; Deshen 1978; Goldberg 1972, 1978; Goldshieder and Friedlander 1983; Handelman and Shamgar-Handelman 1986). What I am saying in this part of the text is that at the time of writing my proposal I had little or no sense of how much these objectified "isms" form a part of Israeli public discourse—the frequent objects of discourse and the terms in which people cognitively "map" the political and social spectrum.

Abstract of Israel) explains its terms in its most recent edition (printed in 1988 about 1987 data), as follows:

Population groups and religion. Tables include, as a rule, the breakdown of the population according to Jews, Moslems, Christians, Druze and other.
When such a breakdown is impossible because of availability or scarcity of data, population is broken down by "Jews" and "Non-Jews—thereof: Moslems" [page 16 of the official English translation of the Introduction to the Tables which appears on p. 27 of the Hebrew text].

And a few lines later it adds: "*Country of Origin* of born abroad—the country of birth, and of Israel born—father's country of birth."

These tables commonly distinguish between Jews from *Europe and America* and Jews from *Asia and Africa,* as well as between Jews and non-Jews. But that is only part of the story. Finer distinctions are sometimes perceived as necessary; some categorizations are questioned; some are seen as relatively insignificant, while others are imbued with great political significance.

As the 1986 statistical yearbook explains (on p. 24 concerning data on immigrants), the system first classifies immigrants according to the country in which the immigrant lived at least one year before immigration, and then groups the countries according to a particular, though by now also habitual, classification: "the U.S.S.R. and other countries of Eastern Europe"; "other countries of Europe and America, including South Africa and Oceania"; "Asia-Africa (excl. South Africa)."

Enormous groupings result. They are intended as more scientific substitutes for the longer-standing labels—Ashkenazi and Sephardi—that appear with frequency in contemporary Israeli speech, but they still basically parallel popular usage and reproduce many of the ambiguities and problems of the Ashkenazi/Sephardi distinction. Most of those counted as from "the U.S.S.R. and other countries of Eastern Europe" would be commonly referred to as Ashkenazim along with most of those from "other countries of Europe and America, including South Africa and Oceania." And most of those from "Asia-Africa" would be typically thought of as Sephardim (or referred to by the alternative term *Oriental Jews*).

But, as demographers and those descended from Spanish Jews always point out, these labels are by no means perfect equivalents. *Sephardi* literally means "Spanish" in Hebrew and, in the strictest sense, *Sephardim* refers to descendants of *Spanish* Jews (not to all Jews from Asia and Africa). There are Sephardim descended from Spanish Jews who ended up in Holland, England, the Balkan peninsula, Turkey, prestate Palestine, and northern Morocco—meaning that some of those officially put in the Asia-Africa category are from Europe in ancestry just like those in South Africa or the Americas (though these latter two populations are put into the Europe and America group). It also means (1) that some of the Jews of Europe consider themselves Sephardim, and (2) that most of those from "Asia and Africa" have no Iberian ancestry at all.

These distinctions and differentiations might look like hairsplitting to a non-Israeli, but in Israel they are definitely not the concern of librarians and statisticians alone. The Jewish/non-Jewish and Sephardi/Ashkenazi distinctions, so pervasive in official counts, command the most political and statistical attention, and the latest government population tables show both how and why.[2]

1. Jews constitute 82.0 percent of the population of Israel. This takes into account the 28,500 Jews listed as living in Israeli settlements in Judea/Samaria and Gaza—i.e., the West Bank and Gaza—but it does not take into account the majority Arab population of the West Bank and Gaza otherwise estimated to be 860,000 and 564,000, respectively—see Table 27, on page 705 of the yearbook. It also includes all of the population of Jerusalem—West and East, Jewish (346,100) and non-Jewish (136,600)—because Israel considers Jerusalem unified since 1967 and an integral part of Israel.

2. Of the 79.3 percent of Israel's Jewish population who were born abroad or whose fathers were born abroad, over half by now come from Asian or African countries. While the vast majority of Jews who moved to Palestine before the establishment of the state came from Europe—especially Eastern and Central Europe—the pattern changed significantly with the founding of the state in 1948. Immigrants came in droves from throughout North Africa and the Middle East—among them notably Morocco, Yemen, Iraq, Syria, Turkey, Kurdistan, Bukhara, and Libya. The Ashkenazim had created the emerging state's structure and institutions, but the non-Ashkenazim were to emerge by the 1970s as the demographic majority.

My Israeli colleagues have not been blind to this change. Just as I had no problem finding sociocultural categorizations within Israel, I had no problem finding Israeli scholars whose own work seemed to justify interpreting all of these distinctions, differences, and categorizations as problematic, and "ethnicity" itself as constitutive of Israel and problematic

2. Appendix 1 is taken directly from two key population tables regularly included in the official annual publication entitled *Statistical Abstract of Israel*—"Population, by Religion" and "Population, by Religion, Origin, Continent of Birth and Period of Immigration."

for "Israeli society." An expected amount of what has been written about Israel over the years is about Zionism—its rise as a political movement, a philosophical movement, a social movement, a nationalist movement; its practically convergent but ideologically competing streams; its relationship to other movements of "national liberation"; and its awkward, often dependent, often antagonistic, relationship with various forms of Judaism (e.g., Avineri 1981; Cleeman 1945; Halpern 1969; Isaac 1976; Kimmerling 1983; Laqueur 1972; Rubinstein 1980; Sachar 1982). In addition, academic and media attention has turned increasingly in the 1980s to groups and events that suggest a rising popularity of religiosity in previously "secular" social circles or at least a rising awareness of religiosity in circles otherwise described as secular (Aviad 1983; Avruch 1979; Deshen 1978; Goldberg 1987; Goldscheider and Friedlander 1983; Kotler 1985; Newman 1981; Segal 1987). Oneness, or at least the notion of returning to oneness, is a common theme throughout this body of work.

But a great deal, too, has seemed to be about the existence and persistence of sociocultural difference and what the state should do about it. In the 1950s and 1960s, many talked and wrote about Israel's "problems of nation building," how these required an institutional infrastructure characteristic of a "modern" society, the "absorption" of hundreds of thousands of immigrants in a very short period of time, and the then perceived need to get these immigrants—especially those from non-European backgrounds—to abandon their "traditional" cultures and become acculturated, responsible citizens in their new "modern" society (e.g., Eisenstadt 1954, 1967; Matras 1965; Shokeid 1971; Shuval 1962, 1963; Weingrod 1965, 1966; Willner 1969). Increasingly over the past ten to fifteen years, politicians, journalists, and academics have begun to expose the institutional discursive and nondiscursive practices that discriminated against non-European immigrants for much of the history of Israel since independence, and that frequently led to the perpetuation of significant socioeconomic and political gaps (Ben-Rafael 1982; Deshen and Shokeid 1974; Eisenstadt 1985; Elazar 1986; Peres 1977; Segev 1984; Smooha 1978; Swirski 1981; Weingrod 1985).[3] Fragmentation and inequality are the common themes in these works.

As I examined much of this material—the colloquial, the official, and the scholarly—it was obvious that much of it seemed to legitimate my looking at "the problem of ethnicity" as I had long seen it. And yet,

3. These are some of the major works but, as the reader may already know, there is quite a large bibliography on Israel and Zionism. Useful references include the bibliographies in Deshen and Shokeid 1984; Eisenstadt 1985; Handelman and Deshen 1975; Kimmerling 1983; Krausz 1980, 1983, 1985; Swirski 1981; Weingrod 1985.

something about that conclusion seemed too facile. As a student of culture, stereotypes, and misunderstandings, I had grown skeptical of first impressions and superficial similarities. Moreover, there was all that talk of Zionism and Judaism that pulled one in the opposite direction. I began to pay attention to changes in my own outlook while I was still in the field, thinking that they might be the product of my interactions with Israelis and, thus, be no longer just an outsider's perspective.

I noticed that by the time the Israeli-Lebanese war broke out in early June 1982, I had been in Israel over a year and my language had changed. When a friend in the United States asked me to describe to him what it felt like to be in Israel that summer of '82, I wrote in the opening paragraph of my reply that I felt "a bit like Hillel [a tower of postbiblical Judaic scholarship], the way he must have felt when challenged by a heathen to teach him the entire Torah [in the narrow sense, the first five books of the Hebrew Bible, though in the broader sense more like the word of God] while standing on one foot." My own and my friends' Zionism had become an issue. I quoted a "leftist," "secular" woman saying in reaction to a news broadcast that "that is not the way it was meant to be, that is not the way this country was supposed to be—we were going to be human and sensitive; we were not going to do what other countries do." I quoted a former New Zealander accusing the British of being more primitive than the Israelis when he heard that the British government had insisted for weeks on a blackout of film clippings from the Falklands/Malvinas Islands war. And I ended with profound puzzlement about the Israeli obsession with their own collective morality—

the disappointment of a visible and undeniable loss of innocence, fear of the self, and a coming to grips on a mass level with the possibility of guilt. I have enormous respect for Israelis in general insofar as they are obsessed with the definition of "ought's" and "is's," the probably unbridgeable gap between them, and their willing resignation to persist in the interminable struggle. In a nutshell, I have never known people more governed by the question of morality.

In less than two years—my foreign accent in Hebrew notwithstanding—I had grown not only to identify with many Israelis but even to see the world, I thought, as they did. I sensed a shift in my focus, away from fragmentation and toward collectivization. I thought I had "discovered" something without which there could not be "the problem of ethnicity" in Israel—that there may or may not be an Israeli collective self at the practical level but that one cannot understand anything social or political in Israel if one ignores "it"; that its empirical referent is vague and constantly subjected to institutional and political manipulation; and that as either goal or reality it is an ever present object of public discourse.

I became interested in Israelis' social classifications, but this time not just in divisions within the society but also, and eventually primarily, in their positing of *oneness*, of shared identity. But how to approach this? Too much about the popular and academic usage of the terms *ethnicity, ethnic group,* and *ethnic identity* seemed socioculturally grounded in the ideology of pluralism that followed the 1960s in the United States. In much of that literature, ethnicity comes across as "stage 2" in the process whereby an immigrant population adjusts to life in the United States. The "ethnic" smacks of difference and underempowerment, of the existence of parts of a society that are not "mainstream" (cf. Chock 1987; DiLeonardo 1984). Though a number of writers suggest they are writing about a more general phenomenon, the tie between ethnicity, immigration, and underprivilege is so strong in our most typical thinking and writing about the subject (e.g., in the *Harvard Encyclopedia of American Ethnic Groups* and in the *Journal of American Ethnic History*) that by calling something ethnicity we invoke mental and emotional associations that may not always be appropriate in many cases where there is, nonetheless, a sense of *peoplehood.*

Ethnicity does come from the Greek word *ethnos,* meaning people, and hence literally means the phenomenon of peoplehood. But is it used that way freely in actual speech and writing? I do not believe so. We regularly refer to some populations as nations or peoples and not as ethnic groups, and to others as ethnic groups and not as nations or peoples. We tend to speak of the *nations* of Europe and the *tribes* or *peoples* of sub-Saharan Africa. We may refer to ethnic groups in Europe or sub-Saharan Africa, but then do we not usually mean groups that are politically, economically, and/or culturally identified as different and problematic by a "mainstream" population (e.g., Glazer and Moynihan 1975)? We might want to agree to call sociocultural divisions among the Jews of Israel ethnic, but are we equally comfortable calling the general Jewish claim to peoplehood in Israel a case of ethnicity?

In recognizing that it was peoplehood (rather than ethnic fragmentation or pluralism) that intrigued me in Israel, I was making two discoveries simultaneously—one about Israel, and one about myself. And they were analytically connected. Israel and I shared (1) a concern with collective identities, and (2) the taking for granted of our objectifications of collectivity to such an extent that it is hard for us even to imagine alternative objectifications until, and unless, challenged to do so.

I shifted gears to a level of analysis that could shed light on both. I became interested not just in *Israelis'* social classifications, but in representation and objectification themselves. They seemed to be issues in my analysis of Israel, but they were also clearly issues in my analysis of the intellectual or scholarly representation of self and other in which I as non-Israeli and non-Jewish author of this book participate. I began to focus, accordingly, on dialogue and discourse, representation and manipulation, control and authorship. The longer I explored the roles they played in the shaping of Israeli society the more I recognized ways in which they shaped my work, too, as *a* representation of Israeli society. It was clear that the book had to be not about "the problem of ethnicity" but, rather, about collective identities as objectifications in need of semiotic exploration, and about the objectification of collective identities by both insiders and outsiders as simultaneously semiotic and political.

FROM ONTOLOGY TO EPISTEMOLOGY

Concern with objectification is both new and old. In the works of Hegel (1967 [1807]), Marx (1978 [1867]), Dilthey (1961 [1910]), and Lukács (1971), we find theoretical, philosophical discussions of subject-object relations, of the disputed identities of subject and object, of the "objectivity" of nature, and of the relationship between objectification and alienation. In twentieth-century popular discourse, at least in North America, perception of objectification seems most salient in discussions of sex and gender—from the references to women as sexual objects to more encompassing treatises on the objectification of women.[4] Sensitivity to the participation of researchers and writers—anthropologists most definitely among them—in the condescending objectification of others has more re-

---

4. I am thinking primarily of two types of discussions of objectification in the feminist literature. In one, of which Simone de Beauvoir's *The Second Sex* (1970) is an excellent early example and Gayatri Spivak's *In Other Worlds: Essays in Cultural Politics* (1987) is a very recent example, women as other, as object, are juxtaposed to men as subject. De Beauvoir's analysis is abstract and general and consonant with George Herbert Mead's (1913, 1934) portrayal of "the social self" where the subject/self has or needs an object/other to be itself and define itself. It is this part of de Beauvoir's work that has been a foundation of much of the feminist discourse of the so-called second wave (cf. Firestone 1970; Rubin 1975; Daly 1978; Griffin 1978; Wittig 1981).

A second, and related, large body of literature—both popular and academic—concentrates on actions and attitudes on the part of men that index a perception of women as sex objects. Note, above all, the literature on pornography, rape, and prostitution (cf. Brownmiller 1976; Barry 1979; Dworkin 1981; Ellis 1984; Faust 1981; Griffin 1979, 1981; Morgan 1980), but the concept is inherent in most areas where feminists focus on women's bodies—from *Our Bodies, Ourselves* (Boston Women's Health Book Collective Staff 1986) to the pro-choice literature arguing for women's right to contraception and abortion (cf. Gordon 1977; Hubbard et al. 1979; Rich 1979; O'Brien 1981; Shorter 1982; Petchesky 1985). Alison Jaggar's *Feminist Politics and Human Nature* (1983) is an excellent philosophical and historical analysis of discussion, changes, and varieties of feminist discourse, with special reference to North America.

cently come from, and promotes, a shift in emphasis from the ontological to the epistemological in our formulation of research problems.

Description is giving way ideologically to explorations of cognitive, social, and historical factors that shape the perception of others. Discourse switches from the *objective* description of social organization, political life, ritual, or agriculture to the at times tortuous propositions about conscious and unconscious role playing by the ethnographer and his or her "informants." At our most penitent stage, we accuse ourselves of objectifying the other as if the other were inanimate and incapable of subjectifying himself or herself. At our most modest, we admit to having been "constructed" by those we set out to study, who in objectifying us turned the ethnographic process into a project of forced resubjectification. Subject and object become terms of analysis of a phenomenon we experience but are always grasping to understand.[5]

Ethnography holds no monopoly on objectification, but few fields confront the practitioner with as much tension between the social and the cognitive "requirements" of research. Immersion in the field requires a willingness to "be born again." The ethnographer stumbles around grasping for the appropriate categories of understanding and the rules by which to distinguish the possible from the impossible. As the ethnographer "grows up," she or he acquires a cohort, a set of roles, and a set of rights and duties determined by her or his participation in the host society. But like a spy, she or he must never fail throughout the process to keep enough distance to objectify the other. The tension makes emotional fragility both a necessary feature and a tool of the ethnographic enterprise.

The trick for the ethnographer is to acknowledge the epistemological contradictions of the enterprise and yet develop criteria of understanding to learn, nonetheless, both about those we try to objectify and about ourselves as objectifiers. If emotional fragility is a condition of fieldwork and a consequent tool of data gathering, then emotional reactions are the most powerful indicators of the sensitivities of the two worlds that meet/clash in us and through us. The introspective analysis of our own reactions—of what we love and what we hate, of what intrigues us "irrationally" and what we simply fail to understand, of what we fear in the society we study and what we fear in our feelings toward the society we study—may ironi-

---

5. I do not assume that I am above or beyond the tendency toward self-flagellation to which I hereby refer. I have a sense of where I stand, and where this book stands, on the practice of objectification in which we as intellectuals and researchers participate. But it will no doubt take others to point out assumptions and practices perpetuated in this text of which I am still unaware.

cally allow us to approximate "reality" better than the perennial attempts
to maximize objectivity by minimizing subjectivity.

These issues loomed larger and larger the longer I stayed in Israel. I
saw my first glimpse of Israel in the summer of 1970 from the Lebanese
side of the Israeli-Lebanese border. I was a college student at the time,
and my father was stationed in Beirut as marketing representative for a
U.S. tobacco company. I remember that day at the border. I stood there,
flanked by an amateur archeologist and a Lebanese army colonel, won-
dering if I would ever see the other side. Tanya, the amateur archeologist,
kept pointing out that on a clear day you can see Haifa.

The Israeli-Arab conflict had felt very foreign. I had spent most of my
life in Latin America and been politicized into fighting inequality, racism,
American imperialism, and government corruption. It made sense to me
then to think of fighting those battles. I could not fathom getting into the
problems of the Middle East. I had already been tear-gassed several times
—between 1968 and 1970—and I was only eighteen. For most of two
summers I lived in Beirut. I spoke French and English throughout. I made
a lackluster attempt to learn Arabic on my own. I never expected to have
to deal with the region again.

Then in the fall of 1977, while luxuriating in Boston's intellectual
life, I befriended a young archeologist with extensive experience in Israel
and plans to move there permanently. As the months passed, I grew increasingly curious about Israel, asked more and more questions about the
grammar and structure of the Hebrew language, and revived those memories of life on the other side of the Lebanese-Israeli border. In December
1978, I visited Israel for the first time. I stayed eight days. I was hooked
but I couldn't quite tell why.

The story then changes, as I grew to be less and less the gawking
tourist and more and more the inveterate participant observer. In March
1979 I returned for a month. This time I had a wedding to attend, a kibbutz to visit, and a Passover Seder to experience. I also had a work agenda
of my own. I set out to meet Israeli anthropologists and sociologists,
and discuss with them whether or not a non-Jew with my background
and interests would be welcome as a researcher in their midst. I was not
dissuaded.

In the summer of 1980, with a small grant from the Trent Foundation, I returned to Israel, this time for two months. I spent five hours
a day five days a week studying Hebrew with about thirty new immigrants at a municipal *ulpan* (intensive Hebrew language learning center)
in Jerusalem. I read the *Jerusalem Post* and *Sha'ar LeMatkhil* (a weekly
newspaper in "easy Hebrew" for adults) avidly. I took fieldnotes at the
ulpan, experienced life vicariously as a new immigrant by following the

trials, discoveries, and tribulations of my classmates. I made contact with middle-aged speakers of Ladino (sometimes known as Judeo-Espagnol, the language spoken by descendants of Jews who left Spain because of the Inquisition and migrated to various provinces of the Ottoman Empire).

I returned to Durham with two goals in mind—to find a tutor to further my learning of Hebrew, and to obtain research grants for the following academic year. In May 1981, armed with a working though still insufficient knowledge of Hebrew and generous grants from the Mellon Foundation, the Social Science Research Council, and the Duke University Research Council, I went to Israel for fifteen months.

For the next four years I lived in Jerusalem, though for part of that time I actually taught at Duke. From August 1982 through June 1984, I was at Duke whenever classes were in session; otherwise I was in Israel. In 1984, I returned to Jerusalem for fourteen months as a Fulbright professor in anthropology at the Hebrew University. During that period I spent thirty-four months in Israel, learned to speak, read, write, and lecture in Hebrew, fell in love, almost converted to Judaism, experienced the fear and the agony of the war in Lebanon, and went through stages of loving and hating Israel.

At some point in the midst of all this I began to "react to Israeli society," and with each negative or emotional reaction I pondered ever more about my construction of the "object." By May 1985, I found myself writing:

The question before me is "simple": Has my obsessive, long-term encounter with Israeli society over the past six years turned me into the anti-Semite I never was? I find myself sharply intolerant of the noisy, brash behavior of most Israeli children. I coin terms of description that are even explicitly judgmental. I get exasperated with the perennial references in the media to the Jewishness of well-known public figures abroad. I lose my patience with my closest friend when she says or does something I dislike that I associate with "israeliut."

For a while I was embarrassed to have these feelings. I was uncomfortable with all the alternatives I entertained in my search for a valid explanation. Could I have simply learned what "Israeli society" was really like? Could it be some latent anti-Semitism coming to the surface? The long-standing fragility of the relationship between Jews and non-Jews made both of these at once reasonable and laughable, likely to attract partisans and to be rejected simultaneously. Yet I felt they both needed to be posed. "Israeli society" and latent anti-Semitism had already become concepts I took for granted. After three and a half years of fairly constant research in and on Israel, I as a non-Jew felt compelled to pose the question about my emotional reaction to Israel.

I sought to become my own ethnographer—to ask of myself the kind of questions the ethnographer typically asks of others—not out of narcissism but, rather, because I sensed it could shed light on Israel. In examining my evolving feelings toward Israel and my discomfort with some of them, I felt I was looking at the dynamics of my "dialogue" with Israelis. I was extending Paul Ricoeur's dictum that interpretation is about "the comprehension of the self by the detour of the comprehension of the other" (Ricoeur 1969:20). I am sure much, if not all, of my research on others is one way in which I attempt to comprehend aspects of myself, but I see no reason for anthropologists to hold a monopoly on comprehension by detour. If Israelis themselves, I thought, were doing that with me, then undoubtedly part of the analysis I was doing on myself came from Israelis' own terms, assumptions, and understandings. To inspect myself as an object in the predication of self and other in Israel today looked like a feasible, even illuminating, point of entry into "Israeli society."

I call the technique heuristic self-objectification. My goal is not to suggest ways of transcending our objectification of others, but rather to enrich our understanding of the processes of objectification and the role they play in creating and maintaining collective identities. I become "the laboratory animal" in the written text, not just in the process of collecting data in the field.

On the conscious use of subject

In thinking, saying, and writing all of this, I am obviously taking the position that it is not only not inappropriate for social researchers to insert themselves in the write-ups of their data but that it is, in fact, advantageous to do so. I am not alone in taking this position, but I am of course aware that most readers of scholarly or scientific texts in the twentieth century will be unaccustomed to the extent to which I do so consciously in this book—and that some will object in principle.

The points I am making in these paragraphs are, however, my take on problems and issues raised increasingly, and with growing academic legitimacy, by a network of scholars pushing for reflexivity in the *writing* of academic texts as well as in the research leading to the writing of those texts (Clifford 1983; Clifford and Marcus 1986; Marcus and Fischer 1986; Dwyer 1982; Crapanzano 1980, 1985; Lavie 1986; Rabinow 1977). The terms *reflexive, poststructuralist, interpretive, dialogical,* and *hermeneutic* fill many of the pages of texts emerging in this discursive network. To those outside the specific concerns of that discourse, it must seem faddish and monolithic in purpose and content. I have heard critics call it navel staring and narcissistic, even the annihilation or disintegration of the object.

In fact, I think that both the proponents and the critics of research and writing that is deliberately more self-aware err by simplifying the nature of the exercise, polarizing textual genres, and assuming that it is a distinctive and distinct approach that *breaks* with tradition in a far more radical way than I suspect is warranted. Who and what is part of this movement? The first nine issues of *Cultural Anthropology* are full of *variant* arguments about textuality, voice (especially the first 1988 issue edited by Arjun Appadurai), ethnographic writing, epistemological critical awareness, dialogue, hermeneutics and, as Michael Fischer puts it in his editorial introduction to volume 3, number 1 (February 1988), "the concern with the prisonhouse of language and its means of self-transcendence." A session entitled "Metaethnography" at the 1987 meetings of the American Anthropological Association in Chicago portrayed itself as critical of reflexive anthropology, but in analyzing anthropological discourse on and in India, Haiti, and East Africa, were the participants not in fact engaging in the kind of critical awareness, albeit historical as well as textual, that many of the contributors to *Cultural Anthropology* seek? And what about earlier writers like Gregory Bateson (*Naven* and *Steps to an Ecology of Mind*), Sidney Mintz (*Worker in the Cane*), or Marcel Griaule (*Conversations with Ogotemmeli*), who knowingly and consciously experimented not just with ethnographic genres of writing but also with the presentation and representation of their chosen "objects"? Where do we draw the line?

I think the push to study ourselves in the act of studying others is the product of the convergence of variant streams of thought, concern, and scholarship that we are experiencing since the mid-to-late 1970s. Literary theory heavily influenced by Roland Barthes (1967), Jacques Derrida (1977, 1978), Paul de Man (1971), and Julia Kristeva (1980) provided one continuous focus of rethinking in intellectual circles. An "interpretive" tradition within anthropology (cf. Rabinow and Sullivan 1979), while not typically focused on the researcher, certainly had the theoretical tools and perspective to put the spotlight also on the researcher.

Geopolitical realities affecting where scholars do their field research have also, I think, had their impact. Shalva Weil, for instance, entitled her most self-focused paper yet "Anthropology Becomes Home; Home Becomes Anthropology" (1987). Moshe Shokeid (1988) found himself struggling to figure out how to relate to Israelis in New York in his book on *Yordim* (Israelis who emigrate from Israel) and his 1987 paper entitled "An Israeli Anthropologist in the Company of Yordim (Israeli

Emigrants)." Robert Thornton has found himself sitting in South Africa contemplating the ethnographic genre in South African academia and its relationship to South African politics. In fact, some of this shift toward reflexivity was anticipated by—even promoted by—various contributions to Dell Hymes's *Reinventing Anthropology* (1969) twenty years ago.

I think the real question is *what to do* with our heightened political awareness and increasingly sophisticated understanding of the tropes in which representation and ideology meet (cf. Pratt 1982). Kevin Dwyer (1982) experimented with dialogue as a strategy for minimizing control and representation. Byron Good et al. (1982) sought to derive practical as well as theoretical insights from exploring reflexivity and countertransference in psychiatric consultations. Smadar Lavie (1986) used it to say something about world politics, Arab-Israeli confrontations, and the descent-oriented "tribal" structure of Beduin people.

I would certainly not say that conditions—be they the concerns of the intellectual world in our countries at any one time or the state of relations between those populations in power and those out of power—*dictate* how reflexive our research is or our writing becomes. But when they converge, it is hard not to see the value, even the need, for a focus on ourselves as objectifiers.

The result need not be confessional in tone. I think Vincent Crapanzano is right. "Tales of observational malaise," he wrote in a 1987 editorial in *Cultural Anthropology*, which has so far seemed almost obsessed with the problem, "so commonplace among American anthropologists, have tended to serve confessional purposes, to point to the possibility of distortion, and to illustrate the contingencies of discovery—and they have offered, I suppose, some comfort to the lonely, disquieted participant observer—but they have usually failed to show exactly how the vantage point of the observer affects his observations, descriptions, and interpretations" (Crapanzano 1987:180). We have tended to address the problem of objectification and otherness in theoretical critiques,[6] but we do not know

6. Over the past two to three years, I myself thought and wrote about the politics and hierarchies of ways we represent objects, ourselves, and others (Domínguez 1987); I proposed intimate connections between what Michel Foucault (1970) called the emergence of Man in the nineteenth century and the early anthropological scramble to salvage "dying cultures" (Domínguez 1986b); and I looked at the realities and illusions of the striving for representational control—for semiotic self-determination—among those perceiving themselves part of an unempowered or underempowered sector of the population (Domínguez 1986c). But most of these articles have been analytic thought pieces, critiques, theoretical arguments for reformulating presumably analytic concepts. In none of these have I been confronted directly with my own participation in the disciplinary tradition of objectification—until now.

what to do—or even if we should do anything—with the observations, "facts," and figures we have gathered elsewhere in studying whomever we chose as the objects of our study. At most we typically apologize for our anthropological *chutzpa,* describe our awkwardness and even incompetence in early stages of fieldwork, and dedicate our books to the people we studied. We may even in the process discover the ways in which the canons of scholarly writing contribute to a perception of self and otherness that we may theoretically decry but in which we participate in practice. But we are still up a creek when we decide, nonetheless, to take the plunge and write about the people we studied. It is a decision that seems to traditionalize us. Here we were articulating all the reasons other people's depictions of people must be intellectually understood as *representations,* rather than as collections of facts, and yet here we are depicting people, nonetheless. But my position is that the discomfort this realization produces can be the impetus for exploring not just what writers and scholars do but what we all, in fact, do—represent and objectify each other. Throwing out my "data" because there is no satisfactory way to transcend *my* otherness or my objectification of their otherness is tempting, but it ultimately begs the questions I believe this problem allows me to address: What is peoplehood? In what ways is it a representation, an objectification? How is it shaped, molded, altered, and perpetuated? And how can it help us learn about the very processes of objectification in which we *all* participate?

In this sense, then, this book is and is not about Israel.[7] It is about

7. The point was driven home even further as I looked at my own struggle to find a title for this book. Never in fifteen years of publishing have I ever had as hard a time coming up with a fitting title. For many months, as I wrote the first draft, I inspired myself by staring at a tentative title page with the lofty, theoretically ambitious, and highly coded words, *The Significant Self: Toward a Predication of Israeli Society.* It reminded me constantly of the audience I aimed to reach—academic, intellectual, international, and philosophical with an interest in language and meaning. I counted on having an Israeli readership but, in my uncertainty about this book's reception, I chose to weave ties elsewhere. But that wording seemed to discount my Israeli audience, as if most of them could not, would not, be able to understand my multiple layers of meaning, and as if their reception did not really matter. The longer I lived with it the more I realized how artificial that felt. That title was deliberately and inappropriately distancing.

I contemplated alternatives. *Israel's Jewish Problem: A Case of Self-Determination* was the catchiest of all, but how could I ignore the baggage those words carried? I tried it out on Jewish and non-Jewish friends, Israeli and non-Israeli. Everyone saw its appeal, but a number of my Jewish friends became very sullen upon hearing it. I do think that in many ways this book is about Israel's problem with its Jewishness—what to do about it, what it should or should not mean in social, political, and daily life, what connection there is, or should be, between its Jewishness and Judaism. Were it not for the unintended allusions to

Israel as a way to ask questions about the objectification of collective identities and, throughout the exercise, to come closer to an understanding
of the process of objectification itself. It is, thus, about discourse and the
constitution of peoplehood, about Israeli society as an objectification, and
about the representation of otherness as a common, though circuitous,
route to representing ourselves. It is about the objectification of specific
collective identities—Israeli Jews' objectification of each other, their objectification of Jewishness, their objectification of Israeli society. It is also
referentially and indexically necessarily about my objectification of them
and what I have learned through them about my objectification of them.
Hence the role reversal with Adam.

---

anti-Semitism, in particular, its implication that there could, or should, be a "solution" to
the "problem," it would have been catchy and appropriate. But how insensitive could I be?
How could I have lived with Israeli Jews all these years and not understand the depth of the
pain and anguish, angst and anger that such a reference would evoke in Holocaust survivors
and their children? How could I ignore the fact that most Jews feel that pain, anger, or fear
themselves not just by identifying with those who died but by seeing themselves as targets?

Creating Facts: Beyond Territories and Government Decrees played amusingly with
words. This time the amused (and not so amused) audience would be exclusively Israeli or
Israeli-oriented. "Creating facts" were the words used by adamant supporters and promoters
of Jewish settlement on the West Bank. Have lots of Jewish settlements and settlers on the
West Bank and you will have de facto annexation by Israel. *Shtachim* ("territories") was the
word used for years after the 1967 war to refer to territory captured in that war, primarily the
West Bank of Jordan. The Begin government, in its push for Jewish settlement on the West
Bank, campaigned fervently and forcefully for the replacement of *territories* by the names
Judea and *Samaria* taken from biblical times and signaling historical Jewish ties to the land.
My intended message—that collective identities, even one as long-lasting as the peoplehood
of the Jews, are perceived with uncanny regularity by those from "within" as constantly
in need of nurturing, of re-creation—would have been swallowed up in all the allusions to
Israel's policies toward the West Bank. *Creating Facts* would clearly be manipulating facts
for the sake of generating an audience.

I contemplated calling it *Eileen's People* because it felt the most honest. But I ultimately decided it would serve *my* needs more than do her honor. She would have been very
uncomfortable with the clear assigning of identity, of belonging, of possessiveness that the
phrase might connote. She was an Israeli and a Jew but, like most Israeli Jews I know, she
spent much of her life trying to find a comfortable way to relate her sense of individual identity to her not-always-joyous perception of the collective identity of which she saw herself,
and was seen by others, as a member.

1 On the Grounds of Dialogue and the Discourse of Power

I F we presuppose the existence of something, can we still be involved in the process by which it is created? If we see ourselves as creating something, do we not perforce deny its prior existence? What sounds like a riddle is actually a paradox in signification: the possibility that through dialogue and discourse we may assume, or at least come to believe in, the existence of something whose very existence is, in fact, continually "created" by discursive acts of signification in which we participate.

The apparent problem in logic is obviously, simultaneously, a matter of social intercourse and political consequence. The existence of "objects" is always supported, challenged, bolstered, or molded by individuals and groups engaged in social and political processes of everyday discourse and institutional life. It may be hard to see how this matters when the object in question is a "concrete" item of undisputed everyday life. It would be hard not to see that it matters when the object in question is a representation of the self (singular or collective).

THE DIALOGUE OF OBJECTIFICATION

Consider a seemingly trivial example. A March 5, 1985, news release issued by the office of the spokesman of the Hebrew University read: "Visiting Fulbright professor examines, becomes part of Israeli society at Hebrew University." A March 19, 1985, article in the *Durham Morning Herald* based on the March 5 news release read instead: "Duke professor teaching in Israel." The former began: "How did a young, Cuban born, American educated professor of Catholic parentage come to teach courses in fluent Hebrew at the Hebrew University in Jerusalem?" The latter countered with "Virginia Dominguez, a professor of socio-cultural anthropology at Duke University, is teaching at the Hebrew University of Jerusalem as a Fulbright Fellow."

I had expected to see the former. I had, after all, agreed to grant the interview on which the text was based. I was surprised and a bit embarrassed the day in early April I went through the mail forwarded to me in Jerusalem by my office at Duke, and found the newspaper clipping from the *Durham Morning Herald*. I had not expected anyone outside the Hebrew University to pay any attention to the news release. I read both texts, however, with nervousness and trepidation. It was not so much that I feared I might have been misquoted; I feared seeing myself in someone else's eyes, discovering what I had said between the lines that I had not planned to say or was even unaware of having said, grappling with my sense of myself after experiencing myself as an other.

The punchline in the *Durham Morning Herald* item—meant to catch the reader's eye—came in the second sentence: "And she is teaching her courses in Hebrew." Unlike the Hebrew University news release which in one breath had mentioned that I was young, Cuban born, American educated, a professor, and of Catholic parentage when it dropped the "bomb" that I was teaching in Hebrew, the Durham paper restricted itself at the outset of its article to the apparently newsworthy fact that I was teaching in Hebrew. It did go on in the third paragraph to mention the fact that I was born in Cuba, and in the second paragraph to state that I have a bachelor's and a doctoral degree from Yale signaling, among other things, that I was educated in the United States. It did not, however, anywhere in the article describe me as young, give my age, or mention that I have "Catholic parentage." We must assume either that these were not considered newsworthy or that they are considered too private or personal to be exposed in an article that did not absolutely require their disclosure.

The North Carolina paper offered a useful counterpoint to the Israeli news release. The Israeli text self-consciously tells a story—previewed already in its headline—about my becoming a part of Israeli society. The format is that of a storyteller who captures an audience's interest by posing an intriguing question and then proceeds to relate the story as an answer to the question. The first of three sections gives biographical details— where I was born and raised, where I attended high school, college, and graduate school, what my father did for a living, and when I first got interested in Israel. The second section, though entitled "First Visit to Israel in 1978," tries to explain what brought me back time and time again over a period of six years. The third section, entitled "Writing a Book on Israel," establishes me as a bona fide researcher and scholar. The story ends with a quotation that ties it back to the title of the piece. It reads:

Prof. Dominguez is beginning to become a little bit worried about maintaining her own objectivity. "I no longer relate to Israel as a tourist. I'm becoming a little bit Israeli. I get angry with some of the latest developments in the news and react to things with the intensity of a native," she said.

There were only four quotes in the two typewritten pages of the news release. After the hour-long interview I had granted, I was curious to see what had been selected to appear in my voice. Clearly the final sentences made sense in light of the focus of the piece at the opener. Interestingly, two of the quotes were things I said about my teaching. The fourth appeared at the end of the first section—a comment about my having developed my initial interest in Israel as a result of having lived in Arab countries as a young woman.

The quotes reminded me of a time sixteen years ago when I was quoted by name in the *Reader's Digest*—a Yale freshman the first year of coeducation—having apparently said to some reporter that we (the Yale women) wanted to be equal but not identical to the men. I remembered being embarrassed not so much by what I had said, but by the fact that it had appeared in the *Reader's Digest* and my peers were teasing me about it. Recently arrived in the United States after four years in Latin America, I had thought my remark perfectly sensible, common sense, even obvious. That it should appear in print at all was a surprise; that it was newsworthy, pithy, or "charming" enough to be picked up by the *Reader's Digest* from the *Saturday Review* was news to me; that in the eyes of my classmates it was the wrong thing to say was totally unexpected. I had participated in an open dialogue with a reporter, become a name and quote in his story, and as a name and quote had been "batted" around—an object—in a discourse of negotiation over the rightful place of women in American society.

The Hebrew University interviewer had been very nice, but her objective had explicitly been to write about me ultimately as propaganda for the Hebrew University. She had asked the questions. I chose and gave the answers. The structure of the dialogue was asymmetrical, but the asymmetry ensured a balance of power in the dialogue itself. I tried to extend that balance to the act of writing itself, by formally requesting to see the text of the news release before the actual release. But the balance I sought was fictive. I wondered how bad the text had to be in my eyes before I would seek ways to contest it.

The question, of course, was, What would make it a bad text in my eyes? I had agreed to be objectified when I agreed to grant the interview. The writer/storyteller, after all, was to tell a story about me. The article would necessarily be short and, thus, the facts used would be selective.

If the writer was any good, there would be a "story" in it. I figured I would be able to check the "facts" and correct any factual mistakes, but I figured as well that I had little chance of altering the story. The story was the storyteller's; it was not mine even though it was about me. The text would be bad in my eyes if it made a caricature of me—portraying me negatively and stressing only a handful of points with little or no mention of the total picture. I expected, however, to be little more than an object in the storyteller's discourse.

The writer/storyteller turned out to be doubly effective. In addition to avoiding any real factual errors, she presented her story in such a way that it really looked like my story. The text refers to "the story" and assigns the authorship directly to me. The second sentence read: "Virginia Dominguez, 33, a professor of socio-cultural anthropology at Duke University in North Carolina who is currently teaching at Hebrew University as a Fulbright Fellow, explains that the story is a rather long and complicated one." The objectification ironically sought to subjectify me. The storyteller sought to deny authorship.

But "the story" in my eyes used me rather than introduced me. The writer could have focused on my research, my impressions of the Hebrew University, my comments about anthropology, or the nature of the Fulbright program, in addition to delving deeper into my personal biography. The story was Israel–focused even though a small portion of my life has had anything to do with Israel. The story described me as having become part of Israeli society, even though institutionally and legally I have never been anything other than a visiting foreigner and subjectively I could not imagine myself living on a long-term basis in Israel. The story focused on the attraction to Israel. The tone is personal, even emotional. The first time my voice appears in the text, in fact, I am quoted as saying "Israel for me became not exactly a forbidden fruit, but something like it." The professional interest is downplayed. I recognized myself in the story but disavowed authorship.

The mutual and simultaneous denial of authorship seemed at once ludicrous and central. In the popular sense, the text, of course, had an author. But in both the narrower and the broader senses of language, authorship was in question.

The written text belongs to a genre of prose, the product of the emergence and development of a given profession. The genre reproduces itself —with rarely more than minor alterations—each time aspiring public relations apprentices and budding journalists study it, learn it, and copy it in order to become competent in their professions. The writing is goal oriented: to get information and to write it up for public consumption.

The writing is judged within the profession according to criteria of appropriateness typically emergent in the development of professional traditions. Some techniques are preferred, some are prescribed, some are to be avoided, and some are considered proscribed.

The news release, as the expression itself proclaims, is supposed to be a genre through which news is released—news, not opinion. "Objectivity" is demanded of the writer; creativity discouraged. Releasing news means transmitting facts. Thus the writer is ideally a helper, a facilitator, but not an author. Two good writers of this genre should ideally come out with very close to identical texts. The interview is seen as a means of data collection, and the text the writing up of the data. There is little reason to even identify the writers by name.

The world of prose has long known writing techniques that displace the sense of authorship. If Mikhail Bakhtin (1983) is right, writers employ certain "artistic-speech phenomena" in order to exert some control over objectification and displacement in their texts. I interpret that to mean that much of language, prose included, is referential—that it is about something whose existence it presupposes but whose ontology it may in fact be creating when it presents it as an object of speech. In its referential function, language presupposes the existence of objects. It also perpetuates their objectification in the continued reference to their existence, shape, form, and content.

Writers' and critics' experience, however, points to a consciousness on the part of most writers of the phenomenon of objectification, and to their grappling with ways to exert more control over the linguistic fact of objectification. Bakhtin, for example, notes that direct speech inserted into prose (such as a dialogue between characters in a novel or short story) serves at once to represent and to objectify discourse. "Such speech," he wrote, "is meant to be understood not only from the point of view of its own referential object, but is itself, as characteristic, typical, colorful discourse, a referential object toward which something is directed" (Bakhtin 1983:250).

Authorship is a conscious issue. A character utters a statement, but it appears in the context of the writer's "speech"—subordinate to the latter's needs. Bakhtin took it further. "The hero's discourse," he wrote, "is treated precisely as someone else's discourse, as discourse belonging to some specific characterological profile or type, that is, it is treated *as an object of authorial understanding,* and not from the point of view of its own referential intention" (ibid.; emphasis added). In contrast, the writer's direct, referentially oriented discourse "recognizes only itself and its object" (ibid., p. 250a). In Bakhtin's terms, the author's discourse—is treated stylistically as discourse directed toward its own straightforward referential meaning. It must be adequate to its object (cognitive, poetic, or whatever). It must be expressive, forceful, significant, elegant, etc. from the vantage point of the direct referential task it fulfills—to signify, express, inform, represent something. And its stylistic treatment is oriented purely toward an understanding of the referent. (Bakhtin 1983:250)

The careful placing of direct speech in a piece of prose, then, stylistically displaces control for the purpose of exerting control over linguistic objectification. The sudden appearance of a quotation in a text not only calls attention to the person whose voice is being quoted, but also calls attention to the fact that we had until then been hearing only *one* voice. The juxtaposition strengthens the image of the writer as little more than transmitter of news, thereby granting the writer more credibility as a reporter. But since both the direct, referentially oriented discourse and the direct speech in a text are of the writer's choosing, the juxtaposition enables the writer to author the text and to disclaim authorship simultaneously.

When the text, as in the case of the Hebrew University news release, is about someone rather than about a thing or an action, the dispute over authorship centers on the objectification of the self. The dispute is not about the reality of objectification. We know that objectification takes place almost unnoticed in natural discourse—that most grammars categorically differentiate doers from those done to, making the predication of subject and object effectively inescapable. And we know, of course, that reference to someone via linguistic signs—be it proper name, common noun, or pronoun—is semiotically an act of objectification, a pointing to *a* representation of the self (cf. Benveniste 1971; Eco 1976; Peirce 1955; Ricoeur 1974). The problem with the objectification of the self that leads to a contesting of authorship is neither its possibility nor its immanence but rather its control.

Grammars dictate neither the precise representations that dominate a story, nor the grammatical categories in which the self is represented. We know that in the form of proper name, common noun, or pronoun the self can be subject of a predicate as much as its object. And we know that only a set of all the possible representations of the self gets signified in any instance of language use. It is the exercise of choice of the mode of representing *me* that the dispute over the authorship of the news release is about.

Apparently, I wish more control over the objectification of my self. I accept the fact of the news release because I recognize the power asymmetry built into my relationship with the Hebrew University. I seek ways both in the interview and in the writing to exert some power over the written product. But the power asymmetry itself leads me in the end to reject the sense of authorship that the writer/storyteller attributes to me. I blame the resulting representation of me on the powerlessness of individuals vis-à-vis sociopolitical institutions.

The interviewer/writer denies any conscious attempt to control the representation of my self. She is just doing her job as competently as she can, using a genre she has learned by which she is judged competent and thus appropriate for her job. She interviews me before she "writes me up" in order to get facts and quotes. She is the writer, but she uses only material she gets from me; thus, in her eyes she creates nothing. She is not the author of my story.

Milton Singer (1980:492) has argued that it is possible semiotically to represent the self as a subject, but that "this is a more difficult problem than the semiotic representation of the self as an object." Umberto Eco has outright denied that the sign-creating subject can be included within semiotic representation—that empirical subjects are either among the possible referents of a message or text or, if presupposed by the statements, have to be read as an element of the conveyed content (Eco 1976:314–17). The problem is that at the gut level many of us still desire a more active role for ourselves as subjects of others' objectifications, and find it difficult to achieve that in the medium of language.

THE PUBLICNESS OF THE DIALOGUE

These issues affect us all, not just a handful of us. Specific senses of self and other do not emerge through individual experience alone, though we may come to feel that they do. And our desire to see ourselves as subjects—as individuals with control over our selves—may lead us to struggle feverishly to try to attain self-determination, or it might lead us to downplay the extent to which we are objectified by others.

But the fact is that objectification takes place all the time—because of language and in language, because of power struggles and in struggles for control. My own experience as a visitor to the Hebrew University is repeated time and time again. Dozens of visitors come to Israeli universities each year, and many have stories written about them. Interviews precede the issuing of most of those stories. Facts dot the pictures painted in these stories. Yet the explicit goal is not objectification at the expense of the interviewees; it is, rather, to enter and affect *public* discourse on behalf of each university. A semistructured dyadic dialogue is simply the means to obtain information with which to write stories for *public* consumption.

"The public" [*ha tzibur*] is a positivity of ordinary language. It is something to be tapped, to be polled, to be sampled. Above all, for the government and the media it is that ever present rather amorphous collective body "out there" which speaks in many voices and must always be taken into account. It matters little that referentially it is at once fuzzy and shifting. The underlying assumptions (1) that it exists and (2) that it is something to contend with make it a fact—in Michel Foucault's terms (cf. Foucault 1970) a positivity—of political and journalistic life in Israel regardless of the epistemological and methodological problem of determining its precise empirical referent. In fact, since government and the media see themselves as "serving the public," the objectification of "the public" is a precondition for their existence.

A sense of "the public" is implicit in acts of censorship. Acts of government censorship often evoke lively and heated debates, especially among those connected to or with access to the media. The highbrow newspaper *Ha'aretz* protests censorship by leaving blank the space on the paper in which the censored phrase, sentence, or article was meant to appear. A great deal of media "noise," likewise, accompanied the censorship in the fall of 1982 of a Hebrew-language play entitled *The Patriot*, which drew explicit parallels between certain Israeli actions and Nazi Germany. The periodic disclosure by the press of books officially banned from the West Bank by the Israeli military authorities is always followed by discussions of the nature and extent of Israel's security problem. The assumption is that censorship is valid, if not ideal, when disclosure would seriously threaten the security of the state. In times of open warfare, few quarrel with the need to grant the military censors complete discretionary power.

But censorship otherwise follows from an assessment of "the public's" sensibilities. *The Patriot* would offend the public. The mere suggestion of a similarity between Israeli Jews and German Nazis would tax the public's tolerance beyond its limits. It is not always the majority of the public whose reaction is taken into account. It is sufficient that it be a sector of the population with the ability to mobilize political power.

Anticipation of public reaction leads to nongovernmental acts of censorship as well. A draft of a paper I wrote in collaboration with a curator at the Israel Museum, for example, was censored by the chief curator and the director of the museum after months of internal debate in the fall of 1984, because in the words of the chief curator there is no reason "to wash one's dirty laundry in public." The paper had already been accepted for publication by a respected and reputable international journal in the human sciences. Aspects of the museum's approach to the mounting of what it regards as ethnic exhibitions had been called into question, and the museum was scheduled to celebrate the twentieth anniversary of its opening at about the same time the administrators feared the article would come out in print. They deemed it inadvisable to let the article enter the public discourse under those circumstances. Both my academic freedom and my freedom of speech were to be sacrificed because of their assessment of the sensitivities of "the public."

Similarly, one of the two reviewers of a paper attempting to estimate the incidence of induced abortion in Israel, used by an Israeli medical journal in the fall of 1980, recommended not publishing the paper for three reasons—the third of which was that "this paper might reflect on the standards of medical services given in Israel nowadays."[1] That the point was a touchy one was evident in the rejection letter sent to the author of the paper. Its second paragraph read: "For your interest, I enclose extracts from the comments sent by two reviewers. I would like to stress that the alleged reflection on standards of practice mentioned by Reviewer II played no part in our decision not to accept the paper." More recently, in 1984, a paper by a different social scientist dealing with the gynecology department at Hadassah Hospital in Jerusalem was accepted for publication in an Israeli, Hebrew-language social service journal *on the condition* that she change a few items that would otherwise reflect poorly on the profession of medicine in Israel.

The act of writing for public consumption thus engages the writer in a mental negotiation with his or her sense of the public. But when the interviewee seeks as I do to exercise some control over the process of objectification itself, the speaker, too, negotiates mentally with his or her sense of the public. The interview/dialogue between two people will contain all the elements of exchange, power play, management, and privatization of meaning that a transactional approach would point out (cf. Paine 1976; Cohen and Comaroff 1976). But the goals of the dialogue— to contribute to a public discourse—strip it of any real sense of privacy.

I ask myself, for example, to what extent I let my experientially derived interpretation of what Israelis like to hear from visitors about their experience of Israel shape my answers to the interviewer's questions. She had asked at the outset of the interview how it was that I had come to Israel, but I was, after all, the one who volunteered the fact that I was not Jewish. I had explained that I had long been interested in ethnicity; she was the one who had perked up upon hearing that and pursued questions about what I thought of ethnicity in Israel. *I* chose not to mention the museum paper at all to the Hebrew University interviewer. I figured she would not print an ugly story in a news release that was to be sent mostly abroad for publicity. And when she asked how Israeli students compared, in my opinion, with students at Duke, I had been the one to preface the re-

1. The colleague whose experiences these were asked to remain anonymous.

sponse with a carefully worded statement about how she might not want to write up what I had to say, since I have some serious reservations about aspects of the Israeli educational system whose effects are evident even in my otherwise bright, affable, and eager students.[2] I clearly had a sense

2. This is neither the time nor the place to review or critique the Israeli educational system. Mine are observations based on (1) teaching a self-selected group of undergraduate and graduate students at the Hebrew University in 1984–85, (2) many discussions with a variety of Israeli and non-Israeli colleagues who teach or have taught at universities, teacher-training institutes, vocational training institutes at the secondary and postsecondary level, and high schools, (3) closely watching the children of my friends and colleagues go through the system at least in the 1980s, and (4) some exposure to the research and analysis of academics like Chaim Adler and Reuven Kahane (sociologists of education at the Hebrew University) and David Harman (for years head of the research division at the Jerusalem headquarters of the Joint Distribution Committee) who have devoted years to improving the system, not just researching it.

I would be the last person to say that the U.S. educational system is flawless. Indeed it is so problematic in what it delivers to many kids, especially those in underprivileged communities to start with, that it would be silly to suggest that it as a whole is better than the Israeli educational system. Both, in fact, have much higher school dropout rates than either country wants; both have disproportionately small percentages of nonelite, "marked" (minority and underprivileged "ethnic") students at the postsecondary level. Both, too, have people who really care about improving the system, coming up with better, often experimental, ideas for education, and implementing reforms. In Israel, at least, I think the most creative, innovative, and effective teaching/learning takes place in programs and centers that cater to those (adults or adolescents) not expected to go through the linearly structured process of acquiring a "mainstream," normative education in Israeli schools and universities. I remain very impressed with the *ulpan* system for teaching Hebrew to immigrants and other non-native speakers, though I am often reminded that it does not usually work as well with others as it did for me (cf. Katz 1982). I am impressed with the U.S.-based National Council of Jewish Women's efforts, openness, and willingness to fund experimental programs in education and with their Israeli collaborators' enthusiasm, hard work, and imagination (e.g., Sharlin 1986). Education has long been a real concern of Israeli social scientists, even among those whose theoretical, internationally known scholarship might not on the surface reveal it (see, for example, Handelman, Sprinzak, and Basker 1981; Shamgar-Handelman and Handelman 1986; Azarya 1983; Goldberg 1984). *Megamot*, the main Israeli social science journal, in fact, started out in 1949 as the *Child Welfare Research Quarterly*, and continues to be published by the Henrietta Szold Institute/National Institute for Research in the Behavioral Sciences with long-standing, even primary, interest in education broadly defined.

But I experienced my own frustration as well as the frustrations of my Hebrew University students, nonetheless. Accustomed to being lectured at, told "facts," and how to think about them and apply them, my students were lost for months in my classes where I stress thinking on one's own much more than learning canonized facts. It was clear to me that I had among the best and the brightest in these courses. They had self-selected themselves, partly because of the perceived heavy reading in my courses and partly, I think, because periodically I'd need to lapse into English, Spanish, or French to clarify points in class. And yet they were unaccustomed to thinking on their own, taking intellectual risks, carefully but firmly critiquing their elders in papers. It became clear to me that the content of what

that some things would interest her and her superiors, that some would drop like seeds on barren land, and that others would be deemed inappropriate for publication. On the last point, she immediately agreed. We both had a sense of a discourse "out there," whose exact shape and boundaries escaped us but at least some of whose sensitivities we thought we knew.

Much harder to sense, however, is the form and extent of the penetration by that discourse of objectification we see "out there" into our own representation of ourselves presumably to ourselves. Dutch anthropologist VanTeeffelen (1977:53) wrote that "Israeli anthropology implicitly expresses concerns similar to post-statehood Zionism." Using analytic concepts derived from Gouldner (1975) and White (1973) to examine sociological and historical texts, respectively, VanTeeffelen argued that basic assumptions provided by Zionism enter into the very dynamics of fieldwork and frame the stories then told by the anthropologist. He went on "to account both for the kind of plot that structures many Israeli monographs and for the actors' style in playing their parts" (Gerholm and Hannerz 1982:18). Gerholm and Hannerz put VanTeeffelen's work in perspective by noting that he found basically the same relation between Israeli Arab anthropology and Palestinian nationalism as between Israeli Jewish anthropology and Zionism. Israeli anthropologists, however, with few exceptions, do not have many kind things to say about VanTeeffelen's work. Almost without exception the charge is that he misrepresented the vast majority of the anthropologists whose work he examined, and that his overall conclusion was derived not from his encounter with his "data," but rather from the ideological baggage with which he entered the scene. The critique is made—again almost without exception—with great emotional investment. For anthropologists who deem it crucial to maintain a certain necessary distance from their field and their informants, to accept VanTeeffelen's claim would be to admit a large measure of individual and collective failure. Most Israeli anthropologists, like their counterparts in the United States, see themselves as liberals, progressives, frequent critics of government policies. VanTeeffelen makes them sound like collaborators of Israeli government policies when they often see themselves as critics.

The problem is both analytic and emotional. The notion of a public

---

gets taught in most Israeli schools (with the exception of some kibbutz schools and some semiprivate schools such as Pelech in Jerusalem) is encyclopedic in intent and presentation. The implicit message and structuring principle seems to me to be an idea of education as the imparting of *information* deemed by those in power to be necessary for a person to have in order to make proper and useful contributions to adult society. How much room can there be for innovation and creativity in any field if students are taught to have so much respect for "a canon" that it is hard for them to imagine that their own thinking could be valuable and useful?

discourse presupposes people talking and writing beyond a single person's control—a fact nobody disputes—but in addition it presupposes (1) the existence of patterns of objectification that are not idiosyncratic, and (2) the dual functioning of all individuals as selves and as others in that discourse. The former without the latter would not necessarily implicate the anthropologist. But the point of the latter is that neither the journalist, the politician, nor the academic is exempt. Each one is, to every other, part of the public that engages in the process of objectification and, to himself or herself, a subject in constant negotiation with the public over his or her own objectification. The implication of the former, thus, becomes that the writer/analyst's texts are largely constructed by patterns of objectification in public discourse itself and that they contribute to the ongoing popular discourse in the same measure that they draw from it. Foucault (1970:364) put it succinctly when he wrote that "the human sciences, when dealing with what is representation (in either conscious or unconscious form), find themselves treating as their object what is in fact their condition of possibility."

AN ACADEMIC ISSUE?

Consider the academic problem of how to go about studying Israel. What is the "object" of study?

Few of us would ever attempt to write a book about an entire country, its social, economic, and political structures and mechanisms, its processes and histories, its public and private events, the daily lives of its people, their aspirations, frustrations, and interpretations. It sounds exhausting just to think about it, and many would consider it simply too mammoth a task. Yet over the years, for professional as well as, I think, personal reasons, Israeli academia has been confronted time and time again with the question of whether and how to do just that. Scope and coverage have been definite issues, but so has the question of how to conceptualize the object of study.[3]

3. Most notable among those who have aimed valiantly for encyclopedic coverage is S. N. Eisenstadt (1954, 1967, 1985). His 1967 book, boldly called *Israeli Society*, was clearly the most ambitious and most assertive, and his most recent, *The Transformation of Israeli Society*, which seeks to update his earlier representation, aims to be equally comprehensive. Yet even in Eisenstadt there is a sense of doubt about having mastered the representation of the object. There is, in the very fact of the 1985 publication, a strong hint that Eisenstadt himself perceived there to be an unfinished quality to the 1967 work or at least to its object of study, Israeli society.

Most Israeli social scientists, in fact, stay away from holism or the claim to encyclopedic coverage. Emanuel Marx's *A Composite Portrait of Israel* (1980) is both a critique of, and an alternative to, the kind of sociological/anthropological holism that might lead a

In 1977, in an introduction to a special journal issue on culture and ethnicity in Israeli society, Israeli anthropologist Harvey Goldberg wrote:

The circumscription of ethnicity, as an *object of study* to its narrowest socio-logical meaning, was not an outcome of the fortuitous interests of sociological

---

scholar to presume that his or her work were comprehensive of a "national whole" (cf. e.g., Handler 1985). It is also, however, a critique of the opposite extreme—what Marx notes as a tendency (especially among anthropologists) to study only sections of a population in a nation-state, and never even attempt to portray the ways in which they index the existence of a working national economy, national polity, or national society.

Studies in Israeli Society, a publication series of the Israel Sociological Society, exemplifies the more typical social science approach to Israel within Israeli academia. Volumes 1 (*Migration, Ethnicity, and Community*), 2 (*The Sociology of the Kibbutz*), and 3 (*Politics and Society in Israel*) reflect Israeli social scientists' view of what they do in and on Israel and what the issues of importance are in their eyes. In them are articles written by a wide variety of Israeli-based academics on related topics, and "comprehensive bibliographies" (words taken from the book jackets) on these three major themes. Their self-representations shed light on the topics most often investigated in and on Israel, but also reveal an unwillingness on the part of most of the contributors to claim encyclopedic intent or knowledge. All three volumes identify the goal of the publication series as the wish to identify and clarify the major themes that occupy social science research in Israel today and publish previously scattered articles in an integrative form.

Accordingly, what gets included in these volumes is revealing. Volume 1 goes on to state that it focuses "on the themes of migration, ethnicity, and community, seeking out the dynamics of conflict and integration in a new society. Topics include such relevant contemporary issues as 'migration and remigration,' 'patterns of ethnic residence,' 'ethnic factions and inequalities,' and 'ethnicity and the labor force.'" It argues that earlier Israeli social science writings dealt with the absorption or assimilation of immigrants, that they were more concerned with various processes "'internal to these [ethnic] collectivities'—the division of labor, class struggle, and the like, or with the processes of change from one type of collectivity to another," but that today the focus is "on cultural ethnicity or cultural pluralism and ethnic social stratification," on explaining "the resurgence of ethnic consciousness and the militancy that accompanies it."

Volume 2 focuses on debates and analyses concerning the nature, changes, and internal politics of kibbutzim and, in the process, identifies the kibbutz as a second major focus of sociological, psychological, and anthropological scrutiny in Israel, even though only about 3–4 percent of the Israeli population actually lives on kibbutzim. Volume 3 is described as "representing a sociological view of political life in Israel that demonstrates the links with other institutional facets of Israeli society, such as the class and ethnic factors at work, the ideological and religious dimensions in politics, and the military variable." It goes on to specify that the volume "clarifies the important processes of change that have occurred in Israeli political life in the last decade, marked by the 'political upheaval' (*mahapakh*) of 1977, the Begin era, and the break in the national consensus since the 1982 war in Lebanon."

More directed than all but the few special issues of the major Israeli social science journals—foremost among them *Megamot*—these three volumes take a middle ground in the discussion of the value, or even possibility, of a totalizing, holistic approach to the study of Israel. Complexities of Israel keeps these scholars from attempting a more holistic depiction of Israeli society, yet few, if any, would argue that Israeli society is just fiction.

investigators, but a *self-conscious research strategy*. Israeli sociologists, in the early 1950's, no less than economists and planners, were faced with the challenge of comprehending the diversity of cultural and social forms in the mass immigration which more than doubled the Jewish population of the country in less than four years. (Goldberg 1977:168; emphasis added)

An internal debate, Goldberg writes, followed the adoption of this research strategy and resulted in the dominance of a particular sociological orientation that he associates with Joseph Ben-David (1953), S. N. Eisenstadt (1953), and Rivka Bar-Yosef (1968). The poles of the debate were (1) "to view Israeli society as built up of a number of different ethnic groups—or to use extreme imagery—'tribes'—each of which is both a social and cultural universe in its own right" (Goldberg 1977:168), and (2) to view Israeli society as "a dominant nucleus of a European based culture (the *Yishuv*) and each of the incoming groups [as] bent on shedding its cultural heritage while participating and gaining acceptance in the sociocultural life of the society's center" (ibid., p. 169).

For a decade and a half, Goldberg writes, the latter view predominated. Critical of its slighting of culture, he notes that it

is largely a version of culture-and-personality theory (Ben-David 1953—reprinted in Eisenstadt et al., 1970), then very prominent in American anthropology . . . [but] since . . . superceded by more refined understandings of the interrelationship of social processes and cultural forms, together with the development of conceptual tools, for the study of cultural systems, such as structuralism, semiotic analysis and other symbolic approaches. (Goldberg 1977: 170–71)

For Goldberg in 1977, the debate was a sociological one, being part of the discourse of sociology and having competing models of analysis derived from competing sociological theories imported from abroad.

Goldberg's exegesis was part of a genre making its way into the academic literature by the late seventies. At times invited by international journals published outside Israel and at times at their own initiative, a number of Israeli anthropologists and sociologists produced texts reviewing the state of the art of one or the other field in Israel (cf. Bernstein 1980; Cohen 1977; Eisenstadt 1984a; Goldberg 1976, 1977; Handelman and Deshen 1975; E. Marx 1975; Matras 1982; Smooha 1984). Most described, compared, and evaluated approaches to particular objects of study without inquiring into the sources of objectification.

Judah Matras departs a bit from the pattern by devoting two out of forty-eight pages of text to the intellectual effect on Israeli sociology of having "developed as part and parcel of the Zionist enterprise" (1982:8).

He is both specific and general. Unlike those in Goldberg's portrayal, his sociologists seem to be citizens first, sociologists second. "It is probably fair to assert," he wrote,

> that Israeli sociologists—perhaps as most other academics—accepted and assumed at face value that the primary political objectives of the organized Jewish community in Palestine and Israel must be a) safety and survival in hostile surroundings; b) survival and rescue of threatened Jews outside Palestine and Israel, and immigration and absorption of immigrants; c) assuring material sustenance and its acceptable distribution; and d) equality and social justice. . . .
>
> For the most part, the undeveloped social vision of Israeli society and the absence of a well-developed corpus of socio-political tenets and traditions have been a "given" for Israeli sociology. Nor has Israeli sociology, whether in research activity or in teaching, been at the forefront of identification, examination, or illumination of unresolved dilemmas in the design of Israeli society, much less taken on the task of pointing to the implications of their resolution one way or another. (Matras 1982:8–9)

But Matras (1982:1) still talks about "the major issues confronting Israeli Jewish society . . . [and] the manner in which Israeli sociology has addressed" them. The sociologist remains in large measure an analyst of issues or objects she or he identifies as existing in the society.

A long-standing vision of Israel as an ideologically constituted and motivated society (cf. Domínguez 1984) has both blinded Israeli sociology/anthropology and paved the way out of its self-made trap.[4] So strong has been the harping on the striving for objectivity that would free social science from charges of ideological bias that the acknowledgment of subjective biases on the part of each researcher has been very late in acquiring legitimacy. As late as 1980, Deborah Bernstein's critique

4. Much about the history of Israel has been seen in terms of social and political movements, their beliefs and plans. Ideology in this context usually means an "ism," with an articulated vision of how society is and should be. These are *objectifications* of what someone like Clifford Geertz (1973) might see as ideologies, not references to loosely interrelated sets of beliefs and values. Robert Paine (1985) grasps this vividly in the subtitle to the draft of his book on religion, redemption, and nationalism in Israel. It reads, "the place of eschatology in Public Ideology in Israel," and beneath it, on the cover page, Paine quotes David Ben Gurion, Israel's first Prime Minister, saying ". . . where there is no vision the people perish."

It is true that in the case of Israel most of those "isms" come out of Eastern and Central Europe along with the majority of Jews in prestate Palestine (the *Yishuv*), and it therefore makes sense that they should perceive objectified ideologies to be actually constitutive of a society. It is only surprising to me when I think about how internally contradictory it feels to so empower objectified ideologies—including socialist ones—in one's description of a society that material, productive, social, and political relations end up sounding as if *they* were the derivative ones.

of Israeli sociology—published in England—met with stiff resistance in Israel although, unlike Van Teeffelen, she herself is Israeli.

Ironically, on the surface, Bernstein's critique hinges on objectifying ideology much like Eisenstadt. She argues quite explicitly that the dominant "school of Israeli sociology provides a prime example of the affinity between the dominant state ideology and a functionalist analysis. They share basic assumptions, make similar claims and ignore similar conflicts and contradictions" (Bernstein 1980:262). She concentrates on five examples:

1. The state leadership, she argues, "presents the pre-state period, in which it achieved power at a time of glorious pioneering, a period of total sacrifice and dedication to the collective. The sociologists follow suit by regarding it as a period in which 'Ideological values' guided all forms of action" (ibid. p. 262).

2. The same leadership pushed the new immigrants to accept the leadership which brought about the country's achievements and to adopt its culture. "The sociologists," she writes, "repeat this demand, using sociological terms such as the learning of new roles and the internalization of new identities" (ibid., p. 263).

3. The politicians and bureaucrats charged with the integration of immigrants, she argues, "treated the immigrants as pre-citizens, as passive dependents, at times as children to be guided, with no independent will or responsibility. The sociologists shared the view that such should be the nature of 'absorption' by introducing the terms 'desocialization' and 'resocialization,' and thus giving their 'scientific' acceptance to the process of infantilization and dependence" (ibid.).

4. The country's official leaders sold an image of a state able and willing to transcend all potential internal cleavages and stressing the equality of all its citizens. Bernstein believes sociologists supported that image "by taking the 'social system' as their unit of study" (ibid.).

5. The "ruling group" claimed that progress and achievement "far surpassed the problems which still remained to be solved. The sociologists end up by implicitly conveying the same message . . . by eliminating from their analysis the dimension of struggle over alternative ways" (ibid.).

In sum, she accuses Eisenstadt and his followers of being ideologically tainted, if not downright ideologically motivated. In doing so, she has, of course, objectified ideology herself and presented a case for how it functions to perpetuate the existing system of power and inequality. Her analysis of *their* objectification of ideology and *their* tendency toward functionalist explanation is itself based on an objectification of ideology and an apparent tendency toward functionalist explanation.

But, clearly, an obsession with ideology as the object of study may,

as in this case, prove beneficial in unexpected ways. It can facilitate recognition of how ideology, too, can serve as a tool for analysis, and in
so doing, enable us to begin to see how a discourse of objectification we
see "out there" penetrates our own—our own representation of ourselves
(presumably to ourselves).

If Bernstein's critique is one example, so, too, are Eisenstadt's most
recent contributions to the study of ethnicity in Israel. On February 11,
1982, at one of the three major scheduled talks of the annual meeting of
the Israel Sociological Association, Eisenstadt surprised most of the audience—including his two official discussants—by proclaiming the central
question in the study of "the ethnic thing" in Israel to be its "ideologization" [ideologizatzia]. Emanuel Marx, the first of the two discussants
—looking somewhat taken aback—acknowledged the change in Eisenstadt's conceptualization at the very opening of his remarks (recorded in
my tape transcription and field notes). He said simply:

When I prepared myself to make this appearance, I thought . . . I would be
between two contemporary biggies on the subject [Eisenstadt and Yochanan
Peres, the second discussant], and that the two of them would pressure me,
and I thought that I would react to this pressure by being very aggressive. But I
have been freed from that because something happened to "Rabbi" Shmuel: he
changed his analysis. . . . Actually I find that what I have to say now to a certain
extent follows [in the spirit of] what he has said.

Eisenstadt's "new" position was confirmed in writing in his contribution to a booklet on "new directions in the study of ethnic problems"
(Eisenstadt 1984a). "Were Israeli citizens to be asked to point to central
problems in Israeli society," he announced, "there is no doubt that the
question of ethnic relations would be stressed as main and central" (Eisenstadt 1984a:5). The question, Eisenstadt asked, was how and why the
public—social researchers included—came to perceive ethnicity in Israel
as central and problematic. In 1984, his answer time and time again was
that ethnicity was (1) turned into a problem, (2) in Israel, (3) by the
"center" of power rather than by those who emerged as ethnic. And sociologists and anthropologists as part of the "center" both played into it and
contributed to it. After all, he pointed out in his February 1982 talk, some
90 percent of the research projects done in Israel use the bureaucratic split
between people from "Asia-Africa" and people from "Europe-America"
freely in their research, and "a great deal of the problem has been created by the explanations." The tone differs from Bernstein's but the call
for individual and collective introspection and self-criticism is much the
same.

The problem is that such introspection can only go part way. We can neither talk nor write about "the world" without objectifying, and we may even be incapable of thinking about the world without objectifying. The point, however, is not that we should avoid objectifying but, rather, that we should strive to understand *that* we objectify, what we take for granted as a result of objectifying, how we participate in more general discourses of objectification, and that our patterns of objectification have practical, social, and political consequences.

CONSTITUTING THE OBJECT

What is, or should be, the object of study when we study "Israel"? Some will argue that it must be Zionism, for it is responsible, in very immediate ways, for the establishment of a Jewish state on the eastern shores of the Mediterranean. Others will argue that it must be Judaism, for without it there would never have been Jews to begin with and, therefore, no Israel. Or, perhaps, that it must be socialism, since it provided the early pioneers with a vision of the Jewish state, its structures and infrastructures.

Those who work on inequalities, stratification, or ethnic differentiation in Israel walk a difficult line. Theirs is work whose objects come from a generalized public discourse, but whose scholarly nature can easily be seen as validating, if not necessarily the worth of those objectifications, at least their existence. What under those circumstances is participation, and what is analysis, or at least observation?

A younger generation of scholars—Israeli and Diaspora Jewish alike —exemplifies this dilemma with special poignancy. Trained in the 1970s and 1980s, they are conversant with Fredrik Barth's (1969) thesis that ethnic groups may primarily be organizations for the management of resources, and that folklore, symbols, and rituals are, at least in part, sociopolitical in function. They may, as in the case of Goldstein (e.g., 1985), Lewis (e.g., 1985), Avruch (1979), and Oppenheimer (e.g., 1977, 1978, 1980), deliberately and consciously write about the role of macropolitical forces in Israel in *constituting* much of the ethnic character of the "group" each has studied. Goldstein writes about "the constituting process of ethnicity"; Lewis coined the phrase "phantom ethnicity"; and Avruch points to it in his concept of "traditionalizing immigrants." They may also, as in the case of Jeff Halper, Shalva Weil, or Shifra Epstein, choose to enter the policy-making arena on behalf of specific "ethnic groups" they believe are, or have been, discriminated against by agencies or institutions of the state.

And yet, almost without exception, they still do their work by focusing on one specific "ethnic" group (or, in a few cases, two over a period of time). Goldstein herself works on Persians/Iranians (1985), Avruch on Americans in Israel (1981), Oppenheimer on the Druze (1977, 1980), Yael Katzir (1976) and Lisa Gilad (1982, 1983) on Yemenites, Yoram Bilu (1987) and Rahel Wasserfall (1987) on Moroccans, Jeff Halper on Kurdish Jews (1976) and more recently on and with Ethiopians, and Shalva Weil on Indian Jews (primarily Bene Israel) (1977a, b, c, 1981) and through her recent jobs on Ethiopians. The same is true of most master's level students in anthropology in Israel. They are, on the one hand, much more aware of the constituting process of ethnicity than was the older generation at the time of researching and writing, but they remain, on the other hand, very much rooted in the constituted vision of Israeli society which regards these groups as given rather than constituted. The dilemma is that, despite a certain amount of intellectual questioning of primordialism or essentialism, they, too, contribute to a constituted vision of Israeli society that has long served the interests of the already dominant sectors of society, when they pursue their studies taking these "ethnic groups" as their units of observation, analysis, and representation.

Throughout the years of working in Israel, I have come to realize just how true some of the things we teach in introductory anthropology courses are—that people around the world really can and do perceive things very differently, including those things we never thought to question, and that short-term research using questionnaires and structured interview schedules can only rarely get at these differences because their own objectifications put a stranglehold on the ability of insiders to guide the researcher to and through their perceptions of society. I have also, however, come to appreciate the fact that obtaining the insiders' objectifications through long-term fieldwork still leaves a researcher with a problem in representation—what to do with the insiders' objectifications? How stable and widely shared are they? And how to represent them?

For my Israeli colleagues, it is a matter of how to deal with the objectifications of *their* informants from one or another sector of the Israeli population. For the outsider, like me, it is a matter of deciding how to relate to a more general public discourse as well as to more specific ones. The challenge becomes how to demonstrate the centrality of the phenomenon of objectification without falling prey to any one of its variant objectifications; how to deconstruct each objectification by focusing on the process rather than a crystallized form; how to assume collectivity while calling it into question.

The pitfalls are many. It is easy to fall unwittingly for the traditional anthropological presumption of objectivity. In 1985, for example, I found myself writing as I first conceptualized this book, that I had "discovered

the problem of the Israeli collective self," that I had cracked *the* code to
"Israeli society." I found myself reacting defensively, perhaps even arro-
gantly, to suggestions by Israeli colleagues that my view of Israel was
interesting but that it felt foreign—not Judaic enough, or not historical
enough, or not experiential enough.

I felt they wanted me to write as an insider, to write what I took to be
the kind of book an insider might write about his or her society—full of
wonderfully rich details on the trees but little way of seeing how different
this "forest" may or may not be from others. I wanted to maintain the
prerogatives of the outsider looking in. I wanted to hold on to the greater
freedom I saw in the role of observer over that of participant. I envisioned
myself as an outsider looking in, aware that I was viewing "them" through
some perceptual grid that was not theirs, but optimistic that the long-term
field experience would allow me to discover how "they" perceived the
world. Thus, I thought, I would be freed from the shackles of only having
one way to view the society. I pictured the insider's struggle with the objectifications in his or her society to be far more valiant but also far more
difficult. I wanted to retain the authoritative voice of the Western ethnographer. I came from years of exploring the strengths and weaknesses of
Barth's claims (cf. Domínguez 1977, 1986a), and saw myself now as harping on Barth's weaknesses—that there is little systematicity or structure
in his scheme, certainly little sense of there being a *system* of classification
that affects the freedoms and constraints specific groups have. I felt I did
not want to mute that critique just because my "informants" tended to
think otherwise.

In all of this struggle to find the right balance, I realized, of course,
that what I do is very much like what Israelis do themselves to themselves
and each other. I have participated in dialogues, used and been used by
their discourses on self and others, sought to retain some control over my
perception of myself and others, reacted to perceptions that went against
my values, and spent a great deal of time struggling to understand how to
deal with "Israeli society." In the process, I picked up some of their terms
and concepts, I assume I ignored others, and certainly changed much of
what I used to think about personal and collective social identities. The
result is that I want to argue strongly that we need to call attention to the
nature of the process more than to claim the absolute correctness of the
picture we may end up painting. That picture will in all likelihood reso-
nate with what many, if not all, of our "informants" feel and think, but
understanding what it is that they and we are doing in creating those pictures—those representations and objects—is ultimately of longer-lasting
value.

My concern in this book, then, is methodological as well as substantive. I am concerned with revealing public discourse to be the mechanism of collective objectification and individual grappling with reflexivity. I will try to show that its substance consists of the objects of that discourse itself, and that the struggle between circles and sectors of the society evident in that discourse—to crystallize certain objectifications and do away with others—lies at the heart of the assumption of peoplehood.

The chapters of this book, accordingly, highlight elements in this portrayal of the semiotic paradoxes of peoplehood in Israel; they do not exhaust them. I have chosen them because of the richness of what their analyses have to offer, not because they are the only sources of illustration of the processes of objectification of an Israeli collective self. Chapter 2 explores the ritual signification of that collective self by examining issues surrounding the marking of Israeli Independence Day. Chapter 3 examines Barth's boundary problem but from a semiotic perspective. The focus here is the influx of Ethiopians who identify themselves as Jews, and what more veteran Israelis' reactions to that influx indicates about their sense of collectivity. Chapter 4 takes the analysis more deeply into language. "Culture" becomes the object of discourse, the carrier of assumptions and the arena in which domination takes place. In chapter 5 we see some of the consequences of the struggle over culture—a search for mechanisms to claim semiotic self-determination and the constraints on those mechanisms. Chapter 6 takes the struggles and uncertainties over ritual, personnel, language, and custom, and situates them in a macropolitical arena in which others, though constructed as such by a self, define and shape the existence of the collective self. Who and what are and have been Israeli society's significant others, how has their otherness been constituted, and what does their otherness signify about the selfhood of Israeli society?

2 On Ritual and Uncertainty

THE thing about rituals we notice the most is that we notice them. They stand out for us. They look different from other actions, out of the ordinary, special. We see them as marked, separate from all those other behaviors and actions that we do not see as worthy of special notice although they may have many of the structural characteristics of the ones we notice as rituals.[1] But in marking them we also spotlight them. They seem in need of explanation, in search of meaning.

1. Noticing and not noticing, I submit, are not accidental. I am reminded of two sets of analytic concepts, from different areas of scholarship, that suggest as much—the now widely used linguistic distinction between marked and unmarked terms or categories and Pierre Bourdieu's identification of, and differentiation among, doxa, orthodoxy, and heterodoxy (Bourdieu 1977). In the former, the terms or categories we refer to as unmarked depict what insiders see as the rule, the norm—whose posited characteristics are not noteworthy. We refer to others as *marked* terms or categories because the way they are used, or referred to, in speech indicates that they are noticed because in some presumably important way they depart from general popular expectations. An example I use in teaching at Duke is that of Duke's basketball teams. The men's team is almost never referred to as Duke men's basketball. *Duke basketball* suffices to indicate the men's team. The women's team is almost never referred to simply as Duke basketball. It is nearly always the *Duke women* or *women's basketball*. The unmarked phrase signifies male players. Duke women playing varsity basketball must then be the marked category, requiring the terminological marker *women* in nearly all references to them.

Bourdieu's differentiation among doxa, orthodoxy, and heterodoxy gets at the paradoxical nature of orthodoxy—that calling oneself or a position orthodox implies the existence of a counterview and of people holding the counterview. Thus, there can be no orthodoxy without heterodoxy, and the terms orthodox and heterodox then signify lack of consensus, i.e., the presence of ideological disputes and contestation. Thus, the orthodox position cannot be what the orthodox believe it to be—that which existed prior to the emergence of dissidence. Both the orthodox and the heterodox positions are interpretations of the past, the present, and the future, taking place in the midst of a recognized ideological,

42

As I approached the analytic problem I posed about the nature of Israeli society, the very concept of peoplehood, and the relationship between the two, I found myself looking for rituals by which they might be signified. It seemed important to be able to point to ritual signifiers of what I posited as problematic semiotic "objects"—to be able to show "concrete" examples of Israelis themselves marking the specialness, significance, and objectification of a broadly encompassing collective self. I wanted confirmation that I was not imagining the positing in Israel of the existence of a significant collective self.

So I picked Israeli Independence Day (Yom HaAtzma'ut) as a marked day I hypothesized would be full of ritual signification. It stood out for me. It attracted me because I saw it as different, out of the ordinary in two senses: (1) it was a named day of annual significance not seen as an ordinary day,[2] and (2) it appeared to be a secularly marked day, not one of many avowedly religious holidays that fill the Jewish calendar. I also assumed I knew its purpose, its primary signification or meaning.

Then I began to look into it. Suddenly I felt like a traditional eth-

---

social, and/or political struggle. Both then are highly noteworthy. What is not easily noted, according to Bourdieu, is that which precedes the rise of a political/ideological split in a community, and *this* he calls doxa.

Note that I am not restricting the notion of ritual to the world of religion. Nor am I comfortable describing them as sacred and simply explaining that it need not be a reference to any formally recognized religious system. I think that even in this expansion of the notion of the sacred, there is a great deal of meaningful baggage that evokes religiosity and restricts our analytic imagination in attempting to understand nonreligious rituals. Robert Bellah's work on "civic religion" has been provocative and, thus, useful (e.g., Bellah and Hammond 1980), but does religion really provide the best terms in which to understand communal, regional, and national civic actions? Liebman and Don-Yehiya's (1983a, b) recent work, adopting Bellah's notion of "civic religion" and applying it to Israel, thus, invites the same critical query.

I believe *marked* or *special* are better terms than *sacred*. They do not index any particular domain of life and yet they allow for a distinction to be drawn between habits, or even customs, and those actions we see as rituals. I credit Edmund Leach (1954) with expanding the notion of ritual beyond the idiom of the sacred, though in my view he deprived the concept of some analytic power by making it hard to see how habit and custom may still be different from ritual.

2. I use the phrase *ordinary day* without necessarily invoking religious notions of ordinary and nonordinary (special, religious, holy, or sacred) days. Any day can be marked as special in any context so long as its specialness is identified and noted. But in the Israeli context it is hard for me (and I presume, therefore, for Israelis reading this) not to "hear" reference to the religious concept of ordinary day in Judaism. *Ordinary day* is lexicalized in Judaism as a *Yom Khol,* to be distinguished from the Sabbath and a host of other marked days—festive and nonfestive—in the Hebrew calendar. I considered not using the term *ordinary day* to avoid confusion, but it seems to me that it captures the very problematic nature of the concepts of secular (*khiloni*) and religious (*dati*) in Israeli life and, thus, warrants inclusion.

nographer studying rituals. I asked for insider exegeses and jotted them down. Then I struggled to decide how to handle the fact that I saw things in that ritual that my insiders for the most part did not. I contemplated the possibility that I was like Dan Sperber (1975) among the Dorze in Ethiopia. He became obsessed with the fact that they would periodically put slabs of butter on their heads and assumed it was his job to find its symbolic meaning. They, the Dorze, almost always answered his questions by saying that they did what they did because they had always done so. Sperber found their actions out of the ordinary; the Dorze did not. Was Israeli Independence Day unproblematic because most Israelis fail to spend much time contemplating it?

I think not. The thing about objects (as opposed to rituals) is that we do not usually notice them. We assume they are what we take them to be and even forget that they have not always been seen that way. I came to the conclusion that Israeli Independence Day was a good example—of what makes something a ritual and for whom,[3] of what makes something an object and for whom, of the assumption of meaning and for whom that assumption is important, and of the construction of meaning and for whom that construction is important.

THE CRITERION OF ENJOYMENT

In 1972, the Israeli Government Information Office commissioned a study to help in the planning of the twenty-fifth anniversary celebration of Yom HaAtzma'ut (Israeli Independence Day). The Israel Institute of Applied Social Research obliged by sampling 1,892 adult Jewish residents in the four major urban areas—Tel Aviv, Jerusalem, Haifa, and Beer Sheva. Questions probed both attitudes toward and participation in the celebration of Yom HaAtzma'ut. Charles Kamen (1977:19), then on the staff of the Israel Institute of Applied Social Research, reported five years later that one of the explicit reasons for commissioning the study was "the fear that people were not enjoying the holiday."

The wording of the questions was explicit. Toward the beginning of the questionnaire, interviewees were asked, "In general, how much did you enjoy what you did on Independence Eve this year?" Later on, following a question about what they specifically did on Independence Eve that year, they were asked, "How much did you enjoy your participation in this activity this year?" And this was followed by, "To what degree do you think this activity contributes to the happiness of the holiday?"

3. Here I credit Victor Turner, especially in *The Forest of Symbols* (1967), for calling our attention to "polysemy" in rituals and symbols and the need to always ask the question "meaning for whom?"

Two years earlier another study conducted by the Israel Institute of Applied Social Research on culture and leisure in Israel had determined that, to 63 percent of those surveyed, Yom HaAtzma'ut primarily meant the enhancement of a feeling of belonging to the nation and to the state, whereas to 30 percent it was primarily an opportunity to be happy (Katz et al. 1972:50). Government officials in most new nation-states, concerned with instilling or promoting feelings of national identity in their populations, would be envious of those survey results (cf. Bocock 1974). But to Israeli public officials in charge of the planning of Yom HaAtzma'ut each year, they were cause for worry. According to Kamen (1977:7), the degree of popular enjoyment had become "the unofficial measure of the 'success' of any year's Independence celebrations."

This view is not a transient one. Year after year the papers, the radio, and the television news broadcasts anticipate the ceremonial passage from the solemnity of Remembrance Day to the happiness of Yom HaAtzma'ut. The former is billed as a day of remembrance for Israel's war dead; the latter, as a day of festivities, celebrations, entertainment. The two form a neat contrast set conceptually. The pathos of a day to remember the dead contrasts with the joy of a day to remember the establishment and survival of the state.

The juxtaposition is not accidental. Yom HaAtzma'ut is celebrated on a certain day each year because it was on that day in 1948 that the leaders of the Yishuv proclaimed the establishment of the state. Remembrance Day is commemorated the day before Yom HaAtzma'ut by design —signaling that Israel's survival is ensured from generation to generation by the ultimate sacrifice made by those who die fighting to preserve its independence.

The juxtaposition is, however, also forced. The design is to lead Israelis to mourn before they rejoice, to make it difficult, if not impossible, for citizens to swing into a festive mood without first putting it all in perspective, and to remind the bereaved that their loved ones did not die in vain. The combination signals a striving for equilibrium, perspective, respect, and a sense of achievement. But it also signals an attempt on the part of state institutions to channel citizens' emotions by clockwork.[4]

4. Leah Shamgar-Handelman and Don Handelman have recently written two related papers that explore ways in which state institutions in Israel have attempted to develop and institutionalize particular representations of the national "collectivity" in Israel. One (Handelman and Shamgar-Handelman 1986) analyzes a process (that occurred shortly after the establishment of the state) of choosing symbols by which Israel would be officially designated. Most of the discussion concerns the workings of the provisional government and early Knesset, in particular its Committee on Symbols/Flag and Symbols Committee. The other (Shamgar-Handelman and Handelman 1986) focuses on the nature of holiday celebrations in Israeli kindergartens and the patterned ways they observed of creating a sense

Children attend school on Remembrance Day, because the government fears that it might acquire a festive atmosphere if children looked forward to a holiday from school. But the government worries if the public does not sufficiently enjoy itself on Yom HaAtzma'ut.

The literature on rituals and celebrations describes and analyzes a wide array of activities and performances—religious and nonreligious, named and unnamed, solemn and rowdy. In many of these events, it is clear that many of the participants enjoy themselves, and that at least part of the objective of the event is to maximize enjoyment. But time and time again, scholars of ritual have identified form and context over and above enjoyment as central features of celebrations. Their emphasis is on the structuring of rituals, the idealization of form, the generation of iterability, and the communication of messages (cf. Moore and Myerhoff 1975, 1977). It has been pointed out that "anti-structure" is structured by its contrast to structure (Turner 1969); that rituals of rebellion are as ritualized as rituals of affirmation (Gluckman 1945); that games are defined by the rules by which one plays (Lévi-Strauss 1966); and that play is a "stepping out of real life into a temporary sphere of activity with a disposition all of its own" (Tambiah 1979:117). The emphasis, even in the study of spring carnivals (Da Matta 1983) or New Orleans Mardi Gras (Domínguez 1986a), is rarely, if ever, on the degree of enjoyment of the event by either spectators or participants. Kamen's acquiescence to measure degrees of enjoyment of Israel's Independence Day celebrations seems superficial, even silly, in terms of that literature.

Kamen's justification appears simple. He writes that he employs " 'enjoyment' as a key variable because of the emphasis on it in public discussions" (Kamen 1977:7). The implication is that the issue exists out

---

of belonging to a collectivity larger than each child's family at the same time that they used a representation of family to create a sense of collectivity. In the introduction to "Shapes of Time," they summarize what they saw as the government's "dilemma." "Before them," they wrote, "was the dilemma of how to subsume, in a single representation, that which the state signified to them and should signify to the wider public" (Handelman and Shamgar-Handelman 1986:1). And later they summarized some of the commentary that appeared in the press as the government struggled to come up with a flag and an emblem for the new state of Israel. "The SC [State Council]," they wrote,

> blew up a flurry of press commentary which raised issues that [according to protocols and press reports] had yet to be articulated by the legislators: the close relationship between the imagery of national symbolism and the formation of national life (G. Schoken, *Ha'aretz*, 18 July [1948]), and whether it was possible to invent national symbols, or whether they "must grow organically with the historical creation of the nation" (M. Troype, *Ha'aretz*, 27 July [1948]). (Handelman and Shamgar-Handelman 1986:16)

there in the public domain, and that the Israel Institute of Applied Social Research just conducts its research according to the discourse on Yom HaAtzma'ut. His emphasis on the results of the survey makes sense as an extension of that Israeli public discourse on Yom HaAtzma'ut.

To an outsider, however, it is the relevance of enjoyment as an issue of "public discussions" that commands attention. Hints of the problem surface in Kamen's introductory and concluding sections when he tries (1) to justify the emphasis on enjoyment and (2) to speculate about the meaning of his data. In the two-page discussion that caps the article, he refers frequently to the problem of socializing people to national values, to the problem of creating appropriate celebratory symbols for Yom HaAtzma'ut, to Israel as a democracy, to the pervasiveness of planning, to the frustration of government planners charged with planning but restricted in the implementation of their plans by the public harping on democracy, and to the demand for instituting a tradition of celebration. The image conveyed is that official institutions spend a great deal of energy planning, on the one hand, and being very ineffectual, on the other. In its mild-mannered way, Kamen's speculation seriously indicts the entire enterprise. "Each year," he writes,

following Independence Day, the national planning committee carries out an evaluation of the success of the celebrations. The planners have thus far not succeeded in introducing activities whose content reflects the symbolic meaning of the holiday, and in having these activities accepted and carried out by the public. This is probably the reason why they evaluate the holiday's success primarily according to whether people enjoy themselves. . . . It is much easier to devise forms of spectator entertainment than to create "meaningful" traditions for participants. (Kamen 1977:15)

The critique resonates with his assessment of public discourse—that the day has an obvious meaning, but that the public marks the day in unreflexive and often inappropriate ways over which the government has little control but for which it is still responsible. What interests me is that embedded in that set of propositions is a questionable but unquestioned premise that the day has an obvious meaning.

What, in fact, does Yom HaAtzma'ut celebrate? Kamen (1977:17) writes nonchalantly that "the celebrations must annually affirm and reassert the achievement of Independence," and he reports that intellectuals and government officials annually voice concern "that the form and content of the celebrations—especially on the Eve—fail to express the significance of the Independence which they commemorate" (1977:7). The phrases echo with the sound of public rhetoric, but convey little referential meaning. Does the former just mean that independence was an achievement and that it was that achievement which must be affirmed and re-asserted annually? Does it not also simultaneously imply the celebration of things deemed achievements brought about by, because of, or simply after independence? If so, what specifically is to be celebrated as an achievement? And who is to determine "the significance of the Independence" that is to be celebrated?

Kamen explicitly draws from Durkheim and Bellah at the opening of his article. "All societies," he began, "commemorate events which, real or imaginary, are imbued with great symbolic significance. Durkheim saw in these commemorations the expression and reaffirmation of the 'collective sentiments and the collective ideas which make [the society's] unity and its personality'" (Durkheim 1965:475, cited by Kamen 1977:5). From Bellah (1972), he infers that the ceremonies of celebration derive from a kind of civic religion—"which may demand [in modern societies where the state is divorced from religion] the loyal adherence which religious ideologies once did" (Kamen 1977:5). Collectivity, unity, and the establishment of a modern secular society are assumed to be what Yom HaAtzma'ut celebrates.

Eliezer Don-Yehiya (1984) offers a more elaborate, two-sided answer. In his analysis of government designs for the celebration of Yom HaAtzma'ut in the first few years of the state, he refers with regularity to "the collective values that [the holiday] represents" and to "national and state objectives" it carries out. The political discussions and activities initiated by the state reflected, according to Don-Yehiya, the governing elite's view of the collective values of the state. The symbolism was instrumental; the goal, the affirmation and strengthening of the collective values of the state.[5] But, says Don-Yehiya, independence days are holidays whose traditions of participation and celebration cannot be imposed on from above, and in the case of Yom HaAtzma'ut it is precisely that sense of collective identification with the values of the state—values that the state fought so hard in the early years to inculcate—that has since been steadily in decline. Like Kamen, he seems to lament the introduction of more individualistic concerns in Israeli society and the way they affect attitudes toward Yom HaAtzma'ut, but he does not, like Kamen, oppose individualism to collectivism. A new version of collectivity, Don-Yehiya (1984:26; my translation) writes, "puts at the center [of its civic religion] not the state and its institutions but rather the Jewish people and their cultural tradition." Unfortunately for his argument, he brings almost no data to

5. I find the terms *symbolism* and *values* so loaded and so polysemic that I try to be more specific in my own references. I use them here, and in discussing Kamen's views, because Don-Yehiya and Kamen use this terminology.

bear on the period past the mid-1950s, mentioning the present only in the three-page conclusion that follows nineteen pages of details on the early years.

Thus, in one case we confront an implicit functionalism that assumes, but does not examine, the signification of collectivity, and in the other we confront a claim—based on only partial historical analysis—about a change in the signification of collectivity. The mixed imagery invites an exploration of the problem of the assumption of collectivity in the discourse on signification. The question remains, What is the object signified?

THE SACREDNESS OF THE PROFANE

The *Jerusalem Post*'s front-page article on the eve of Yom HaAtzma'ut 1985 listed the events—official and unofficial—expected as part of that year's celebration of Israel's Independence Day. It briefly mentioned dancing, campfires, picnics, receptions, and entertainment programs. It then went on to detail the "central state ceremony" to be held in the evening at the start of Yom HaAtzma'ut at Jerusalem's main military cemetery, where twelve especially selected Israelis light twelve beacons near Theodore Herzl's grave. This was followed by the president's and the prime minister's televised addresses to the public, dozens of entertainment events in different localities throughout the country, special services in synagogues, exhibitions at military bases and institutions of higher education, the president's reception for special groups of Israeli military commanders, the televising of the World Jewish Bible Quiz for Youth, the president's reception for the foreign diplomatic corps, Jerusalem Mayor Teddy Kollek's reception open to the public, the awarding of the Israel Prizes, the organized running of a half marathon in Jerusalem, fireworks, a treasure hunt and folk dancing at a centrally located park expecting seventy thousand picnickers, and a Gush Emunim march in the West Bank.[6] The headline of the *Jerusalem Post* article read, "State's 37th birthday offers something for all" (*J. Post*, April 24, 1985, p. 1).

---

6. Gush Emunim, literally translated as the "block of the faithful," is a group—or rather, a social movement—within contemporary Israel that has of late attracted a great deal of media attention both in Israel and abroad. Its members are, by self-definition, religious and nationalist, but unlike the mainstream supporters of the National Religious Party (which is religious and actively Zionist, too, in its political platform), those of Gush Emunim believe in taking active steps to repossess/reappropriate those geographical areas "given by God to the Jewish People," even if it requires confrontation with Arabs living in the West Bank (which Gush Emunim regards as Judea and Samaria and, thus, part of the biblically designated Promised Land). Gideon Aram (1986) has recently completed an interesting and rich dissertation on the Gush Emunim for the Hebrew University, but in addition a variety

The day before, however, a friend had looked troubled and announced sardonically that Yom HaAtzma'ut "is awkward because it is the only secular holiday in Israel." The conversation had gone on at my initiative to explore whether Israelis know how to celebrate nonreligious holidays, whether one should refrain that day from visiting the Old City in East Jerusalem, and whether or not the movie theaters would open or the buses run. The openness and diversity of modes of celebration suggested by the article in the *Jerusalem Post* sounded more like awkwardness, uncertainty, and disorganization when I listened to my friend's remarks. The question Kamen felt no need to ask became more and more intriguing.

There are many Jewish holy days, and they are all marked with varying degree in the "secular" Israeli calendar. They differ in sacral rank, degree of observance, strictures, exegesis, and likelihood that non-Jews would be familiar with them. Reams and reams of text and commentary discuss and anticipate almost every imaginable issue of orthodoxy and orthopraxis connected with each of those holy days. Uniform observance does not follow, but the long-standing hermeneutics on their meanings and appropriate observance provides the willing participant with a ready-made script he or she need simply follow. There are, of course, variant scripts—by geohistorical origin, philosophical attitude, and institutional affiliation—but, to use Wittgenstein's (1953) concept of family resemblance, the particularities of each script are dwarfed by the overall family resemblance. There is little doubt that their significance is Jewish, that their temporality is determined by a ritual cycle, and that special rituals allow each Jew the opportunity to join in the collective affirmation of the connection between each of those days and the special relationship they claim as Jews with God.

But Yom HaAtzma'ut is billed as a secular holiday. There are no prescriptions or proscriptions concerning its celebration in either the written or the oral law. Thus, there are no guidelines or rules to be followed, no words of wisdom passed down over the centuries regarding either its

---

of journalists, writers, and other academics have recently spent time trying to figure Gush Emunim out (e.g., Newman 1981).

Who and what the Gush Emunim members are is an important question, but I worry that in focusing on these marked groups of religious and/or political zealots, observers of Israel may be assuming that religion is an issue in Israel only for the "religious," and that "religious nationalism" is a radically different thing from "secular nationalism." Robert Paine's (1983, 1986, 1987) most recent papers on Israel echo this doubt of mine and expand on it. To focus exclusively on named social movements or political parties is to ghettoize a problem that reaches far beyond the ideologies of bounded groups (cf. Aviad 1983; Deshen 1978; Goldberg 1987; Goldscheider and Friedlander 1983; Herman 1970; Rubinstein 1980, 1984). Hence, I worry about all the media focus on Meir Kahane and Kahanism.

meaning or the appropriate modes of celebration. Whereas the absence of tradition grates on all new nation-states, the intended Jewishness of the state of Israel aggravates the problem. The more than three thousand year history of Jewish life has witnessed the annual celebration of about a dozen Jewish holy days century after century. Around all, even the ones which may have been perceived as secular at the beginning, there developed rituals of celebration, a prescribed and preferred structuring of time, and a sense of their Jewishness. In the context of highly structured, ascribed holy days handed down from generation to generation full of tradition, Yom HaAtzma'ut is an intrinsic problem. For one thing, it is not clear whether it is a Jewish holiday; for another, it has only so far been celebrated forty-one times. Jews—and not just Israeli Jews—simply have little experience with it.

The problem is not merely what the White House faces each year when it must decide what kind of outdoor festival or entertainment it will sponsor in the capital on July 4; nor is it merely the problem newer nation-states face in choreographing military parades and/or multiethnic festivals with the hope of solidifying disparate populations and rejoicing in the passing of yet another year of national independence. There remains in Israel the central question of how to celebrate a secular holiday of national significance when one is used to celebrating only religious holy days of collective significance.

The difficulty had already surfaced in the parliamentary debate of 1949 which preceded the establishment of Yom HaAtzma'ut as a legal holiday. How active was the central government to be? How quickly should it push toward the institutionalization of a particular tradition of celebration? While some urged strategies to crystallize a tradition of celebration, others preferred a laissez-faire approach. The examples drawn on in the debate were frequently Jewish religious holy days.

The issue remained alive in the 1950s in the public discussion of ways the population could participate on an individual and group level in the celebration of Yom HaAtzma'ut. Four suggestions dominated discussion. Three have little to do with Judaism except in indirect ways—displaying the Israeli flag outside people's homes, decorating facades of buildings and private homes, creating and disseminating a greeting appropriate only on that day. But the fourth derived directly from the experience of Passover, one of the Jewish holy days par excellence.

The idea was to establish and promote the custom of celebrating Yom HaAtzma'ut with a special ritualized dinner in every household—a kind of Yom HaAtzma'ut Seder. This idea was not just casually mentioned once or twice. In 1951–52, writer Aharon Megged was commissioned by the Education and Culture Department of the Israeli Army to write

a "Haggadah," modeled on the Haggadah for Passover, that would re-
count the story of how the modern state of Israel came to be established.
The result, published in the special Yom HaAtzma'ut edition put out by
Ma'ariv on April 30, 1952, follows much of the written style and form of
the standard Passover Haggadah, though it deliberately makes little reference to God. In 1956, the Ministry of Education and Culture went so
far as to put out a collection of prayers, readings, and songs it considered
appropriate for the occasion, and even suggested a special menu for the
day (Neriah 1956). In 1978, the Thirtieth Independence Day Celebrations
Inter-Ministerial Committee sponsored the reissuing of the 1956 pamphlet and the publication of a Hebrew-English *Seder Hatefillot Leyom
Ha'atzmaut* (Order of Prayer for Independence Day) put out by the World
Zionist Organization's Department for Torah Education and Culture in
the Diaspora (*J. Post*, May 5, 1978).

In terms of the *Jewish* calendar, Passover was no doubt a good model
for Yom HaAtzma'ut. Triumphantly and defiantly, Jews have followed
the Jewish religious calendar in marking a week each year as the annual
commemoration of events that opened an "activist" stage in the collective
Jewish experience. Thematically, the holy day annually reenacts the passage of the biblical "children of Israel" out of Pharaonic Egypt away from
a life of collective bondage and toward a life of collective freedom. The
themes of passage and freedom were deemed appropriate for the celebration of Israel's Independence Day. Hanukkah, the festival of lights which
commemorates the Hasmonean (Maccabean) struggle against the Greeks
during the Hellenistic period, has similar themes and was, logically, frequently referred to in the Knesset discussions leading to the establishment
of Yom HaAtzma'ut. But it has disadvantages vis-à-vis Passover. For one
thing, it is considered a minor festival in rabbinical interpretation and
popular traditions. For another, the Hasmonean struggle itself was downplayed for centuries by the sages, following Talmudic tradition which
chose to stress the miracle of the cruse of oil in the Temple as the significance of the holiday. That interpretation of Hanukkah—that the Hasmonean's success was "not by might, nor by power, but by [His] spirit"
(Zech. 4:6)—jarred with the sense Israeli political and military leaders
had that they had won independence with the sweat of their brows. Ben
Gurion would eventually say so explicitly—that "the state of Israel was
founded not on the strength of a U.N. decision but rather on our own
strength" (*Davar*, April 20, 1953; my translation from Ben Gurion's Yom
HaAtzma'ut speech to the nation).

Calendrically as well, Passover is closer to Yom HaAtzma'ut than
any other major Jewish holy day. It begins on the fifteenth day of the Jew-

ish month of Nissan and ends on the twenty-second. Yom HaAtzma'ut follows just thirteen days later. If we examine the calendar, moreover, it becomes obvious that Passover is linked to Yom HaAtzma'ut by a series of intervening marked days all set according to the Hebrew calendar though not all biblically derived. From the fifteenth of Nissan to the fifth of Iyar, there are actually eleven marked days on the Israeli calendar. These include (1) the seven days of Passover; (2) the day immediately following Passover (Isru Khag) which serves as a transition from feast time to "normal" time, celebrated traditionally by Moroccan Jews with open houses in the evening and picnics during the day, and for more than ten years the date of a mass outdoor "ethnic" festival in Jerusalem (the Mimuna) (cf. Goldberg 1978); (3) four days later, Holocaust Day; (4) on the fourth of Iyar, Israeli Memorial Day (Day of Remembrance for Israeli War Dead); and (5) finally, on the fifth of Iyar, Yom HaAtzma'ut. In addition, for the religiously observant the first of the month of Iyar—a Rosh Hodesh—is another marked day. The number of marked days sets the period aside as one where little work is done and schools are for the most part not in session. The result is a holiday (holy day) atmosphere for much of the period which includes Yom HaAtzma'ut.

But the calendar attests to the awkward secularism of Israel's Independence Day in another way as well. Yom HaAtzma'ut was set according to the Hebrew, i.e., biblical, calendar. It falls on the fifth of Iyar, not on May 15 of each year. Two members of the 1949 Knesset did propose adopting the "foreign" calendar and making May 15 the day for celebration. They argued that it would be more effective internationally because that was the day the rest of the world marked as Israel's Independence Day. But the majority of the Knesset voted, nonetheless, against the proposal and for adoption of the Hebrew calendar as the basis for determining the precise day of celebration (*Divrei HaKnesset*, 1949, p. 350). Don-Yehiya (1984) claims that, in the early years of the state, explicit efforts were made to stay away from items, symbols, and practices they identified as having Christian origins. Thus, early Israeli nationalism had to turn to Judaism when it sought alternatives to Christianity and Islam.

The calendrical juxtaposition does not, of course, automatically turn Yom HaAtzma'ut into a religious or even Jewish holiday, but it makes secularism a noticeable issue. Secularists rejoice that it remains a day of uninterrupted public transportation, television programs day and night, and no expectation of verbal or physical conflict between the religious and the secular. On the other hand, the religious sector points to a tradition in Jewish history of transforming "secular" holidays into Jewish holy days. At least one reputable rabbinic scholar, in arguing that "as the years

pass, a tradition of observance is beginning to crystallize" in Israel, fore-
casts that "in time Yom HaAtzma'ut will certainly take its place alongside
Hanukkah and Purim" (Klein 1979:145).

The problem is one of knowing or unwitting collusion. Secularists
may be wary of the synagogue services on Yom HaAtzma'ut, and of the
intentions of the Chief Rabbinate when it issues a special guide for observance and guidelines for synagogue services. But other major activities of
the day evoke far less vocal reaction.

The most poignant example is the institution of the World Jewish
Youth Bible Quiz which, since the early sixties, has been a regular feature
of the celebration of Yom HaAtzma'ut. The contest is billed as an opportunity for Jewish teenagers from around the world to come together in a
spirit of friendly competition that requires them to learn the Jewish Bible
and be proud of revealing their knowledge. There are secular aspects to
the contest, but the religious ones dominate the encounter.

Quite secular is the spirit of nationalism aroused by the structured
competition between youths of different countries—"Israeli wins Bible
quiz" (*J. Post*, April 26, 1985); "As expected, the three Israelis took the
top honours" (*J. Post*, April 19, 1983); "Israeli wins Bible Quiz by scor-
ing 100" (*J. Post*, April 22, 1980). Arguably secular is the Zionist message vividly communicated by the fact that the contest always takes place
in Israel and always on Yom HaAtzma'ut. But an element of religiosity
creeps into that Zionist message each year when the contest rewards the
highest-scoring Diaspora participant with the title of champion of the
Diaspora—a consolation prize full of veiled paternalism toward the accomplishments of Diaspora Jewry in the area of religious knowledge. The
subject matter of the contest, of course, is knowledge of texts deemed
sacred in the Jewish tradition and treated as such by participants as well
as examiners. The fact that all the young male participants wear *kipot*
(skullcaps), at least for the duration of the contest, and that even the secular prime minister Shimon Peres wore one when he appeared on stage to
ask contestants the final question indicates a general willingness to index
the sacredness of the Bible.

The secular-religious mix here is deep-rooted. The Bible is taught
in detail and for years in secular as well as religious Jewish schools.[7] A

7. The state of Israel actually runs three separate "public school" systems—one depicted as secular and for Jews (though non-Jews are not necessarily excluded from them),
one depicted as national and religious and for Jews, and one "for the Arab sector." There
are others, in addition to these three. The kibbutz movement runs its own schools as does
the "ultra-Orthodox" population, and there are a few individual private schools (e.g., the
Anglican school in Jerusalem, the American school in Kfar Shmaryahu) catering primarily
to non-Israelis. The state has some defined institutional relationships with both the kibbutz

popular poster in Israel promotes and justifies archeological digs with a picture of a test tube inside an ancient broken pot. The caption reads: "The future is where our past is." An item in the April 1978 paper informed its readers that schools and kindergartens would reopen after the Passover recess "with a special programme designed to heighten Jewish and Zionist consciousness to see pupils through to Independence Day" (*J. Post*, April 30, 1978). Paine's (1983) "irreverent" observation about totemic time comes vividly to mind—that Israeli nationalist and religious life converge in invoking a concept of time that is more totemic than historical, that the past that counts dates back 2000–3000 years and that the intervening years are for the most part considered transitional, liminal, of little interest on their own without the biblical and the Zionist period to flank them. The argument is that religiosity and secular Zionism both need the Bible, hence the collusion on Yom HaAtzma'ut.

The lighting of the beacons on Mount Herzl seems equally bidimensional and convergent. Don-Yehiya (1984) notes that the customary lighting of the twelve beacons at the official opening ceremony evokes both secular and religious interpretations. Drawing from the Enlightenment and Revival literature of "romantic nationalism," some infer an indexing of renewal, awakening, and growth in the symbolism of light. On the other hand, the lighting of the beacons has been taken by others "as a revival of the ancient Jewish custom from the period of the Second Temple of lighting beacons or bonfires on hilltops to inform dispersed Jewish communities about the sanctification of the month" (Don-Yehiya 1984:14). The possibility of both interpretations has been frequently alluded to in official speeches and ceremonies. Already in 1950, Speaker of the Knesset Yosef Sprinzak spoke about "the beacons of Israel's freedom" being a revival of the "ancient custom of bringing [raising, making] light" (*Davar*, April 23, 1950; my translation).

But the collusion is also evident in contexts that are often not easily interpretable as deliberately politically motivated. In May 1978, in a piece reporting the reissuing of the 1956 Yom HaAtzma'ut "Haggadah" and the publication of the Hebrew-English Seder for the day, Moshe Kohn wrote:

> While most Jews everywhere (except those who are hostile or indifferent to Israel) continue to grope for a special way of celebrating Israeli Independence

---

schools and the ultra-Orthodox schools, but they remain officially independent. Aharon Kleinberger (1969) provides useful background information on the history of the politics of education in Israel.

Day, those who define themselves as "national-religious" mark it as a religious occasion that is almost, but not quite, on a par with and after the pattern of our original national-liberation festival, Pessah [Passover].

This is most conspicuous, of course, in kibbutzim and moshavim affiliated to the National Religious Party and in the synagogues and homes of NRP-minded urban people.

It can also be seen, though, in moshavim and urban centres populated by many tens of thousands of observant Jews whose political loyalties lie with Mapai-vintage Labour, the Likud, and even the Democratic Movement for Change. (Kohn, *J. Post*, May 5, 1978)

But then he added that "many so-called secular settlements have long been experimenting with forms of Independence Day celebration that have a quasi-Pessah [Passover], even quasi-religious nature, just as their Pessah celebration itself has taken on an ever-stronger traditional, religious tinge" (ibid.).

One example of such a celebration is the decade-old Seder held annually on Yom HaAtzma'ut in Jerusalem's Mevakshei Derekh, which seeks to be a nonorthodox and egalitarian congregation. Their 1984 Yom HaAtzma'ut Seder attracted

several hundred members . . . and their friends, . . . [took place] in the congregation's as yet unfinished building in the San Simon quarter, . . . [included] a memorial for the fallen in Israel's wars, . . . the halel prayer, . . . a meal consisting of food which they had brought, . . . tales of the pre-State army, and . . . a round of communal singing. (Alexander, *J. Post*, May 11, 1984)

Rabbi Jack Cohen, one of the founding members of the congregation, explained that the tradition of the Seder had been started "as a result of a search for a meaningful way to observe the holiday" (ibid.).

Quotations from sacred texts and allusions to Judaic themes have, moreover, long added to the awkward secularism of the public discourse surrounding Yom HaAtzma'ut that appears in the self-labeled secular press. A column in the *Jerusalem Post* in the spring just following the 1973 Yom Kippur war, for example, takes its title from a well-known passage in Ecclesiastes ("A Time to Celebrate, and a Time to Mourn"), begins with a quotation from an ancient Jewish prayer, and ends with explicit references to the applicability of lessons from Judaism. It reads:

There are things to celebrate and a suitable time and way to celebrate them, and there are things to mourn and a suitable time and way to mourn them. To do each in its time and way requires the balance of perspective that historical Judaism—the totality of the generations that produced us—has always displayed. Let us learn what they knew, apply it to ourselves, and commemorate our dead in

the suitable time and way and celebrate our regained sovereignty in Eretz Yisrael
in the suitable time and way. (*J. Post*, April 22, 1974)

The same day the paper quoted then prime minister Golda Meir, who
called

for the deepening of Jewish education, an increased awareness and understanding of the Jewish faith and heritage, upon which, she believed depends "the
spiritual continuity of our people and the reservoir of commitment and strength
for the future of Israel." ("Meir in Independence Day message: Israel ready for
'credible compromise,'" *J. Post*, April 22, 1974)

In a more recent example, Charles Liebman of Bar Ilan University
explored Israel's problem with Judaism in a three-page article in the *Jerusalem Post* intended as a commentary on Yom HaAtzma'ut, and in 1985
David Krivine dwelt on the nontheological dimensions of Judaism in a
special Yom HaAtzma'ut column entitled "Taking Stock at 37" (*J. Post*,
April 24, 1985). To Liebman, the issue was "the basic dilemma of Israeli
society, which most Israelis stubbornly choose to ignore"—that

without a Jewish component to its national culture, that culture lacks historical
roots and cannot provide a sense of common purpose or the rationale that makes
sacrifice and struggle meaningful. With a Jewish component, its national culture
becomes ethnically particularistic and alienating to a sizeable minority of its
population. (Liebman, *J. Post*, May 5, 1978)

To Krivine, the issue was that "we [Jews] have always, since the dispersion, wanted to have our cake and eat it . . . [even though] Judaism isn't
only a theology." Judaism is, he wrote,

also a social code tailored for a distinct nationality. In order to be an Orthodox
Jew you have to live in a Jewish society ruled by Jewish laws. The Jews tried
to do that in a Gentile environment. They tried to create a state within a state,
they willed themselves into ghetto life—and suffered the consequences. (Krivine,
J. Post, April 24, 1985)

In all four examples, Judaism emerges as a nondisappearing issue of Israeli
secularism.

A DAY OF RECKONING

The problem of the awkward secularism of Yom HaAtzma'ut has
not, nonetheless, interfered with the emergence of undeniably secular

modes of celebrating the country's independence alongside the questionable ones. Privately, after all, Israelis have been going on family picnics
in large numbers on Yom HaAtzma'ut for well over twenty years. They
have given singing, eating, and even at times dancing parties at home since
the establishment of the state. And they have for years hung Israeli flags
from apartment balconies, garages, even automobile antennas with the
frequency with which one would find mugs, bumper stickers, T-shirts, and
sweatshirts with a school name on an American college campus. At the
institutional level, there have been firework displays, outdoor concerts,
and receptions for foreign dignitaries.

The list conveys a sense of activity, a busyness about the day that
seems to contradict the oft-heard line I quoted at the outset—that Yom
HaAtzma'ut is awkward because Israelis don't know how to celebrate
secular holidays. On the other hand, many Israelis do not perceive "busyness" to be a marker of special days. In jokes and cartoons, they frequently
characterize themselves as terribly busy people. Busyness would not make
any particular day stand out.

The claim of awkwardness refers to the *nature* of the activity on Yom
HaAtzma'ut, not to its quantity. The charge is implicitly a comparative
one. In contrast to long-standing holy days, each marked and commemorated with a particular activity that has become over the years both its
metaphor and its metonym—putting on a Seder on Passover, fasting on
Yom Kippur, sounding the Shofar on Rosh HaShana, building the outdoor
sheds for Sukkot, dressing up in costume on Purim, and building bonfires on Lag B'Omer, to name a few—Yom HaAtzma'ut has seen modes
of celebration come and go. The two most prominent examples are the
staging of a military parade on Yom HaAtzma'ut and the banging of heads
—including those of perfect strangers—on the street with a noise-making
plastic hammer.

In the 1950s and most of the 1960s, the government staged a military parade on Yom HaAtzma'ut every year. The three major cities—Tel
Aviv, Jerusalem, and Haifa—rotated as sites for the annual event. Large
crowds greeted the soldiers and the hardware that was put on display.
Unabashedly, government officials and military commanders repeatedly
mentioned the Israeli army's strength and achievements on and around
Yom HaAtzma'ut. In 1951, to reinforce Israel's claims that Jerusalem was
and would be its capital, the parade was deliberately held in Jerusalem
(*Davar*, May 11, 1951). In 1957, again by design, the parade showed
off Soviet and Czech weapons captured by the Israeli forces in the Sinai
campaign (Don-Yehiya 1984:13).

Then in 1968, a year after the victorious Six-Day War, the army chief
of staff recommended canceling the annual event and holding a military

parade only every five years. The government agreed. A parade was held as planned in 1973, but the one that was in the works for 1978 was scratched after an intense public debate and the one scheduled for 1983 was squashed within two weeks. By spring 1988, of course, with its army actively using force to suppress the Palestinian intifada, Israel needed no more symbolic show of power.

The demise of the military parade as a marker of Yom HaAtzma'ut can be dated to public discussions and governmental cost-accounting. In 1968, Haim Bar-Lev, then army chief of staff, focused on the cost of the parades as an argument against holding the event annually. The Six-Day War had been costly; with the capture of the West Bank and the Gaza Strip the territory under the army's charge had risen dramatically and the opportunity cost of staging a parade would be prohibitive. In addition, the country had proven its military capability to itself as well as to the rest of the world. This was not explicitly stated so much as it was alluded to between the lines.

By 1977 the double message was more explicit, but the national economy was also in much worse shape. On August 2, 1977, shortly after then new prime minister Menachem Begin announced on a visit to the United States that a military parade would be held on Yom HaAtzma'ut the following year, the newspapers were full of items and editorials about the inadvisability of a parade. It was pointed out that the cabinet voted for the parade out of deference to Begin, that the estimated cost of the parade—150–200 million Israeli pounds (the equivalent at the time of some $10–20 million)—was shockingly high, that it made no sense especially because the army was simultaneously being asked to cut back on expenses, that officers feel they lose time in training when they practice for parades, that "we no longer have to pinch ourselves to remember that we have an army and how good it is," and that "the argument . . . of the need to parade our power both before ourselves and before our enemies is equally spurious" (editorial, *J. Post* August 2, 1977). A country whose citizen soldiers and their immediate families constitute such a large part of the population, it argued, "has no need for such vicarious exhibitions of military might" (ibid.). Growing public expressions of concern over the worsening foreign debt and the then steadily climbing rate of inflation combined with an uneasiness about the flaunting of military prowess to squash the idea of a military parade very quickly. No one could muster enough support for the staging of a military parade even though it was the thirtieth anniversary of Israel's independence. By August 9, 1977, the paper reported that "the realization that the parade proposal was not popular has induced the prime minister, government sources said yesterday, to propose instead a parade of veteran fighters." It did not matter in the end that it was the Likud—its more nationalistic image notwithstanding—and not Labor, that was in power.

Not surprisingly, disclosure in the fall of 1982 that Prime Minister Menachem Begin wanted to mark Yom HaAtzma'ut 1983 with a military parade raised eyebrows. Conditions that had led to the canceling of the 1978 parade not only had not improved; they had deteriorated almost across the board. The inflation rate seemed out of control; the balance of deficits continued to worsen; the invasion of Lebanon in June of that year had incurred enormous military expenses and, in opportunity cost, great civilian expenses. The army had already shown its prowess, but it now had a much greater territory to hold and defend. Journalists and politicians were quick to estimate the cost of a full-fledged military parade. But with the announcement of Begin's decision—coming almost exactly a month after the massacre of Palestinians by right-wing Christian Lebanese in Sabra and Shatilla refugee camps in an area held by Israel in Lebanon—the question of Israel's image loomed large in politicians' and journalists' public reactions (Kahan Commission 1983). Jerusalem Mayor Teddy Kollek stated that he had supported the staging of military parades up until 1968 to show Israel's willingness to defend the sovereignty and unity of Jerusalem, "but that there is no sense [point/taste/reason] in holding it in the present situation (*Ha'aretz*, October 24, 1982, p. 7). Bar-Lev added explicitly that "today Israel is depicted abroad as a militaristic country . . . and that a military parade can give its critics further support for their claims" (*Ma'ariv*, October 25, 1982, p. 2). The timing of the announcement by Begin barely four weeks after the massacre in Lebanon and the demonstration in Tel Aviv calling for a committee of inquiry, in which an estimated four hundred thousand people participated, simply stunned much of the Israeli public. A poll conducted by the Modi'in Ezrahi Research Institute at the end of October and first week of November among a representative sample of 1,255 adults in Israel revealed that two-thirds of the population was opposed to the staging of a military parade in 1983

Table 2.1. Relative Popularity of the Proposal to Hold a Military Parade on Yom HaAtzmau't in 1983 (answers to the question, "In your opinion, should there be a military parade this coming year?")

	Pro-Likud, %	Pro-Labor, %	All, %
Definitely yes	23.1	5.0	14.6
Yes	27.0	10.5	16.8
No	22.3	24.4	24.7
Definitely not	25.1	59.6	41.6
Undecided	2.5	0.5	2.3

and this included 47.4 percent of pro-Likud voters (cf. table 2.1). An editorial in *Ha'aretz* (November 11, 1982 p. 13), opened by saying: "The
Knesset Committee on Symbols and Ceremonies did well to decide to rec-
ommend to the government not to hold a military parade on the 35th
Yom HaAtzma'ut next year. . . ."

HAMMERING IT OUT

The association of the toy plastic hammer with Yom HaAtzma'ut
is by all accounts quite unrelated to the staging of military parades on
Independence Day. It is, for the most part, a grassroots phenomenon. No
one seems to know how or why it got started, and no government decision
was responsible for its introduction. Moreover, none of the Israelis I have
asked can date with any ease the year the phenomenon began. No one
recalls seeing the plastic hammers before the mid-sixties—1965 or 1966
at the earliest. Most recall seeing "lots of them" in use on the streets first
in 1968–69.

And yet already by the mid-seventies the papers referred to them as
if they were long-standing indices of Yom HaAtzma'ut. Two articles in
the *Jerusalem Post* on the atmosphere on the streets of Tel Aviv on Yom
HaAtzma'ut 1975 both mentioned them. Sarah Honig wrote at the opening of her piece, "Canned music, festive street lighting, fireworks and the
perennial plastic squeak hammers will again this year typify Independence
Day celebrations in this city" ("Joy with economy tonight in Tel Aviv
streets," April 15, 1975; emphasis added). And Sraya Shapiro included
them in her two-paragraph description of the ambiance:

"Dizengoff" was distinctly unpleasant on Independence Day last week.
Loudspeakers blared "pop" songs, mostly in English, some in French. But people
were not interested in dancing. Mostly young, some sat in the cafes, others
perched on the iron railings at the crossroads, most strolled. Many of the young
men looked theatrically villainous, hair long, shirts open down to naked waists.
The girls wore trousers of various lengths, widths and colours.
    There were also whole families, the babies in prams. *Plastic hammers
came down on heads.* Hawkers sold sweets, buns; one displayed a tray of silver
trinkets. ("Independence Day and 'the good old days,'" *J. Post*, April 4, 1975;
emphasis added)

In a 1978 item which announced an apparent waning of the popularity of the plastic hammers, they were still labeled traditional. The reporter wrote that "toy manufacturers report that *the traditional plastic
hammers,* now about eight Israeli pounds each, aren't much in demand"
(J. Siegel, "Thirtieth Independence celebration begins tonight in quiet

mood," *J. Post*, May 10, 1978). The 1985 newspaper articles on and about Yom HaAtzma'ut still included not only verbal references to the hammers but even drawings and cartoons.

Despite variations in popularity from year to year, the hammers have come to be associated with Yom HaAtzma'ut. In the late afternoon, before the sundown that marks the end of Memorial Day and the beginning of Yom HaAtzma'ut each year, one already sees young children playing outdoors with their plastic hammers—banging the hammers against a wall, a tree, or each other. By eight or nine in the evening, the downtown streets are so crowded with groups of youths carrying plastic hammers that many adults avoid going out to avoid getting hit. Bald men are apparently particularly attractive targets.

When asked why they do it, many fourteen, fifteen, and sixteen year olds shrug their shoulders. It is fun, they say; it's what one does on Yom HaAtzma'ut; it's the one day of the year when kids are allowed to hit grownups without getting punished. The hammers are also whistles, but one rarely sees them being used as whistles.

The emergence of the plastic hammer as a marker of Yom HaAtzma'ut coincides in an eerie fashion with the gradual demise of the military parades. There was an obvious overlap between the two in the late sixties, and the euphoria that followed the victory in the 1967 war definitely led to a more joyous celebration of Yom HaAtzma'ut in 1968 than was usual.[8] An enterprising entrepreneur must have read the public mood as playfully proud and peddled the hammer with increasing success. But while institutional considerations brought an effective end to military parades, no institution ruled on the advisability of the plastic hammers and the cost remained insignificant. Plastic hammers caught on.

The question is whether my temptation to see the plastic hammers as a substitute for, but also a continuation of, military parades is justifiable. Is this symbolism? All of the questions Sperber (1975) asks about our tendency to find symbolism when something otherwise looks strange to us immediately come to mind. Must the plastic hammers necessarily have meaning other than as harmless toys? Were it not for the specific use to which they are put on Yom HaAtzma'ut and the connection most people in Israel now see between the plastic hammer and Israel's Independence Day I, too, would not resort to the claim that there is symbolism here. But

---

8. One vivid way to sense the impact of war on Israeli soldiers is to compare three particularly powerful texts—*The Seventh Day* (Anon. 1971, recorded by a group of young kibbutz members) on the 1967 war and Amia Lieblich's *Tin Soldiers on Jerusalem Beach* (1978) and *The Spring of Their Years* (1987)—written in the aftermath of the 1973 war and the 1982 invasion of Lebanon respectively.

is the act of hitting people with a hammer not an act of at least veiled aggression? The fact that the hammer is made of plastic and hurts no more than a tap on the head with a piece of paper makes it *feel* like play. The fact that it is almost without exception children and youths under twenty to twenty-two who use them leads us to dismiss it as children's play. Yet it is adults who often buy the hammers for their children and allow themselves with humor to be hit by plastic hammers; thus they give the custom a generalized legitimacy. Is this so far removed from Pierre Bourdieu's (1977) concept of symbolic violence?

The term *darwin* is used in Israeli army jargon to label a torturing kind of tease, an order or a threat that gets dropped only at the last minute. The plastic hammers are known not to hurt, but the act of hitting with the hammer still evokes a physical reflex we have little control over —as if in defense of our bodies. In this sense, it seems a classic case of *darwin*.

Is this an "appropriate" celebration of Yom HaAtzma'ut? It is mostly pre-army youngsters who use the hammers. Is this their way of participating in the defense of their country? Does it show their ability to be tough, to hit perfect strangers, and adults for that matter? Does it show that they, like their older fellow citizens, put up a good show of force but are in the end soft-hearted?

It is not a central question for public discussion, but it is a periodic one. In her May 10, 1978, *Jerusalem Post* article, where she reported the diminished demand for plastic hammers, Judy Siegel added, "celebrants will apparently express their feelings of brotherhood other than hitting each other over the head." Cartoonist Yaacov Kirschner (*J. Post*, April 23, 1985, p. 12) threw in his two bits. One character said to the other, "Tomorrow we mourn the men and women who died so that this country could live. And the next day we celebrate Independence Day with parties, picnics, and squeaky plastic hammers. That's why we're all a little 'nutty'. . . . This society has too many ups and downs . . . for normal people to take!"

The custom appears to be neither sex linked nor status linked among Jews in Israel. I have never seen fancier plastic hammers nor heard of them. I have, however, never heard of any Jewish youths walking through East Jerusalem hitting Arab passerby with plastic hammers, nor going to Arab villages in the Galilee to hit their Arab residents with plastic hammers.[9] The hitting is done by Jew to Jew, with few exceptions. Most Israeli Arabs—however comfortable some may be with their Israeli citizenship

9. A Palestinian-American friend tells me, however, that she has seen Palestinian children playing with plastic hammers just like the one I picked up on Yom HaAtzma'ut—as one of several toys they seemingly play with year round.

—do not exactly celebrate Yom HaAtzma'ut and, thus, do not participate in the "play."[10] Residents of East Jerusalem, like other residents of areas captured by the Israeli army in the 1967 war, see themselves under occupation and, therefore, are even less likely than Arab citizens of Israel in the Galilee to participate in any "playful" celebration of Israeli Independence Day. The result is a bit ironic: the play is only knowingly with Zionists, but so is the aggression.

I see in all of this an uncanny similarity to military parades. Both are done in the spirit of celebration or festivity. Both display the ability to use force. Reflections on the fact that the Yom Kippur war in October 1973 came on the heels of the 1973 Yom HaAtzma'ut parade led many to question the argument that military parades help deter foreign aggression against Israel. In both cases, the captive audience is internal. And the dynamic in both cases is oppositional and dialectical—between play and aggression.

For much of public discourse, the problem is not, as Kamen (1977) perceived it, how to find modes of celebration that appropriately match the "obvious meaning" of the day. The problem is how to grapple with the meanings that seem to be conveyed by some of the ways people celebrate.

Two 1976 Ha'aretz articles summarized it in their titles. One lamented "Twenty-eight years of search"; the other asserted that "The symbol has not yet been found." In 1985, the press was still printing soul-searching articles about the possible meaning(s) of the day. Yosef Goell wrote explicitly in the Yom HaAtzma'ut issue of the Jerusalem Post about "The trouble with Zionism," and David Krivine argued that "running up the flag and playing Hatikva are not enough; nation-building is a Herculean task . . . [and] we have failed to meet those obligations" (J. Post, April 24, 1985, p. 10). Avraham Feder's response pointed to the heart of the problem. "On the occasion of Independence Day," he wrote, "*The Jerusalem Post* published two prophetically critical pieces, Yosef Goell's 'The Trouble with Zionism' and David Krivine's 'Taking Stock at 37' which might easily have been entitled 'The Trouble with the Jewish People'" (J. Post, May 14, 1985, p. 10).

In similar spirit, Sraya Shapiro wrote in 1975 to incite the old-timers who continually express dissatisfaction with what Yom HaAtzma'ut has become to think twice about "the problem." After describing the noisiness and disorganization of the street "rejoicing" in Tel Aviv, she continued:

Snobs and persons of quieter disposition meet privately to celebrate the day. They drink and talk politics, and remember "the old good days." Look-

10. For some vivid descriptions of how some Israeli Arabs experience Yom HaAtzma'ut, see *Every Sixth Israeli* (Hareven 1983).

ing back to the "old good days when people were really concerned" is human nature. But with us it has become a national scourge. As if somebody had deliberately wished to undermine public morale by appealing to the natural delight in grumbling. . . .

Recalling "the old good days of national unity" is also a game snobs like to play. Who remembers the "dissidents"? We are a nation rent by headstrong sectarians with irreconcilable aspirations. We unite only when the danger we know exists all the time is clearly and recognizably imminent. As happened in 1973.

And even in 1947. A testimony to that time, printed in one of Efraim Talmi's anthologies, recalls that the greatest surprise for people in Galilee was that "the Arabs really fired." (*J. Post*, April 20, 1975)

Complaints about how people celebrate mask, in Shapiro's opinion, the problems with the sense of collectivity that many assume the day celebrates.

The fact is that periodic innovations in modes of celebration tend to derive directly from people's dissatisfaction with what it is that is getting communicated to them. A vivid example was an unusual "picnic demonstration" organized for Yom HaAtzma'ut 1974 by a protest movement of demobilized soldiers who sought to comment on what Yom HaAtzma'ut ought to signify. One of the organizers of the 2.2-kilometer civilian march explained that "in view of what happened . . . [they would] stage a civilian march which in great measure is designed as the antithesis to last year's overblown military parade" (A. Rabinovich, "Picnic-demonstration on Independence Day," *J. Post*, April 23, 1974). In addition to the march, the group scheduled entertainment by popular singer Naomi Shemer and other performers, Hyde Park–style open air debates, public singing, and guided tours along the ridges overlooking Jerusalem. Blatant militarism was not a dimension of the Israeli collective self that they sought to encourage or even validate. A similar strategy was adopted by Gush Emunim but on the other side of the political spectrum. Their march through part of the West Bank sought to signify their belief in, and lobbying for, the legitimacy of Eretz Israel HaShlema (the whole land of Israel—including the West Bank).

It is in this vein that we see the Yom HaAtzma'ut problem with, toward, and among Israeli Arabs. In the early years of the state, the Israeli army used to organize Yom HaAtzma'ut celebrations in Israeli Arab areas displaying flags and forcing schoolchildren to participate in official ceremonies (Don-Yehiya 1984:18–19). Some writers critiqued the "lack of good taste" shown by the government and the army in imposing those celebrations (cf. *Davar*, April–May 1950). The argument always seemed to be about the advisability of the celebrations, but the underlying issue remained the problem of determining the role of non-Jews in the Jewish state.

Saad Sarsour has put his finger on the tensions and sensitivities surrounding the celebration of Yom HaAtzma'ut in Israeli Arab areas. "Like any other country," he wrote,

Israel too has values and symbols with which the citizens of the country are supposed to identify. . . . The schools in Israel are supposed to arrange an encounter between their pupils and the symbols of the state at ceremonies, events, holidays and special days. The Arab school cannot ignore the existence of the country's symbols, and the Arab pupil in Israel must learn to know the symbols of his state . . . but the Jewish-national character of these symbols creates difficult educational problems, for these symbols do not mean the same for the Jewish and non-Jewish citizens of the country. (Sarsour 1983:122–23)

Yom HaAtzma'ut puts Arab schools "in a quandary." Not to mark the day as a special day might "intensify [the Arab pupils'] estrangement from the country instead of promoting their sense of belonging and loyalty to it." It might also "arouse suspicions among the Jewish public" and, though Sarsour does not say so explicitly, it might get the school in political and financial trouble with the state's Ministry of Education. So the schools "as a rule comply" with the ministry's instructions "to celebrate that day and to stress to the pupils the achievements of the state and the achievements of the Arab sector in Israel" (Sarsour 1983:122–23).

The problem is simultaneously a Jewish and an Arab one. On April 16, 1978, a note in the *Jerusalem Post* reported that "the Beth HaGefen Arab-Jewish Centre here has cancelled plans for the state's 30th anniversary celebrations because of lack of funds." A May 10, 1978 contribution (A. Kemelman, *J. Post*), reported that residents of the Arab village of Tira "of some 12,000 located in the Triangle a few kilometres north of Kfar Saba [would] take the day off and businesses [would] be closed [the following day—Yom HaAtzma'ut], but [that] that [would] be the extent of the observance of Independence Day." A young man was quoted as saying that "it doesn't have any interest for us." An item on May 3, 1979 (I. Block, *J. Post*), announced "simply" that "the territories [were] quiet on Independence Day [with an] Arab student shot in lone West Bank incident." The first non-Jew to light an Independence Day beacon on Mount Herzl was a Druze,[11] and he was chosen only in 1975 (*J. Post*, April 10,

11. Druze (sometimes spelled *Druse*) are part of the non-Jewish population of Israel, officially considered a minority but also always officially considered separate and distinguishable from the majority of Israel's non-Jewish citizens who are called Israeli Arabs. For a sense of how the Druze fit into Israel, please turn to chapter 6, "On Authorship and Otherness," and to Oppenheimer (1978, 1980).

1975). The first non-Druze Israeli Arab to do so was chosen only in 1984 (*J. Post*, May 3, 1984).

The inclusion of non-Jews in regional and national celebrations remains at its infancy and is being couched in terms of ethnic pluralism. The afternoon celebrations in the Negev town of Yeroham in 1983 included "a festival of thirteen ethnic folk-dance groups including Druse and Circassians" (*J. Post*, April 15, 1983). And the week of festivities to mark Israel's thirty-fifth Independence Day celebrated in Druse villages in the northern Golan Heights was "devoted to Druse traditions" (*J. Post*, April 21, 1983). But a big question mark remains on the scene. Is Yom HaAtzma'ut not a Jewish holiday?

THE PROBLEM OF REFERENCE

In the analysis of language, strictly speaking, we have long witnessed debates and discussions over the role of the problem of referentiality in the problem of meaning, but popularly most of us assume that the meaning of a word, phrase, or proposition is what the word, phrase, or proposition stands for. And it is often with great difficulty that we relate to contrary or alternative formulations when we first encounter the issue in the philosophy of language. If meaningfulness does not necessarily entail the existence of a referent, where then do we locate the locus of meaning? That meaning might be intrinsically shifting, that it might not be contained in a word or phrase, or that it might be something other than given seems to defy common sense. We do, after all, commonly speak of things having meaning and of the meaning of something.

The leap to things outside the sphere of language makes sense within the terms of this common referential "theory" of meaning. We speak not just of words, phrases, or sentences meaning this or that, but also of flags, frowns, smells, rituals, and marked days meaning this or that (cf. Firth 1973; Sperber 1975; Turner 1967). We look up meanings of words in dictionaries, and ask experts about the meanings of symbols and rituals. We often acknowledge our relative ignorance about the meaning of something, but we rarely challenge our popular assumption that it means something. The idea that Yom HaAtzma'ut has an obvious meaning is rooted in just such an assumption.

It would be easy, of course, to argue against such a view by pointing to the mass of arguments, changes, and discussions that I have documented throughout the length of this chapter, but we would be missing the point altogether if we simply dismissed as irrelevant the assumption that Yom HaAtzma'ut has an obvious meaning. It is *because* people presuppose that Yom HaAtzma'ut has a given meaning that they go about unwittingly assigning, and thus creating, its meanings. The seeming paradox exemplifies the problem of authorship introduced in chapter 1: that the presupposition of the existence of an object precludes recognition of the discursive act of creating the object, even in the midst of the act of creation itself.

Analytically, we know of the phenomenon in the strictly construed linguistic literature on referential indexes, otherwise known as shifters. Despite the common description of the meanings of linguistic signs in terms of their presumed "semantic referential value," certain signs, we have come to learn, have no semantic-referential meaning independent of the context of usage. Peirce (1932) designated them by the term indexes, and Silverstein (1976:27) described them as "those signs where the occurrence of a sign vehicle token bears a connection of understood spatiotemporal contiguity to the occurrence of the entity signaled." Those that do not convey any semantic-referential meaning are known as nonreferential indexes. A good example is the use of a suffix -s in the Muskogean languages of the southeastern United States in the inflected verb forms of every nonquotative utterance made by women (Haas 1944). The appearance of the suffix in no way affects the referential value of the utterance, and yet its presence or absence conveys information about the sociological sex of the speaker.

Referential indexes, on the other hand, are signs that do convey referential value but whose referential values are constituted by the speech event itself. Locative deitics (this and that, here and there, these and those) and first- and second-person pronouns are classic examples of shifters. In each case, the actual context of usage is an integral part of the meaning of the term.

As such, terms of this type can be both presupposing and creative. They can presuppose aspects of the speech situation as perceived by the speaker—the existing relationship between speaker and hearer, the position of both speaker and hearer within the larger society, the particularities of the historical moment in which the speech event takes place. They can also create aspects of the speech situation that are not automatically presupposed, as in the demarcation of the boundaries of a social group through selective use of *we* and *they* in the discourse.

In the case of words like *left* and *right* used in political discourse, the relationship between presupposition and creativity is more dialectical than complementary. When a speaker refers to "the left" or "the right," he or she presupposes the independent existence either of people or of a political position with a given set of views, and yet in many instances (cf. Dominguez 1984) the meaning of *left* or *right* is created by the speaker in a given context of usage. In such cases, as in the discussions of the meaning of Yom HaAtzma'ut, awareness of the creation of meaning is severely limited by the presupposition on which it rests.

Substantively, it is in the dialectic between presupposing and creating an obvious meaning for Yom HaAtzma'ut that we see the struggle over objectification of the collective self in Israel. Introducing Judaic themes into the celebration of Yom HaAtzma'ut rests on the presupposition that the relevant collectivity celebrating its acquisition of independence derives its very existence from the laws and beliefs of Judaism. Introducing ritualized shows of force rests on the presupposition that the relevant collectivity celebrating its acquisition of independence derives its very existence from its ability and willingness to use violent means to protect its independence. Introducing deliberately non-Judaic modes of celebration rests on the presupposition that the relevant collectivity celebrating its acquisition of independence derives its very existence from its departure from Judaism. And abolishing ritualized shows of force rests on the presupposition that the relevant collectivity celebrating its independence derives its very existence from its commitment to peace and growth.

In few, if any, cases do the inventors or promoters of a custom, ritual, or image for Yom HaAtzma'ut see their acts as creative acts of objectification of *one* collective self over several other possible ones. The self-avowed search is for *appropriate* modes of celebrating, not for what to celebrate. And yet the process itself, intrinsic to and manifest in public discourse, turns out to be the struggle over what to celebrate—over whether the significant self is to be defined religiously, whether the significant self is a Jewish one, whether the significant self is a military state or a peace-loving people. So long as a sense of awkwardness exists about modes of celebrating Yom HaAtzma'ut, we will know that there has been no resolution concerning the character of the relevant collective self, but we will always be able to use it to uncover the major competing objectifications of that presumed self.

3 On the Boundaries of Self and the Limits of Tolerance

THAT the problem of collective self-definition extends beyond the confines of ritual is evident in the dialogue of objectification over the "Falashas"—Ethiopian Jews—since the mid-1970s. Are these Ethiopians really Jews? Can Israel afford politically and socially to acknowledge them as Jews? Can Israel afford politically and socially not to acknowledge them as Jews? Does color matter in Israel? Are they really "primitive"? Do they stand a chance of achieving upward mobility in Israel? And more poignantly: Can Israel avoid repeating the mistakes made in handling the immigration of non-Ashkenazi Jews in the 1950s? The dialectic between presupposition and creativity generates an enormous public discourse, far less about the Ethiopians than about Israeli society.

The Ethiopians are entering Israel at an "opportune" time. Writing in 1980 for a special volume put out by the Israel Sociological Society on "Migration, Ethnicity and Community" in Israel, Alex Weingrod explained that

a comparison with the studies of the 1950s indicates how different Israeli society has become. The changes appear at different levels, and they are at times ironic. For example, studies throughout the 1950s emphasized the mass immigration to Israel of hundreds of thousands of Jews from European and Middle Eastern countries; the "immigrants" described in this volume are (of all things) Israelis returning to Zion after a lengthy sojourn overseas. The key sociological concepts in the early studies were absorption and institutional dispersion, whereas the studies in this volume emphasize such matters as cultural ethnicity and ethnic social stratification. To cite yet another example, scarcity of resources characterized the Israel that Eisenstadt described in 1953, while the present collection depicts a society with comparative material abundance. (Weingrod 1980:6)

Writing in 1984, Eisenstadt and Lissak commented on the deep concern today in the general Israeli public with "the social status . . . of
groups originating from different countries." "This constant widespread
interest," they wrote,

has two main sources of sustenance: a) strong pressure that is brought to bear
by many sectors of the general public—above all by people who immigrated
to Israel in the 50s—to hasten the redress of distortions in their social status
that, in their view, were created upon their arrival here and b) the basic understanding on the part of the public, and particularly of various elite social groups,
of the need for more equality among groups that have different ethnic origins.
(Eisenstadt and Lissak 1984:3)

Ashkenazi and Weingrod put it succinctly in 1984 when they prefaced
their remarks about the problems of color encountered by Ethiopian Jews
in Israel. They wrote:

Contemporary Israel is a pluralistic and multi-ethnic society. As a state founded
on the ideal of the equality of all Jews, it has made efforts to blur differences
between the various Jewish cultures absorbed into the fabric of society. More
recently, an ideology of "cultural pluralism" has been emphasized, and ethnic
celebrations and identification have become legitimate. (Ashkenazi and Weingrod
1984:44)

As a result, massive funding—much of it from the United Jewish Appeal but much as well from Israeli government sources—is being directed
to "the absorption of the Ethiopians." The note on the "Ethiopian Absorption Project" in the 1983–85 *Biennial Report* of the National Council
of Jewish Women conveys the tone. "The recent absorption of Ethiopian
Jews," it began,

has proven to be one of the most challenging tasks facing Israel since the 1950's
when it absorbed massive immigration from various countries. The NCJW
Research Institute has responded to this challenge with an interdisciplinary two-
pronged project, initiated in 1983, aimed at studying and facilitating the integration of Ethiopian Jewish immigrants into the Israeli educational system and
promoting cooperation between research and the field through a special steer-
ing committee to assure a continuing exchange of ideas and findings. (National
Council of Jewish Women 1985:12)

As a result as well, efforts are being made to encourage the Ethiopians
to preserve their own music and dance in the Israeli context and to exhibit
it proudly at public events. Within months of the mass airlift to Israel at

the end of 1984, for example, a group of fifteen to twenty young Ethiopians associated with the Community Center in Nazareth Illit had already
established a folk dance troupe with the help of a well-known Ashkenazi
folk dance troupe organizer who lives in Jerusalem.[1] At the 1985 Mimuna, Ethiopian singers, musicians, and dancers held center stage longer
than any other "hyphenated Israelis." Special arrangements brought bus-
loads of Ethiopian immigrants to the event to experience the pluralism and
unity intended by the organizers of the Mimuna. On June 10, 1985, the
International Cultural Center for Youth, in Jerusalem, formally opened its
photographic exhibition on Ethiopian Jewry to the public with a series of
speeches, an informative slide presentation about Ethiopia and its Jews,
and a performance by the Nazareth Illit folk dance troupe. The Minister
of Absorption and the head of the Center for the Integration of the Heritage of Oriental (non-Ashkenazi) Jews in Israeli society both attended and
extended congratulatory greetings.

And yet, the overall tone of the Ashkenazi and Weingrod report is
what I would call moderately negative. They claimed that there was a
sense of crisis and failure surrounding the process of Ethiopian absorption, though they moderated their conclusion by granting that "the Israeli
officials responsible for the absorption programs are dedicated, experienced, and intelligent persons . . . [and that] they are consciously concerned not to repeat the mistakes and failures that were made during the
mass immigration of the 1950's." The problem, they argued, was that
"certain key features of the absorption system are not working properly,
and [that] these systems need to be reconsidered and changed" (Ashkenazi
and Weingrod 1984:49).

The "puzzle" or "paradox" Ashkenazi and Weingrod point to is,
however, far deeper than they allow. Fear of repeating mistakes made
in the 1950s is as internalized and sincere as the continued depiction of
the relationship between Jewish immigrants and Israeli Jewish society as
a process of absorption. Presupposition that they are Jews goes hand in
hand with strategies to teach them rabbinical Orthodox Judaism. Concern
with the illiteracy of many of these arrivals in any language goes along
with a continued harping on how well their children do in school. The
presupposition that they may encounter color prejudice against them creates an atmosphere in which color is highlighted. Concern not to invoke
the negative connotations of primitiveness in Israeli society goes along
with policies and actions that index the inference that they are primitive.
The dialectic is nowhere more evident than in what appears in the press.[2]

1. Nazareth Illit is a fairly new settlement of and for Jews in the vicinity of the long-
time Arab city of Nazareth in the Galilee.
2. I focus on the press here because it offers breadth of coverage and the possibility

From Falasha to immigrant

The Ethiopian story must be told in two parts. In the fall of 1984, the Israeli government, backed financially by the United Jewish Appeal, airlifted thousands of Ethiopian Jews from refugee camps in the Sudan to Israel. Operation Moses, as it was dubbed, marked the end of one story and the beginning of another.

The *Jerusalem Post* archives department opened a file on Falashas in April 1974.[3] Over the ensuing six years, fifty-four items taken from the *Jerusalem Post* were inserted into the file, along with one item on the Falashas which appeared in *The New Republic* and another from the *Intermountain Jewish News*. The opening of the file and the number of items in it characterize the era. Falashas—the name used in Israel throughout the 1970s and early 1980s to refer to Ethiopian Jews—had become newsworthy enough to deserve a separate file but were scarcely a pressing issue in Israel.

Two facts emerge clearly from an examination of the file. Throughout the period, the predominant theme in the paper is the question of their Jewishness. And the predominant interest in putting the spotlight on the Falashas and keeping it there seems to have come from certain sectors of the American Jewish community.

In 1972, Israel's then Chief Sephardic Rabbi Ovadia Yosef ruled that the Falashas were Jews. Drawing on the opinions of Israel's highly respected first Ashkenazi Chief Rabbi Avraham Kook, former Chief Rabbi Yitzhak Herzog, and the respected fifteenth-century sage—the Rad Baz of Egypt—he wrote: "The Falashas are undoubtedly of the Tribe of Dan . . . and their verdict is the same as that of a baby caught up amongst the *goyim* . . . we are ordered to save them from assimilation . . . and to quicken their immigration to Israel" (cited by L. Rapoport, *J. Post*,

---

of piecing together a chronology of representations of Ethiopians in Israel among non-Ethiopians in Israel. Other anthropologists have found themselves in the past three to four years conducting specialized fieldwork among the new Ethiopian immigrants out of interest and concern as well as financial need. The Jewish Agency, the Ministry of Education, and the Ministry of Immigrant Absorption have all set up special applied research projects offering employment to anthropologists. Members of the Israel Anthropological Association and the Jerusalem Anthropology Group have sponsored panels and workshops aimed at government bureaucrats, health professionals, social service personnel, and journalists. Among the most active in the past couple of years have been Chola Itzigsohn (e.g., 1983), Rina Ben Shaoul, Jeff Halper, Shalva Weil, Tsili Dolève-Gandelman. General interest in Ethiopian Jews shows up in publications such as those of Kessler (1985) and Waldman (1985).

3. The existence of the file facilitated my research, but coverage—at least by the early 1980s when I began my research—was never exclusively, or even primarily, in the English language *Jerusalem Post*. I refer to the *Post* more than to other Israeli publications because of the already existing file I located at the *Post* archives.

April 12, 1974). It was stated, however, that the Falashas would have to undergo a process of ritual conversion before intermarrying with other Jews. Too many rabbis questioned their status as full-fledged Jews.

Ovadia Yosef's ruling spurred both a certain amount of public discussion and a certain amount of government action. By 1975, an interministerial committee had recognized the Falashas as Jews under the Law of Return, thus declaring them eligible to benefit from the subsidies and privileges extended to all Jewish immigrants to Israel. By 1977, the Labor government had reaffirmed that decision. The activity contrasted with what Adin Steinsaltz, noted Israeli rabbi and Talmudic scholar, had encountered in the mid-1960s. Speaking of his own interest in the problem of Falashas in 1966, he reported early in 1974: "I wanted to force some *halachic* discussion [then] about the Falashas, but all I got was evasions. They didn't want to deal with it" (Rapoport, *J. Post*, April 12, 1974).

Yosef's ruling signaled a willingness to make the Ethiopians an appropriate theme of public discourse. It signaled neither the resolution of the problem nor the organized immigration of the Falashas. According to Rapoport in 1974, the minute number of Falashas then coming to Israel were referred to the Ministry of the Interior which checked their credentials. "It is a necessary precaution," he wrote,

because there are many non-Falasha Ethiopians who try for a share in the aid going to the Ethiopian Jews. Nevertheless, the Falashas here say that several Christian Ethiopians have succeeded in convincing the Falasha support committees here that they are Jews. (The Falashas say they number 113 in Israel. Hazi Ovadia says there are 350 here.) (Rapoport, *J. Post*, April 12, 1974)

On January 12, 1979, in his second long article on the Falashas for the *Post*, Rapoport lamented that none of the official declarations of the 1970s had done much to bring the Falashas to Israel. "There was no serious plan to bring the Ethiopian Jews to Israel," he wrote, "only some half-hearted attempts, which had failed miserably. . . . Many reasons were given for this," he continued, "but critics maintained that the main reason was simply that many officials were against bringing 'these primitive black Africans' to Israel." Civil rights activist and Knesset member Shulamit Aloni agreed. Early in 1977, she told the Knesset that there had been a "conspiracy of silence" about the Ethiopian Jews, and she blamed "racist attitudes" among National Religious Party and Labor Party officials. Golda Meir herself seems to have concurred with the allegation that color prejudice was widespread in Israeli society. Rapoport (*J. Post*, January 12, 1979) quotes a rabbi and official of the Religious Affairs Ministry: "Golda used to say that they would be miserable here, objects of prejudice."

About a third of the items in the Falashas file at the *Jerusalem Post* archives up to mid-1980 are letters to the editor which appeared in print. Almost without exception, they call, often passionately, for the full acceptance of the Falashas as Jews and for their mass immigration into Israel. A large number were written by American Jews, and some specifically came from people associated with the American Association for Ethiopian Jews. Racist accusations are explicit in some, indirect in others.

Eytan Ben Sheriya wrote from Santa Monica, California, in 1976:

We must look deep into our hearts and souls and ask ourselves if we are willing to put forth the same heroic efforts for the Falashas of Ethiopia, as we have in such matters as the Soviet Jews and Entebbe. This would be a great step forward in recognizing our great multi- and interracial heritage, completing the ingathering of representatives of all our people, and answering the gravely disturbing charges of racism raised against us not only by our enemies, but by some of our friends as well. (*J. Post*, October 25, 1976)

Professor Howard Lenhoff, signing as vice-president of the American Association for Ethiopian Jews, Jerusalem, complained about an item that had appeared in the paper. He wrote: "Sir,—Your story on the Black 'Jews' of Rhodesia (February 15), who claim to be Jews yet profess to 'believe in Christ as the Messiah,' was very quaint. But these people should not be confused by your readers with the true Black Jews, the Falashas of Ethiopia" (*J. Post*, March 5, 1978).

The at least implicit accusation of racism did not, however, go by unnoticed. A Tel Avivian, F. Hichenberg, saw fit to comment on it in response to Rapoport's 1979 article. "Finally," he wrote in his January 25 letter, "may I point out that, in Jewish tradition and Halacha, there is not, and never was a 'race' or 'skin colour' concept. The problem with the Falashas is that they have been cut off for a very long time from Jewish learning and tradition, but that is not their fault. And this sort of thing is reported to have happened to light-skinned Jews too."

Falashas then in Israel seemed to disagree. At a press conference on October 28, 1979, Avraham Yardai, head of the Association of Ethiopian Jews, accused the Israeli government and the Jewish Agency of a "racist" approach to solving the Falasha problem, and announced their plan to hold demonstrations in Jerusalem and Tel Aviv to protest what they called government racism and "ten months without a single oleh [immigrant] from Ethiopia" (*J. Post*, October 29, 1979). The October 30, 1979, *Jerusalem Post* editorial argued that "while this may be an overstatement, the Falashas' bitterness is certainly understandable."

As late as 1982, however, the sense was that it was American Jews who had become obsessed with the Falashas because of the experience of the American civil rights movement in the 1960s. Leon Hadar wrote (*J. Post*, March 12, 1982) that "Israelis who regard the issue of Ethiopian Jews as a marginal one will be surprised to learn that the plight of the Falashas is becoming a major topic on the agenda of the American Jewish community." In contrast, an Israeli diplomat who had served in Addis Ababa informed a *Ha'aretz* reporter in December 1982 that "the Falasha problem is still not top priority for the [Israeli] government" (Arzielli, *Ha'aretz*, December 17, 1982, p. 15; my translation).

A curious reflection of the unequal interest could be seen as well in Falasha participation in that year's Mimuna. Along with five other "groups," they had requested, and been allotted, a large tent on the grounds of the park itself to the side of the main stage. A local active and dedicated American-born anthropologist frequently acted as instigator, coorganizer, and broker for the Ethiopians with Israeli offices and institutions. In fact, a major portion of the exhibit consisted of five large cardboard posters mounted with color photographs that the anthropologist had taken a few years earlier in Ethiopia and more recently in Israel. One poster depicted general features of Ethiopia. Another consisted of pictures of Falasha synagogues—explicitly included so as to stress their Jewishness. A third depicted men's work, and a fourth, women's work. The fifth and last contained photographs of Falashas in Israel—children, "living," and a Falasha soldier in the Israeli Army. Mimuna-goers walked by and looked on with varying degrees of interest. They were there, but they were no more lured to the Falashas than to the Kurdish or Georgian tents. And they certainly did not flock to them the way they did to the handicrafts at the Black Hebrews' tent.[4]

The Falasha story began to change by mid-1983 as more Ethiopians managed to make it to Israel. A series of articles in *Present Tense* magazine late in 1982 claimed that some two thousand Falashas had reached Israel between 1981 and 1982. The American Association for Ethiopian Jews commissioned anthropologists Michael Ashkenazi and Alex Weingrod (1984:1) to study "the process and problems of absorption of Ethiopian immigrants in Beersheva." Fellow anthropologist Jeff Halper prepared a more general report on the governmental and institutional handling of the same absorption process. The question became less academic and more

4. Black Hebrews are Afro-Americans who believe that Judaism was originally an African religion and that the ancient Hebrews were much more African in appearance than most of those who call themselves Jews today are. They have mostly entered Israel on tourist visas over the years. Importantly, while their presence was never really welcome, it is Meir Kahane's anti-Arab activities, and not the Black Hebrews, that generated a legitimated discourse on racism in Israel—and this only since 1983–1984.

immediate: How was Israeli society going to react to the presence of Ethiopians as Jewish immigrants to Israel?

The spotlight turned on the native and veteran immigrant population in Israel side by side with the government. On June 1, 1983, we find Arye Dulzin, chairman of the Jewish Agency, asserting that Falashas who arrive in Israel are treated "with the same care and respect as every other oleh." The Jewish Agency had come under pressure because of press reports charging that the Falashas were being discriminated against. "The elements spreading these rumours," he added, "are not unconnected with local political party bickerings, but outside elements are also involved" (*J. Post*, June 2, 1983, p. 3). By early fall 1983, the Jewish Agency and the Ministry of Absorption had consciously begun to engage the Israeli public on the question of the Ethiopians. An ad in the paper invited the "general public" to a "study day and exhibition" in Jerusalem. The implicit, perhaps even unintended, question was who would be the subject of discussion. The big bold letters in the announcement read "Study day and exhibition for Ethiopian immigrants"; the fine print said the study day would be "on the subject of 'A Social and Cultural Expression of Ethiopian Immigrants.'"

The same question arises from coverage of an "incident" in the northern town of Safad. It was reported that certain ultra-Orthodox residents of Safad had threatened to prevent the entry of Ethiopian immigrants into their neighborhood, even if it meant doing so physically. "Within a few days," the February 7, 1984, item in the *Jerusalem Post* said, "most of Israel was convinced that there was an outright confrontation between the black skinned Jews of Ethiopia at the Safad Absorption Centre and the black garbed religious Jews of the *haredi* [ultra-Orthodox] sect in the town." In pursuing the matter, the reporter had discovered that "the mayor was correct. There isn't any trouble. . . . There is, however, a certain amount of fear, and it was this fear that gave rise to the activities of Moshe Blau, a man of the *haredi* community who wrote letters to the various government offices and to the media." The man did not represent the community formally, and was even reprimanded both by his own rabbi and by the chief rabbi of Safad. The issue that had brought him to action was also a practical one: he and others claimed that the building in which the absorption center was then located had been promised to the ultra-Orthodox Agudat Israel by the Housing Ministry a year or so earlier. But as D'vora Ben Shaul of the *Post* put it,

what was [really] evident in Safad was a lot of people who are deeply concerned over this recent flurry of attention. . . . Many of the *haredi* community feel that the absorption of the Ethiopian Jews is a test of their own faith and their own Jewish identity. They say that if they cannot live with these so very different Jews, then they themselves must reassess their own attitudes. . . . That's what one finds in Safad today . . . thoughtfulness and a desire to prove that Jews are one people. (February 7, 1984, p. 5)

By spring 1984, local anthropologists had entered the public discourse surrounding the Ethiopians. The *Post* not only printed an item about the tenth annual conference of the Israel Anthropological Association on the day it was to take place, but it detailed the way in which the conference was to "highlight the absorption of Ethiopian Jews in Israel" (February 6, 1984). The next day, two of the speakers were quoted— Michael Ashkenazi on how the conventional bureaucratic absorption process "is not suitable for Ethiopian Jewry," and how "they are made to feel utterly dependent, even though the professed aim of the absorption officials is to make them independent"; and Jeff Halper on how "Israel is not interested in pluralism, but rather in being a homogeneous European society" and how "there is a replay of the absorption process of the 1950s, planned and executed by clerks who reject the Falasha culture." Jewish Agency and Absorption Ministry reaction reiterated the emergent theme. Yoram Dori, a Jewish Agency spokesman, told the *Jerusalem Post* after the conference that they "have developed a project especially suited to the Ethiopians and [that they] are consciously avoiding all the mistakes that may have been made in handling the last wave of refugees in the 1950s" (*J. Post*, international edition, February 12–18, 1984, p. 8).

BETWEEN RHETORIC AND DISCOURSE

Comments about avoiding the mistakes of the 1950s became more and more numerous—in official and academic study days, public speeches, interviews, and letters to the press. Fear of repeating those mistakes is deep-rooted, and the commitment to avoid them quite sincere. The problem that emerged as the months went by was that the translation of the slogan into action was spotty and unpredictable. Few could outline exactly what those mistakes had been in the 1950s that could now be avoided, and even fewer seemed to detect the ways in which comments, policies, and incidents followed in the footsteps of the 1950s, or could suggest ways to avoid them.[5] Jewishness remained a political and institutional problem.

5. Academic treatises increasingly critiqued "the ethnic gap" and the Labor government policies in the 1950s. There were plenty of texts—newspaper items, government reports, articles in *Megamot*—that almost invited critique (see, for example, Segev 1984; Ben-David 1953; Goldberg 1972; Shokeid 1971; Swirski 1981). But, when advice was sought

Large numbers of the new arrivals were indeed illiterate in any language, and came from rural African villages which did not have high-tech items in their midst. The perennial question asked by immigrant countries also remained: Are the short-term benefits of clustering the immigrants geographically outweighed by the negative social impact of the long-term segregation it may create?

The fragility of the problem is evident in the words of Yehuda Dominitz, long-time director-general of the Jewish Agency *aliyah* (Jewish immigration) department. After interviewing him for a feature in the March 16, 1984, *Jerusalem Post* magazine, reporter Liora Moriel wrote that "like many other officials, Dominitz believes that the main problem is that do-good Israelis 'stir up matters' that would otherwise never come up." He was straightforward with her. The Ethiopian Jews, he argued, must undergo symbolic conversion because "they were on their own, far from any other Jewish community, so that it is not possible to determine if there were not some born to non-Jewish mothers. They themselves are very sensitive to the subject." But, Moriel reports, "he does not agree that this is a humiliating experience. 'This connotation is ours, not theirs,' he says. 'They accepted this with understanding and there were no problems.'" Then, less than a month later, in an item on how Ethiopian immigrants are being "sent to weak areas," Moriel quoted him again. "Dominitz," she wrote, "expressed optimism that his department will handle the new type of immigrant well: 'We'll have to spend more and put in more effort, perhaps we'll even make mistakes, but we'll try our best,' he said" (*J. Post*, April 8, 1984, p. 3).

Nearly a year later the good intentions still went along with frequent slips. In mid-March 1985, for example, Yisrael Cohen, spokesman for the Ministry of Education and Culture, responded to an opinion piece on the absorption of Ethiopian immigrants that had appeared in the *Jerusalem Post*. It was necessary, he wrote, "to dispel some popular misconceptions." "Ethiopian Jews," he began,

or the Beta Yisrael, are not our poor relations. They are Jews just like the rest of us and a closer look at what is happening now inside the Ministry of Education and Culture will expose the picture of "teaching Ethiopian children to say *shabbes* instead of *shabbat*," for what it is: a vulgar misrepresentation.

Probably one of the most outstanding achievements coming out of this aliya —and which was accomplished out of a deep awareness of the mistakes made during the 1950s—is the formation of the Public Council for Ethiopian Education. . . . The council is composed of Ethiopian Jews. The chairman of the steer-

---

about alternatives, the question suddenly seemed much harder to answer. What exactly had the mistakes been?

ing committee of the ministry for Ethiopian education is the director-general himself, Eliezer Shmueli. . . .

The deputy director of the religious education department, who was put in charge of Ethiopian students enrolled in religious education, is Ya'acov Hadani. Mr. Hadani was born in Morocco and does not wear a black kaftan, nor does he force little Ethiopians to wear them. He sees his work with the community as of great national and religious importance and is in constant contact with the council. . . .

Recently we held a study day on the topic of Ethiopian aliya and I would like to quote one of our district directors on how to "treat" the Beta Yisrael: "When I heard I was going to receive an influx of these new immigrants, I made a list of all the things that had happened to me as a new immigrant child from Morocco and promised that this wouldn't happen to the Ethiopians. This is how I operated then and I continue to do so now. You only have to treat them with respect and love." (J. Post, March 14, 1985, p. 10)

The picture drawn by some five hundred Ethiopians who came to Jerusalem ten days later was, however, significantly different. From all over Israel, they came to Jerusalem to demonstrate in front of the Knesset against the Jewish Agency, the Chief Rabbinate and absorption authorities. The demonstration was licensed by the police and organized by the Association of Ethiopian Immigrants, which claims to be the only one of a dozen Ethiopian immigrant groups in Israel to have been initiated by, and to be led by, Ethiopian immigrants themselves. According to the paper, the immigrants declared that they were grateful "for some aspects of their treatment here, [but] expressed dissatisfaction with the 'patronizing' attitudes of some Agency and Absorption Ministry staffers they deal with on a daily basis" (J. Post, March 25, 1985, p. 3).

Their charges included that they were "near-prisoners" in the hotels and absorption centers in which they were being temporarily housed, that their meals were set inconveniently at fixed times, that they were not allowed to have visitors, that they were "not consulted" in their own absorption process, that their wish to find permanent housing preferably in big towns and cities was not being met and that they were instead being settled in far-off development areas, and that the Chief Rabbinate continues to demand that they undergo ritual immersion to "become full Jews" (ibid.).

Despite the good will and intentions reiterated frequently in the rhetoric, actual Israeli reactions were mixed. (1) A senior Absorption Ministry official was reportedly "profoundly hurt" by the Ethiopians' decision to demonstrate, arguing that the ministry consults regularly with a group of eighty Ethiopians. (2) Eliezer Jaffe of the Hebrew University School of Social Work—who has been actively following the "absorption process"

—told the *Jerusalem Post* that most of the 80 Ethiopians consulted by the Absorption Ministry are in fact employees of the Jewish Agency who "are afraid to speak out about problems for fear of losing their jobs [and that] they speak as employees, not as consultants." (3) The Chief Rabbinate sent an aide to one of the chief rabbis to speak to a delegation of about fifty Ethiopians dispatched to the Rabbinate by the Association of Ethiopian Immigrants after the demonstration. The aide reiterated and tried to explain the Chief Rabbinate's position. (4) The Jewish Agency dispatched no one to meet with the other delegation of about fifty Ethiopians sent to the Agency after the demonstration. "Ironically," the *Jerusalem Post* reporter added, "many Agency officials were busy yesterday at Kfar Hamaccabiah, where they organized a conference of volunteers to help settle Ethiopian immigrants . . . [and it] was attended by hundreds of Ethiopians" (ibid.). The *Ha'aretz* (March 25, 1985, p. 3) piece on the demonstration ends with the remark, "but at noon yesterday there was no one at the Jewish Agency. All had gone to Tel Aviv."

There is much about the struggle over how to handle the Ethiopian immigrants that can be gleaned from these four reactions. To begin with, the coexistence of multiple voices, institutional as well as unofficial, calls into question the idea of national consensus on the matter of the Ethiopians. In fact, putting it so mildly may invite criticism that I have not fully understood the extent of the conflict between the religious establishment and the liberal, self-avowedly secular sector of the population on the question of the Ethiopians. But the nonbinary nature of the public's reaction to the "absorption" of the Ethiopians clearly signals that many native and veteran Israelis are neither so liberal and secular nor so religiously intolerant. The point is that there is a conscious sense in the population at large of grappling with the question of what to do with the Ethiopians so as to avoid a repeat of the 1950s, and some of the positions taken by some sectors of the population result in active conflict. To put it any sharper is to ignore the bulk of public discourse.

Consider the attitudinal differences that characterize the four reactions described above. The Absorption Ministry senior official's reaction almost caricatures the classic "Yiddishe mama" syndrome. Its personal, even emotional, tone evokes the image of a parent consciously or semi-consciously seeking to exert control over a child by appealing to his or her feelings of guilt. Eliezer Jaffe's reaction echoes a long-standing antiestablishment tendency to side with the underprivileged. The Chief Rabbinate responded with apparent sensitivity to the Ethiopians' concerns but remained steadfast in its position. Its attitude is not officially uncaring but it comes across as deeply paternalistic. In comparison, the Jewish Agency responded with apparent insensitivity while formally engaged in a project designed to help the Ethiopians integrate smoothly into Israeli society.

To take it one step further, underlying the Absorption Ministry senior official's comment seem to be two interconnected propositions: (1) that government has a duty to ease the absorption of the Ethiopians, and (2) that Ethiopian immigrants have a duty to be grateful. From Jaffe's reaction, we can infer the propositions (1) that citizens have both a right and a duty to criticize government policies when they see fit and (2) that government institutions have the power and the infrastructure to perpetuate themselves by minimizing the range of criticism they allow from within. The Chief Rabbinate's reaction follows from the propositions (1) that the Chief Rabbinate has a role to play in shaping domestic policy in the Jewish state, (2) that it is its duty to ensure the continuity of the Jewish people by serving as gatekeeper, and (3) that the preservation of an authentically Jewish people is a matter of higher priority than the minimization of social conflict. The Jewish Agency's reaction includes the proposition, already spelled out above, that government—or more generally official institutions—have a duty to ease the absorption of the Ethiopians, but it seems to rest as well on the proposition that when push comes to shove the "absorbing" institutions should rely on their own experience rather than heed the wishes or suggestions of the Ethiopians themselves.

At this level, the messages differ significantly from the liberal, even self-flagellating, tone of the public rhetoric. In nearly all of the propositions, a statement is made about the necessary and proper role of government, and in nearly all of them the message is that government institutions must remain the doers and the new immigrants the done to. It is here that paternalism remains rampant and that many of the assumptions made in the 1950s about the non-European immigrants persist to justify paternalism.

The examples are numerous. A May 3, 1984, item in the *Jerusalem Post* quoted the head of Youth Aliya extensively. Addressing educators in Tel Aviv, Uri Gordon called for the establishment of a joint staff that would include national government institutions, the Jewish Agency, and the Union of Local Authorities "to decide on an absorption policy for the Ethiopian olim" (immigrants, plural of *oleh*). "The joint staff," the paper continued, "would decide where the olim should be sent, taking into account employment opportunities, appropriate schools, housing availability, and opportunities for social absorption." Then, as if explaining why this is so necessary, it mentions that Gordon said that "the move to Israel . . . takes the olim from the 16th century to the 20th, and the sudden change throws some of them in deep culture-shock." One paragraph later, more of the same: "Few of them have seen an automobile before, and they have never been taught concepts such as length, width and height. When asked questions about themselves they tend to clam up, never having encountered a questionnaire before." Although Gordon still added that "often the problem is of our own making, as when the Ethiopians are sent to a place just because the Housing Ministry has flats available there," the image he painted of the Ethiopians is one of primitive people with far greater trouble managing on their own in Israel than almost any other group of immigrants.

Gordon's theme was much the same late in December 1984 when he explained to the press why Youth Aliya had turned down an offer by secular kibbutzim to take in Ethiopian youths. In his letter to the kibbutz movement's umbrella organization, he wrote that the Ethiopians "have come from an undeveloped country to modern Israeli society." "So," he continued, "the culture shock they experience is more than they can deal with." To settle in "an open, secular society, not governed by Jewish religious law" would cause them even greater problems. "Psychologically and sociologically, the damage," he claimed, "would be irreparable." He added, however, that after several years in Israel the Ethiopians would be able to choose the way of life they want (*J. Post*, December 30, 1984, p. 3).

That the discursive message leads to paternalistic policies, despite the overall liberal rhetoric, is evident in many of the other items that appear in the press. Consider the following story, printed on May 31, 1985, in *In Jerusalem*.

Ethiopian couples at the Mevasseret Zion Absorption Centre received instruction in birth control for the first time this week. The neighbourhood Tipat Halav nurse, with the help of an interpreter, lectured husbands and wives on the use of the Pill and presented a slide show, demonstrating its proper use.

The Ethiopians' reaction to the lesson was mixed. One couple, Devora and Ephraim, politely rejected the idea.

"To learn (about birth control) is o.k.," said the mother of five, "but to take, no."

They added that none of their friends is interested in using birth control.

Others, particularly those with very large families (10–12 children), appeared to welcome the idea.

The lesson evoked a considerably harsher reaction from the English speaking residents of the centre who have developed close friendships with the Ethiopians since they were asked to adopt them when they first arrived six months ago.

"There isn't a single family that hasn't lost a child or parent or sibling in Sudan or Ethiopia," said one. "They're now healing, and are eager to have children. The message of birth control at a time like this is cruel and inappropriate."

Others object on religious grounds. "There are halachic considerations to be followed by these very religious people in determining who should use birth control and what method of birth control should be used," said Rabbi Ronald Roness, rabbi of all the Jerusalem area absorption centres.

When word first surfaced that Ethiopians would be receiving education in birth control, he asked for and received permission to address them first.

"To be fruitful and multiply is one of the most important mitzvot [commandments] we have," he said through an interpreter.

"If, however, there is a danger to the woman's health, means of protecting her through birth control are to be used, only after consulting a rabbi and a doctor."

He offered to call in Rabbi Yosef Adana, the Ethiopian rabbi, for couples interested in halachic consultation.

No pills were distributed, and absorption centre sources insist that the lesson was intended for older women who are in poor health and have very large families.

Residents still raise questions about the lesson. *Why a method of birth control so complicated?* Others wondered who had made the decision that Ethiopians need such counselling.

"I was told that the demand for the class came from the Ethiopians themselves," said Roness. "But I find it difficult to believe that Ethiopians from all over the country spontaneously asked for birth control at the same time." (Joel Rebibo, "Ethiopians learn about the Pill," *In Jerusalem—J. Post Local Supplement*, May 31, 1985, p. I; emphasis added)

Two weeks later, the same reporter reported that absorption centers housing Ethiopians were being chemically treated to prevent the spread of malaria, and that residents of one Jerusalem-area center charged that they were lied to about the reason for spraying and were given insufficient safety instructions. The paternalism was readily noted by North American residents of the same absorption centers. A computer programmer from Kansas City reportedly complained that "we're adults and deserve to be treated accordingly" (Rebibo, *In Jerusalem*, June 14, 1985, p. II). Another complained to the director of the absorption center only to be told, "it is not your home, it belongs to us." When the reporter confronted the director of the Health Ministry's community health department with the facts, she agreed that it was wrong not to inform the immigrants why their homes were being sprayed, but she would not call off the spraying operations even though (1) there were no known cases of non-Ethiopians in Israel contracting the disease, (2) health officials admitted that the Anopheles mosquito is rare in Israel today, and (3) there has for years been public condemnation of the spraying of newcomers in the 1950s with DDT.

"Resocialization"

Rivka Bar-Yosef's now classic 1968 article about the adjustment process of immigrants focused on psychological and role changes immigrants undergo. Three aspects of that article shed light on the phenomenon of the "absorption" of the Ethiopians, albeit in an unexpected fashion. In using the terms *desocialization* and *resocialization,* she suggests a way of conceptualizing the integration of immigrants that points to the simultaneously destructive and constructive nature of their transformation. Desocialization, she argues, is that part of the process of adjustment after immigration that is characterized by the disintegration of the person's role system and the loss of social identity. Resocialization "is then the tendency to re-establish the role-set, to rebuild the connection between the self-image and the role-images and to achieve a real and acceptable social status" (Bar-Yosef 1968:34). The problem, as she phrases it, is the immigrant's, and the changes, also the immigrant's.

But in the picture she draws, there is, in addition, a strong prescriptive undercurrent. An "immigrant oriented society," she writes,

usually accepts the immigrant on conditional terms and provides a socially accepted "moratorium" during which social judgement concerning the position of the immigrant is suspended. It expects that after the lapse of the "moratorium time" the immigrant will emerge with a full-fledged system of roles and a social identity meaningful in the terms of the new society. (Bar-Yosef 1968:21)

Existing institutions of the absorbing society—government and nongovernment—should then be sensitive to the difficulties encountered by the immigrant and not exert undue pressure on the immigrants at least during the early postimmigration period.

Bar-Yosef's argument must be understood within the context of Israeli sociology in the mid and late 1960s: there was then some concern that something had gone wrong in the absorption of non-European Jewry in the 1950s and early 1960s, but there was no generalized public, institutional obsession with avoiding the mistakes made in the 1950s. Bar-Yosef, accordingly, called for more sensitivity but continued to put the onus on the immigrants.

The question, of course, is how "natural" the processes of desocialization and resocialization are. When the immigrants in the 1950s were told time and time again by teachers, politicians, social workers, and government clerks that in order to become Israelis they were going to have to abandon many of the customs, dress habits, food choices, and popular music of the countries they had left behind (cf. Segev 1984; *Ha'aretz edot hamizrach* [Oriental Jews] file for the 1950s), they were put under external pressure to desocialize. And when they were put in *moshavim*[6] and taught how to farm in Israel, how to organize themselves internally, and how to market their products, they were put under external pressure to resocialize. The same could be said about living in development towns, or apartment buildings in city neighborhoods, becoming factory workers, being recruited into the army, and being wooed by political parties. It would be tough to argue that any of the resulting patterns of desocialization or resocialization could be abstracted from the Israeli situation of the 1950s and early 1960s and used as a model of immigrant adjustment processes in other immigrant societies.

The paternalism and lack of respect alluded to in the frequent references today to the mistakes made in the 1950s refer to an attitude on the part of the then native, or at least veteran immigrant, population toward what Bar-Yosef calls "desocialization"—the idea that the faster it occurs the better it is. It is this aspect of the attitude toward immigrants, at least in the case of the Ethiopians, that *has* changed, especially in the rhetoric of public discourse.

What has changed, however, only in form and not in substance is the pressure to resocialize, to use Bar-Yosef's term. The problem is different from the problem of the 1950s, but the result may be that Ethiopians are being subjected to even more pressure than many, if not most, of the immigrants of the 1950s. It is here that we see the extent to which the problem is the "absorbing society's" rather than the immigrants'.

The evidence is everywhere—in the newspapers, on the television screen, in the composition of panels at universities, and in study days at government offices. It is simply so important to avoid the mistakes of the 1950s that the Ethiopians must be shown to be smart, highly adaptable, quick to learn Hebrew, easily upwardly mobile, and basically contented with the way they are being treated in Israel. As a result, the media report on items that would not appear newsworthy to an outsider, they are quick to print any story that suggests successful integration or upward mobility, and they will very frequently, if not always, include an Ethiopian immigrant on an interview program or panel discussion. The content of those items points to Israelis' perceptions of the nature of Israeli society.

6. *Moshavim* are rural localities organized as cooperatives "where the purchase of agricultural equipment and the marketing of produce are collective, but consumption and most of the production are private" (1986 *Statistical Abstract of Israel*, p. 17). This is to be distinguished from kibbutzim which are also rural localities but where both production and consumption are collective. Structurally between *moshavim* and kibbutzim are collective *moshavim* "where, in addition to the cooperative characteristics of the regular moshavim, the production is collective and only consumption is private" (ibid.).

Take, for example, an article published in the *Jerusalem Post* on August 1, 1984. The piece was entitled "Rena Elias: The 'first Ethiopian sabra' [native-born Israeli, presumed Jewish]," and included a photograph of a young teen-age girl with a phone in one hand, a paper in the other, and a pad of paper in front of her. In the second paragraph of a four-column story, the reporter wrote, "Rena is as Israeli as they come; she is friendly and outgoing. She loves sports and music, and Eilat. She knows no Ethiopian language, only Hebrew. She is now perfecting her English, in her summer work as telephone operator for the Project Renewal office, funded by the British Jewish community" (p. 3). Later, it adds that she wants to study psychology after the army and that she likes meeting new people and learning new things—"broadening my horizons." Another dream of hers, it reports, is to travel, especially to England and Italy. "She is fascinated by the Roman ruins, remnants of old hidden glory." The article notes that she goes to high school in Ashkelon, that her favorite subjects are chemistry, biology, and math, and that one of her two brothers goes to a school for gifted children in Jerusalem while the other goes to school "near home." Toward the end of the piece, after briefly mentioning the history of Israel's grappling with their Jewishness and her parents' own experience with the religious authorities, it adds that "to make sure that the more recent immigrants from Ethiopia don't have to face the trials he [the father] faced, Elias now works for the absorption of Ethiopian Jews here." That reportedly led him (1) to take a special course at Beth Hatefutsoth (the Museum of the Diaspora, on the campus of Tel Aviv University) "so that he could guide groups of Ethiopian Jews around the museum in their own language," and (2) to form an Ethiopian choir "to preserve the songs and culture of Ethiopian Jewry." Then in the last paragraph it concludes, "Rena says she has never encountered any problems arising from her Ethiopian descent. In fact, she believes that the new generation of Ethiopian *sabras* will be as smoothly and completely integrated as she has been."[7]

On August 10, 1984—nine days later—*Kol Ha'Ir*, a weekly Jeru-

---

7. Journalistic and popular books about Israel usually include reference to the concept of the *sabra* and how, before it came to be used to refer to native-born Israelis, it referred to the fruit of a local cactus—"tough on the outside, soft and vulnerable on the inside." There is no doubt a certain amount of external fascination with Israeli Jews and with how different they are, or are supposed to be, from their Diaspora predecessors and counterparts that explains part of that image of the nature and importance of the *sabra* in Israel. But it isn't all externally constructed. Tsili Dolève-Gandelman's (1987) piece in *Judaism: Viewed from Within and from Without* entitled "The Symbolic Inscription of Zionist Ideology in the Space of Eretz Israel: Why the Native Israeli Is Called *Tsabar*" gets at this issue better than anything else I have seen so far.

salem paper then free of charge, included a photograph of three teenagers sent to former president Yitzhak Navon's house to hand deliver the document confirming his membership in the newly formed Knesset. Neither the heading nor the caption mentioned that one of the three youths was an Ethiopian, but the picture focused on the Ethiopian dressed in army uniform (p. 17). On March 7, 1985, the generally highbrow newspaper *Ha'aretz* published a photograph of a Purim celebration which prominently displayed the Ethiopian participants, and noted that an Amharic version of the Scroll of Esther which is read yearly on Purim had been used for the first time in [Israeli] history (p. 8). On March 15, 1985, a photograph in the *Jerusalem Post* was captioned: "Young Ethiopian immigrants from Kfar Sava absorption centre on a 'get-acquainted' visit to the Discount Bank branch at 86 Rehov Jabotinsky in Ramat Gan this week. Through an interpreter the workings of a computer terminal are explained to them" (p. 15). And that was not the first photograph that I at least have seen in the *Post* of Ethiopians next to, or learning about, a computer. On January 11, 1985, another photograph featured two young men at the Yemin Orde Youth village wearing Adidas jackets.

On March 24, 1985, a *Jerusalem Post* article about a forty-five year old man who came to Israel in 1966 and is billed as Israel's first Ethiopian bus driver was entitled "An Ethiopian success story." The story refers to how he first lived on a kibbutz, how even as a small boy he had wanted to learn Hebrew, how he met and married another Ethiopian immigrant, how in 1967 he took a vocational training course for automobile mechanics and worked for a while at the garages of the Egged bus cooperative in Ashkelon and Beer Sheva, and how he finally took further training and became a regular bus driver. About his children, it says "simply":

Binyamin and Anna have three children: Tikva, 11, plays the piano and wants to be a doctor; Geula, 10, plays the flute and wants to be a teacher; and Ilan, 6, wants to be a bus driver like his father. The girls go to public school while the boy goes to a religious kindergarten. "Why? So he'll learn. Maybe he'll grow up to be a rabbi." The girls study Judaism as part of their extracurricular activities (p. 3).

On April 7, 1985, the *Post* sports reporter submitted an item on the inaugural Netanya Road Races whose opening line began, "Nearly 100 Ethiopian new immigrants from absorption centres in Netanya and the Emek Hefer area have registered for Tuesday's inaugural Netanya Road Races" (p. 7). Only later does the article mention that organizers expected some one thousand adults and youths to take part. On April 9, the *Post* carried a photograph of four Ethiopian children playing with snow. The caption read: "Young Ethiopian olim relish their first touch of snow at Kiddieland in Tel Aviv's Luna Park [an amusement park]. The snow was brought from Mount Hermon." The next day the same photograph appeared in *Ha'aretz*. That caption was a bit longer. The first sentence explained that snow had been brought from Mount Hermon and an artificial snow mountain had been built at the amusement park for the enjoyment of children as well as adults. The second sentence read: "Children who immigrated not long ago from Ethiopia enjoyed themselves thoroughly and were hosted at the artificial snow mountain" (p. 2; my translation). On the fifteenth of the month, a *Ha'aretz* headline read: "2000 Ethiopians will participate in the Holocaust memorial assembly at Lokhamei HaGeta'ot kibbutz" on Holocaust Day.

Then, as if to explain what all of the above leads to, on May 7, 1985, the papers reported the findings of a poll commissioned by Youth Aliya chairman Uri Gordon. The *Post* headline read "Most young Ethiopian olim are 'happy' " (p. 3). The article began:

> One hundred and forty-nine out of every 150 young Ethiopian olim living in Youth Aliya facilities in Israel are happy, according to a recent poll.
> Ninety per cent of those questioned expressed themselves positively, saying things like, "I'm living in a dream," or, "for the first time in my life I feel I belong to a land and a people."
> Youth Aliya chairman Uri Gordon, who commissioned the poll, said the result shows that, despite all the problems they face, the Ethiopians have adjusted well. Their traditional diligence, high motivation, good temper and ability to make do with little material comfort has eased their absorption, he said. (*J. Post*, May 7, 1985, p. 3)

The paper mentions that all of the 1500 Ethiopian teenagers housed in Youth Aliya institutions were polled, and that only 10 percent claim they would not have come to Israel "if they had known beforehand of the trials they would have to endure making their way to Israel." The most negative remarks quoted were that "some complained that employers 'prefer whites to blacks' and that 'Israelis want blacks only to play basketball.' " Even where the picture was not totally rosy, the rosier parts were included. For example, when it reported that 30 percent of the teenagers said they felt Israelis treated them like equals "in certain aspects but discriminated against [them] in others," the next sentence pointed out that "even those agreed that they were treated with more respect and fairness than in Ethiopia." And when the piece reported that "Sabbath desecration, lack of respect for synagogues and prayers, denigration of Israeli leaders, parents and teachers, bad manners and intolerance" bother these Ethiopian Jews, it added: "On the other hand, they were enthusiastic about seeing a 'Jewish army,' a 'Jewish police force.' They were also pleased by the abundance of food, scientific achievements and organized studies."

The happiness theme appears at least as important to non-Ethiopians as it may be to Ethiopians. Suicides and attempted suicides have long worried functionaries at the "absorbing" institutions. Already in March 1984 Yael Kahane, who some years ago spent a year living among the Jews in Ethiopia, noted a morbid interest in Israel with suicides and suicide attempts among Ethiopian Jews in Israel. "The newspapers," she told a reporter, "build new stereotypes which are very serious, very racist." She mentioned an article about the shelter for battered women in Herzliya and complained that the first sentence mentioned a young Ethiopian woman. She referred to a television program which discussed the Ethiopians' color problem. But the issue she considered most damning "is the one which blazed across the dailies recently, claiming that there were six attempted suicides in the Beersheba absorption center. . . . Like in other instances of public opinion management, people remember that Ethiopians are prone to suicide" (*J. Post*, March 16, 1984, p. 5).

Her charge against the media seems defensible. Days after Operation Moses was halted by an unfortunate leak in early January the papers reported that a twenty-two year old Ethiopian had committed suicide by jumping out of a window of the main hospital in Beer Sheva (cf. *Ha'aretz* January 13, 1985, p. 6). On the other hand, it is clearly not just the media that show interest in the phenomenon. The Psycho-social Services Department of Youth Aliya, for example, employs a local anthropologist at least in part to examine the problem.

In fact, when they are not slipping back to "the mistakes of the 1950s," many of the institutions that come in contact with the Ethiopians seem engaged in an Israeli version of Affirmative Action. The *Ha'aretz* story about the March 25, 1985, demonstration in Jerusalem explicitly mentioned that the police handled the Ethiopian immigrants with kid gloves. A *Jerusalem Post* report in mid-January on the visit of Education and Culture Minister (and former president) Yitzhak Navon to several educational institutions quoted him as stating "that the Ethiopians must be sent to established communities in Israel and that to the extent that it is up to his ministry, the Ethiopians would be enrolled at well-established, prestigious schools" (January 16, 1985, p. 3). In mid-March, 1985, the director of Machon Meir, a center of religious learning in Jerusalem, announced that special arrangements were being made "to recognize the traditional elders of the Ethiopian community as rabbis." Three, he added, had been taking special courses for three months, and "plans are under way for another ten to begin a one-year programme, which would also include Jewish history, religious thought and Bible." But he "stressed that at the same time, the institute would respect the traditions of the Ethiopians" (*J. Post*, March 13, 1985, p. 2).

Thus, it is no surprise that the Jewish Agency, the Ministry of Absorption, and the Education and Culture Ministry employ hundreds of social workers, psychologists, and *somchot* ("practical social workers" without professional training who are charged with helping, teaching, and supervising a specific number of Ethiopian immigrant families). In April, 1985, *Ha'aretz* reported that 400 *somchot,* 100 interpreters, and 100 social workers and psychologists were working with a population of 7000 Ethiopian immigrants on behalf of the Jewish Agency. The exact number of those involved, including desk clerks, health officials, teachers, and anthropologists, is probably closer to a thousand. But perhaps the most vivid example of the spirit behind what I am calling Israel's Affirmative Action policy for Ethiopian immigrants appeared in late May 1985. Liora Moriel, a Beer Sheva–based correspondent for the *Jerusalem Post*, posted a story entitled "In Ben-Gurion University course: Ethiopian kids become the real teachers" (May 30, 1985, p. 3).

The news part of the story was minimal. "An unusual anthropology course," it began, "is enabling students at Ben-Gurion University of the Negev to get credit toward their BA while helping Ethiopian children with their homework several hours a week." The course was conceived by a local anthropologist, has an Ethiopian adviser ("one of the first Ethiopian Jews to study at an Israeli university"), has an enrollment of sixteen, and works with sixteen Ethiopian children. The mood-setting part of the story filled in the rest. "The idea," the anthropologist is quoted as saying, "is to teach a regular course in anthropology with such topics as cross-cultural conduct, acculturation and cultural relativism in a scientific way, without stereotypes . . . and to deal with the subject matter not only theoretically but also to go out and learn in the field." The Ethiopian adviser added, "I hope time will do the trick and that not only will the Ethiopians learn from the Israelis, but the Israelis will learn from the Ethiopians—things like manners and respect." Teaching is an end goal as well as a means, but in the structure of the course the teaching is bidirectional: the teachers are students and the students teachers.

Presupposing and creating

The experiment may work in a limited university setting, but in the wider public the idea of bidirectional teaching is problematic. No one doubts that the Ethiopian immigrants have a great deal they can learn *in* Israel; the question marks concern what they might learn from Israel *about* Israeli society.

It is no accident, for example, that on the first Friday after full disclosure of the mass airlift and the leak that brought it to a temporary end both the *Jerusalem Post* and *Ha'aretz* printed consciously reflexive stories. But two of them, one in each paper, caught my eye: both explicitly couched their reflections in educational terms. The *Ha'aretz* piece was entitled "What do the Falashas learn?" (January 11, 1985, p. 15); the *Post* item, "Without prejudice" (January 11, 1985, p. 7).

The *Ha'aretz* columnist referred to the experiences of a twenty-one year old Ethiopian immigrant and his peers. In the second of five columns, we note the first jab at the "absorbing" institutions. These young people—some four hundred and fifty, most of whom have had grammar school and partial high school educations—it says, would like at least to finish high school, but vocational training is what awaits most of them. By the third column, we learn that "they feel the budding of an ethnic conflict." "Most Israelis are good," the twenty-one year old explained, but "there are a few bad ones who mess us up. The sabras gave us a present. A new name. Negroes [*kushim*]. They know we don't like the word and they [still] throw it out at us." By the fourth column, we note that the Department of Adult Education has given clear instructions to immigrant learning centers—"to teach things without saying which is better, to just say that that's how it's done in Israel." The man in charge of adult education for the Ethiopians explains: "That's the motto. Not to pass judgment. Not to give brownie points. If culture is literature, refrigerator[s], electricity, and gas, then Israeli culture is richer. But if we talk about culture as human relations—manners, quietness, respect, diligence, pleasant disposition—then we're the primitive ones." Then the columnist turned to the content of a morning class at the learning center. The most fascinating class, she claimed, was the one on Judaism. For an hour and a half, the teacher went over Bible stories, Jewish law and lifestyle, and different styles of interpreting the law. Then she quoted him: "Everyone is Jewish. We're all brothers. We don't have secular people and religious people. There are only people who are more observant and people who are less observant, and the more observant are not better than those who don't observe at all." And yet one student still asked why it is that the government does not close down the roads and demand observance of the Sabbath. Government, ethnic conflict, inequality, poor manners, and a split over the role of religion in Israeli society—that, she implies, is what the Ethiopians are learning about Israeli society.

In the *Post* column, the message is more explicit. At this time, it read, when "charges of racial prejudice have been bandied about with total abandon," we should regain some distance and examine our prejudices. Who, if anyone, in Israel is racist? "Mercifully," reporter Yosef Goell wrote, "racial prejudice, to the extent that it exists at all, is very low on the list of Jewish, Zionist and Israeli sins." Thus, he claimed that "it is certainly legitimate to oppose Gush Emunim on political grounds. But to charge them and their nationalist-religious supporters with racial prejudice is simply nonsense." Problematizing the acceptance of the Ethiopians in Israeli society, he implied, derives from "a hide-bound reactionary ultra-Orthodoxy's prejudice against *goyim* in general and against any attempt by some of those *goyim*, god forbid, to infiltrate the Chosen People without the ritual sanction of the ultra-Orthodox priesthood." But, he insisted, it is not racism. "As Jews and as Israelis," he asserted with assurance, "we are guilty of many sins that beset the human race. We are as prejudiced as any other people, but most of our popular prejudices are aimed at our fellow Jews and Israelis." Then with mustered optimism, he turned once more to the arrival of the Ethiopians in Israel. He concluded:

> There are ups and downs in the ethos of all peoples. For me, and for many others, the Israel of the '70s and early '80s is a painful down period in our moral ethos, as compared with the more difficult, but more exhilarating, early days of Zionism and of the state.
> Hopefully, the arrival of our Ethiopian brothers, who are so much in need of sympathy, and of a friendly helping hand into Israel and into the modern world, should again bring out what is best in us. (*J. Post*, January 11, 1985, p. 7)

The reflections take on an air of defensiveness, even premature defensiveness. Many seem to be based on the anticipation of criticism arising from the "absorption" of the Ethiopians. The criticism itself warrants soul-searching, but the anticipation of criticism warrants explanation.

When outsiders watching how Israel "deals" with its Ethiopian immigrants accuse it of racism, paternalism, or bureaucratic tribalism, many Israelis formally ignore the accusations. After all, Israel has been accused of racism for years—on the floor of the United Nations as well as at meetings of other international bodies. That the accusation has usually focused on Israel's attitude toward Arabs rather than toward dark-skinned peoples is irrelevant here. What is relevant is that many, if not most, Israelis expect outsiders to criticize Israel even when they feel the criticism is not warranted. The historical legacy of fighting anti-Semitism has led many Jews, including Israeli Jews, to expect anti-Semitism from non-Jews. And for many it is hard not to jump to the conclusion that criticism from the outside arises out of latent, if not explicit, anti-Semitic feelings. Thus, outside criticism demands public relations work on the part of the Foreign Ministry, but there is little evidence that it leads to internal soul-searching within Israeli Jewish society.

The matter is somewhat more delicate when the critical outsiders are

Diaspora Jews. Some extremists do dismiss their criticism by accusing the Diaspora Jews who express their discontent of being self-hating Jews, or worse yet of having assimilated into non-Jewish society. But there is little evidence that that is the most common view. The fact that Jews in the Diaspora contribute millions of dollars annually to Israel and lobby for Israel in their home countries makes them Israel's trusted allies.[8] Should they or should they not have the right to criticize Israel the way it is assumed that Israelis have the right to criticize their own country? Many Israelis feel they don't, but that it is logical that they should feel they do. And yet the argument often is that Diaspora Jews are at least as much the product of their non-Jewish societies as they are the product of Jewish communities. Thus, American Jews might be overly sensitive to the specter of racism because of the legacy of American racism and the post-World War II movement to eradicate it. Their charge against Israel, many Israelis say in private, has little to do with Israel itself. Thus, the conditions barely exist for a two-sided dialogue over objectification.

At least as delicate, as I have already noted, is the issue of criticism of Israel on the part of the Ethiopian immigrants themselves. Everyone would like the Ethiopians to be happy in their new homeland. Everyone would like the process of "absorption" to be as fast and smooth as possible so as to avoid the inequities many attribute to the mistakes made in the 1950s.[9] Most expect mistakes to be made, but seek to minimize their damage or occurrence. The question is whether brand-new arrivals have the ability to understand the country well enough to make valid and useful criticisms. The anthropologists and their students may remind others of the special advantages "participant observers"—new immigrants as well as anthropologists—have in seeing what the long-time residents take for granted. But the doubt lingers beyond those small circles.

My point is that it isn't the outsiders, the Ethiopian immigrants included, who have forced the dialogue about the nature of Israeli society. But that it is, rather, native and veteran Israelis themselves who do so, because the immigration of the Ethiopians forces discussion of particu-

8. The Israeli invasion of Lebanon in 1982 shook the basis of that previously unchallenged support but did not destroy it. The horrible wave of violence and shooting of Palestinians in the West Bank and Gaza that began early in December 1987 is once again rocking the boat, though I suspect—based on past experience—that most Diaspora Jews will continue to support the state of Israel even as they criticize its military actions in the occupied territories.

9. The average non-Ashkenazi Jewish household earns about 80 percent of what the average Ashkenazi household earns. Statistics show little progress in bridging this gap (see the statistical abstracts as well as the more specialized publications put out by Israel's Central Bureau of Statistics).

larly sensitive—and unresolved—issues in Israeli society that concern the nature of the significant collectivity. The issue of the Jewishness of the Ethiopian immigrants comes in the midst of concessions to the Orthodox and ultra-Orthodox establishment concerning the role of religion in the state of Israel, including the government's agreement to debate the question of whether to delegitimate non-Orthodox conversions to Judaism that have taken place in the Diaspora.[10] The issue of respecting Ethiopian culture comes in the wake of nearly fifteen years of vocal accusations by non-Ashkenazi Jews against the Ashkenazi establishment they blame for the mistakes of the 1950s. The intent to facilitate, if not ensure, upward mobility for Ethiopians comes in the footsteps of parallel discoveries of an apparently stable socioeconomic gap between Ashkenazi and non-Ashkenazi Jews in Israel. And the issue of racism comes in the aftermath of years of being the brunt of Nazi racism (with which most Israelis still associate the word), and years of being told by others that their attitude to Arabs is or has become racist over the years.

The critiques that matter are those from within. What the Ethiopians themselves say or do is picked up by Israelis exploring what all this means about Israeli society. It would matter little that they did or did not demonstrate against injustices if the charges did not fall on fertile ground. And underlying all of this is the assumption that there exists an "absorbing" society with characteristics that become manifest in the reception the Ethiopians are getting in Israel. But as in the case of Yom HaAtzma'ut the presupposition makes it difficult for the "natives" to see the perpetual act of creating that society in and through the discourse that presupposes its existence. In so doing, the mistakes of the 1950s are themselves discursively absorbed.

10. The November 1988 "resolution" of the "problem" of their Jewishness—the latest as this book was going to press—still leaves them marked. After numerous formal protests, even hunger strikes, especially in 1985 and 1986, Ethiopian activists in Israel won the support of a number of key politicians, but practically no marriage registrars or rabbis seemed willing to marry them as Jews unless they first underwent the ritual immersion ceremony. The November 1988 appointment by the Chief Rabbinate of the Sephardi Chief Rabbi of Netanya as a *special* marriage registrar for Ethiopian Jews was welcomed by supporters of the Ethiopians because he does not require them to undergo ritual conversion prior to marriage, but it also signalled the continued unwillingness of most rabbis to do away with that requirement.

4 On the Construction of Culture

THE reader might at this point be thinking that I am a typical anthropologist after all—choosing to study a "people" and focusing on aspects of them (or it) often perceived as peripheral to the internal construction and organization of their society. As one Israeli friend frequently puts it: Does this not lead to such an emphasis on form and structure that it leaves little room for content?

But what is the *content* of people's lives? Is it the same thing as the content of *a* people's life? And what does it really have to do with their assertions of peoplehood? Many non-Barthian students of ethnicity (e.g., most of the contributors to Glazer and Moynihan's 1975 *Ethnicity: Theory and Experience* and many of those in DeVos and Romanucci-Ross's 1982 *Ethnic Identity*) seem to assume (1) that ethnic differentiation follows from cultural differentiation, (2) that culture is the shared content of a people's life, and (3) that it is the experience of that content that produces what is variously referred to as primordial ethnic sentiments or a sense of emotional attachment to a group in whose culture one participates. But looking at the Israeli material, these assumptions look simplistic —both too static and too apolitical.

Do all people(s) have or claim a culture? Who defines what culture is, what is or ought to be the content of people's lives? Does it make a difference if the question is about people or about peoples? And does the nature of people's culture say something about the nature of their peoplehood?

Consider an elite Jerusalem family's celebration of Yom HaAtzma'ut in the spring of 1982. The account that follows is based on very detailed and extensive notes I took when I got home that night. An American friend visiting from the States had been invited to a "barbecue" at the home of long-time friends Dani and Dina—he an Israeli who had spent a number of years in the States in his youth, and she an American with a strong Labor Zionist past who immigrated to Israel in her twenties. I, as Jake's friend and hostess, was invited to join him.

We arrived just after 8:30 in the evening, and were greeted by Dani, Dina, Dani's mother, and two well-known and well-connected somewhat older friends of theirs, Eli and Leah. After the formal introductions were made, Eli turned to me and said, "You're from Cuba." I looked a bit surprised that they knew anything about me, but Dina explained that she had been telling them about us. We spent the next few minutes discussing Cuban films—I, a "Cuban," and they, film buffs. The conversation proceeded in English. Then, he turned to me again and asked, "You're going back to Cuba?" I explained that I had left Cuba in 1960 and that I now lived in North Carolina. Jake added that I taught at Duke University, and Eli immediately asked what it was that I taught. Then he went on:

This is quite an interesting place for anthropologists. My parents brought Margaret Mead here in 1952. My mother used to know her well and invited her. So she spent some time here, gave a few lectures, and actually gave us some good advice on what to do. You see it was an interesting period. It was when we were settling all these blacks. And at the time the general policy was to make them immediately Israeli, to take off their *tembelim* [a derogatory reference to items of clothing North African Jews brought to Israel with them in the 1950s]. She told us that she thought it was better to let people have their own cultures, and years later when it became clear we had a pressure cooker I thought a lot about what she had said. But you see we also had this other problem. To get people to know how to use modern technology we had to teach logic and mathematics, too, analytical thinking that they didn't have, [that] doesn't exist in those cultures. I remember in 1950–52 a fellow who came from India or the Far East— I don't remember which—wrote a letter in the *Post* saying that Israel then was a totally European culture. People read Schiller, Shakespeare, Racine, but why didn't they read [an Indian author whose name I did not catch]?

Nodding in agreement, Leah added, "We just didn't." And making what I thought would just be polite conversation, I remarked, "And they, too, especially Indian culture, have a very rich culture."

What followed surprised me. Noisily and assertively he exclaimed, "Rich? No!" His wife softly but immediately disagreed, but he pursued the subject. "No!" he went on,

They have some sculptures and art, but that's about it. No! That's not a rich culture. That's why we had to be a Western country. But actually we saw that pretty early on. In 1954–55 we got a group together to start the Ethnographic Film Institute. . . . The idea was that we wanted to get to these people practically when they got off the boats.

He quoted an "old friend" about how "you'd [then] meet these people even a year after they'd arrive in Israel and they just wouldn't remember things, wouldn't really know how they used to do things." He concluded, "they just wanted to have nothing to do with all that." When I remarked that "there seems to have been a return to it [roots, the past] in the last few years," he retorted that it wasn't authentic. Then he added, "I think we really made a mistake. We didn't allow people to think that there could be more than one culture here. I think that was the main mistake."

Dani and Dina remained on the whole quiet throughout most of the evening's references to culture, as did my friend Jake. But when in the middle of a more general conversation, Dani and Dina's young teen-age daughter came in carrying her plastic hammer after gallivanting in the streets with a group of about eight boys and another seven or eight girls that evening, Jake remarked, "It's fascinating to see all the different cultures in this room even though everyone's here [in Israel]" and that the girl could easily fit into his son's junior high school class in Washington. And as Jake and I were leaving, Dani and Dina made a few apologetic remarks about Eli, noting that he was a bit opinionated but that he was still a very versatile and interesting man—a former pilot, a part-time journalist, a filmmaker, and so forth.

The explicit references to North African Jews as blacks took me by surprise, though I realized it was a literal translation of the Hebrew term *shkhorim* which is often used to refer to olive- or brown-skinned Israeli Jews. The at times implicit, and often explicit, hierarchical evaluation of human cultures sounded as if it was straight out of many of the 1950s documents and letters that I was in the midst of reading.[1] And yet there was in what he had to say a strong sense that the handling of culture had been a big mistake in the Israel of the 1950s, and that some aspects of the "less rich" or "less advanced" cultures were worthy of preservation at least on film. I wondered if his was a fairly typical Ashkenazi attitude toward the relatively new policy of legitimating cultural pluralism. His basic assumptions had changed little, though he mouthed the "correct" line.

The problem jumped out at me once again while teaching a year-long course at the Hebrew University in 1984–85. The course spent the first two trimesters developing analytic tools and a comparative basis for the study of ethnicity, and spent the final trimester on the question of ethnicity in Israel. About halfway through the year, I introduced alternative theories of pluralism and gave examples from outside Israel. But then one of the students asked if she could apply it to Israel to see if she

1. These were from the *Ha'aretz* files in the *Ha'aretz* archives in Tel Aviv.

understood the differences between the models and approaches discussed. I agreed. Within five minutes, so many voices had been raised in class, so many arguments were going on simultaneously, and so many of the students were involved in the action, that I could barely hear myself speaking at the top of my voice. The question that so agitated them was whether Israel was closer to the kind of "plural society" that M. G. Smith (1960, 1965), Leo Despres (e.g., 1975), and Kuper (1972) write about than to the "humanistic pluralistic" society that William Petersen and Michael Novak (1982) favor. Petersen and Novak's articles presented an enticingly positive view of pluralism, while Smith's painted a society where a demographic minority barely keeps the society together through its own exercise of power and domination. Clearly from the pictures painted, it would be nicer to be able to claim that Israel was a society with humanistic pluralism.

But did the picture fit? Novak claimed that adopting a policy of humanistic pluralism entailed (1) conceiving of political rights as inherent in individuals, not in groups, (2) granting individuals freedom to choose how much or how little to make of their "ethnic belonging", and (3) encouraging voluntary organizations that nourish "sentiments, aspirations, and practices of group life as they choose" (ibid., p. 4). There was little argument about the third of these points applying to contemporary Israel, but the first two were deeply controversial.

Are individuals in Israel, Jews as well as Arabs, accorded political rights without regard to their group membership—or Jews as Jews, and Arabs as Beduin, Druze, Circassian, Israeli Arabs, or residents of the territories acquired by Israel in the 1967 war? The Israeli Declaration of Independence explicitly says that citizens of Israel are equal under the law without regard to differences in religion or group identification. And yet, they pointed out, Jews and Druze are required to serve in the armed forces while Israeli Arabs are not, and many rights granted to Israeli citizens, including those from the social security system, specify that they pertain only to those who have served in the Israeli army.

Do individuals, they debated, really have freedom to choose how much or how little to make of their "ethnic belonging"? Does an Israeli Jew of Yemenite ancestry really have the freedom not to be a Yemenite in Israel?[2] Can an Israeli of Moroccan origin ever stop being Moroccan?

2. Some very poignant songs to this effect were included in the musical *Yaldei HaKrakh* (officially translated as "Children of the City")staged by young native-born Israelis of Yemenite ancestry in Israel in 1982 under the sponsorship of Bet Lessin Theatre. Most of the songs in this collection were strong social and political commentaries on how they see Israelis not of Yemenite ancestry treating those of Yemenite ancestry. Titles include "Yemenite will remain Yemenite," "King of the Cassettes," "All our respect to the Biluim [the pioneer Zionist

Could it really be that the only ones who seem to be able to drop their hyphenated identity are those of strictly European background? What they could all agree on was that Israelis liked to describe Israeli society as pluralistic, and that they intended it in the positive sense of the word. Beyond that there was little agreement.

At the heart of the matter was the problem of "culture." Frequently referred to, it was still loosely bandied about with the assertiveness one might expect of an anthropologist referring to his or her research. It surfaced in references to pluralism, manners, theater and the arts, and education. It appeared value neutral in references to culture shock, intercultural encounter, and cultural expression, but deeply value laden in references to cultural events or cultured people. It seemed to pop up in myriad conversations, policy statements, and arguments, but while the words were the same the arguments they supposedly bolstered frequently led to competing conclusions.

---

settlers]," "Eight People to a Room," "I was born in Rosh HaAyin," "Everyone says hello to me," "Letter from an army recruit," and "Mixed couple." The music is deliberately modern pop in rhythm and melody and far from the musical styles their parents or grandparents grew up with in Yemen—consequently, also, far from the musical styles stereotypically associated with "Oriental Jewry" in general and Yemenite Jews in particular.

The Yemenite-origin population of Israel (about 50,000 born in Yemen and 116,000 officially counted as native-born of Yemenite origin) has long had a disproportionately marked profile in Israel. Operation Magic Carpet—the code name for the transfer of the Jewish population of Yemen to Israel by plane right after the creation of the state of Israel—became a mission of pride for the early Zionist government and has since become almost legendary in historical accounts of the modern state of Israel. The Yemenite Jewish population was important to those actively participating in shaping "Israeli society."

But the message is very mixed. It is not uncommon to hear Israelis—Ashkenazi and non-Ashkenazi alike—refer to those of Yemenite origin as (1) very hard-working, (2) very nice, and (3) very gentle (implying a tendency to avoid confrontation, conflict, or aggression). There are also, however, frequent references to their body size and shape (always seen as small and with petite frames), to their customs as charming (quaint?), and to how bright they must somehow fundamentally be to have come so far in only thirty to forty years. Many people—those of Yemenite origin included—remember Ben Gurion's comment years ago that the Zionist project will have succeeded the day Israel has a Yemenite army chief of staff. I have heard people say that the Yemenites are "our own Beduin," that the Yemenite Jews are something like "a surviving remnant" of Jewish life in biblical times, and that "the Yemenites are the closest thing to the way Jews were before the Diaspora" and that, therefore, their pronunciation of Hebrew, their family values, their customs, rituals, and musical styles are the most *authentically* Jewish of those found among Jews around the world. "Authentic," however, goes hand in hand with "primitive" in most of these images. For a rather different portrayal of Yemenite life and settlement in Israel—intended to correct both sins of omission and sins of commission—please turn to Nitza Druyan's academic (historical) representations of Yemenite Jews in Israel (especially her 1981 book entitled *Without a Magic Carpet*) and to her growing participation in political or at least public forums on ethnic discrimination, "Oriental Jewry," or specifically Yemenite Jewry in Israel.

I pondered over Roy Wagner's remarks in *The Invention of Culture* —that the anthropologist

calls the situation he is studying "culture" first of all so that he can understand it in familiar terms, so he knows how to deal with and control his experience. But he also does so in order to see what calling this situation "culture" does to his understanding of culture in general. Whether he knows it or not, and whether he intends it or not, his "safe" act of making the strange familiar always makes the familiar a little bit strange. (Wagner 1975:11)

The anthropologist has traditionally regarded culture as the object of analysis and, simultaneously, the assumption of analysis. Seldom, including in places where the native inhabitants themselves refer to culture, have we treated it as the sociohistorical product of a particular process of objectification.[3]

Yet in contemporary Israel, politicized academics, writers, and professionals of North African and Middle Eastern Jewish origin frequently focus on culture (*tarbut*) in their critiques of the Ashkenazi establishment and in their designs for bridging the gap between "Oriental" Jews and Ashkenazim. The media consider it newsworthy to report on Eisenstadt's comments about "Israeli culture"—that "the so-called Oriental communities do not want to establish an Oriental culture here . . . [but that] they want to be integrated into Israeli culture and society and to bring with them some of their own traditional symbols" (interview on the Kol Israel—radio Israel—on August 12, 1984, reported on by the *Jerusalem Post*, August 12, 1984, p. 2). And since 1975 a special department within the Ministry of Education and Culture, entitled Center for the Integration of the Heritage of Oriental Jewry, has operated on a budget of over a million dollars a year promoting the expansion of non-Ashkenazi art forms and knowledge of the customs and history of non-Ashkenazi Jewish communities. Culture is obviously both assumed and fought over.

There are specific power struggles and historical explanations for the relative higher and lower statuses accorded different cultural traditions in Israel, but I want to suggest here that behind it all is the paradox of peoplehood and the awkward but crucial relationship that exists between the Jewish people and Israeli society as semiotic objects. Can *a people* really exist without *a culture* by which they can be identified and distinguished from others? Can *a people* really be culturally pluralistic? And,

---

3. A forthcoming volume tentatively entitled *Nationalist Ideologies and the Production of National Culture*, edited by Richard Fox and published by the American Ethnological Society, argues and illustrates this point well.

if part of the Zionist project is the cultural and social reunification of the Jewish people (after centuries of dispersion), what form will (or should) that Israeli Jewish culture take, who will decide what to promote, on what do they base their arguments, and what do the arguments reveal about the assumption of peoplehood? The frequent Israeli discourse on ethnic groups and ethnic differences takes on, in light of these questions, a special significance. For it is not just about relative deprivation and relative privilege; it is about acknowledging difference while asserting sameness.

THE IDEOLOGICAL CHARGE

In the speeches and writings of many appointed as well as self-proclaimed spokesmen for non-Ashkenazi Jews, there is by now a common running theme—that a particular *ideology* of culture has prevailed in Israel in the twentieth century and that it has idolized an idealized representation of the lifestyle, the visual and performing arts, the technological know-how, and the standards of value of a group of Central and Western European countries. The point is not just that North African or Middle Eastern music is not broadcast on the radio nearly as much as is European classical music; the battle flares up beyond that at the metalevel with arguments about the proper or acceptable meanings of *tarbut* (culture) and the proper or acceptable uses of *tarbut*.

The charge is at four levels simultaneously and parallels the levels at which other critiques of discrimination (such as the feminist critique of American literature) have been waged over the past fifteen years. I shall identify these as (1) elucidating semantic and pragmatic (linguistic) patterns of discrimination, (2) supplementing/broadening the conception of the object so as to include the previously ignored or neglected writers, pieces, or customs, (3) elevating the status/worth of the sector of the population that was previously (and often still is) discriminated against even at the expense of the dominant sector, and (4) exposing institutional strategies by which structural socioeconomic inequalities are neglected or disguised when cultural differences are stressed.

On April 13, 1982, for example, Shimon Shitrit—one of the organizers of the 1982 Mimuna—contributed a piece entitled "Between Political Folklore and Cultural Depth" to the special supplement on the Mimuna printed in *Ma'ariv*. "Over the years," he wrote in his second paragraph, "external folkloristic elements such as clothing and food have come to be stressed" in the celebration of the Mimuna as opposed to almost any of its deeper aspects. The result, he argued, is that the Mimuna has become a negative symbol for many, in fact, a symbol of superficiality.

Nearly a year later, *Ha'aretz* published a story with a slightly different twist to the same message. André Elbaz, a Moroccan-born artist and filmmaker, resident of France, had come to exhibit some of his material in connection with that year's Mimuna. The thrust of the interview was that there is a deep-rooted inequality in attitudes toward the creative or historical products of Ashkenazim and Sephardim. "When people speak about the Ashkenazim," he was quoted as saying, "they use the word culture while when they speak about the Sepharadim they use only [the term] heritage." Agreeing at least in spirit, Shimon Shitrit explained, "the Ashkenazim are sick and tired of hearing people talk about 'the problem' of the 'backward' and 'primitive' people, while the Sepharadim are sick and tired of waiting for a solution."

The issue was the subject of a lively discussion on May 23, 1985, at a meeting of intellectuals, professionals, and writers of Sephardic ancestry held at the Zionist Confederation House in Jerusalem. The excuse for the meeting was the publication of the third issue of *Apirion*, a journal dedicated "to literature, culture, and society" whose expressed aims are

1. To express the mediterranean trends in Israeli culture in relation to the Jewish legacy.
2. To offer a way of expression to mediterranean and middle-eastern intellectuals, in order to enhance comprehension with our neighbours. (*Apirion*, no. 3, p. 30)

About sixty people attended, over half native French speakers. Outside the meeting hall itself, on a table to the left of the door, were copies of the new issue of *Apirion*—available for sale, along with mimeos, brochures, and xeroxes of material put out by the two-year-old organization that essentially called the meeting—the Mizrah el Hashalom (East for Peace) movement. In those handouts, its founders and members are repeatedly referred to as "a group of Israeli intellectuals, educators, students and activists in suburbs and zones of development of Oriental origin," and they list among their main aims the wish to do everything in their power "to help achieve the political, economic and cultural integration of Israel within the Middle East."

Those founders of Mizrah el Hashalom interviewed by Daniel Gavron for the *Jerusalem Post* in 1983 made it clear then that the question of culture was of vital concern to the movement. Poet Shelley Elkayam, then twenty-seven and a seventh-generation *sabra*, dug right into it. "An *eda*," [4]

4. The usual reference of the word *eda* (plural, *edot*) is a section of the Jewish population according to region of origin, especially those from Asian or African countries. For further elaboration beyond this chapter, please turn to chapter 6, "On Authorship and Otherness."

she began, "is a small, quaint group with a folklore, but the majority of Israelis, including those born in Israel, are *mizrahim*, orientals. How can the majority of the population be an *eda*?" The European Jews, she noted, laid claim to a "culture," or a "way of life," whereas the Oriental Jews had been saddled with a "mentality." This, she insisted, was not a mere play on words, but rather an indication of the way the European Jews looked down on their Oriental compatriots (*J. Post*, July 8, 1983, p. 3). Not surprisingly, the scheduled topic for the May 1985 evening was "Israel in the Mediterranean Cultural Environment."

Three poets, two academics, and a middle-level government bureaucrat participated on the panel. One of the poets simply read one of his own poems; one read from her own work and then talked at some length about the problem of defining culture; the third just talked. As the evening began, it became clear that analytic questions about the appropriate definition and attributes of culture preoccupied the participants, at this stage, at least as much as the details of a (or the) Mediterranean culture they were promoting.

The bureaucrat from the Ministry of Education, who spoke first, claimed that he was very pleased that his office had helped create and finance *Apirion*, though he still viewed it as a kind of experiment since it was not yet clear to him that there was enough of a market for such a journal in Israel today. Israel, he said, was a mosaic. Thus, there is a need for many avenues of cultural expression, and *Apirion* was a perfectly legitimate one. He had not heard of Mizrah el Hashalom until that evening, and so he politely focused on *Apirion* instead. But what he stressed in discussing the viability of such a journal was the "fact" that "there isn't *a* cultural struggle in Israel." There are, he claimed emphatically, cultural struggles in Israel. The point escaped me somewhat. He seemed to be arguing for a nondichotomous view of the struggle over culture, but I remained surprised that he, as a middle-level government official, would so easily use the term *ma'avak* (struggle) in reference to that night's scheduled topic in public. The politicization of culture appeared to be his not-so-implicit preoccupation.

The formal program opened up with Erez Biton who, in addition to being the editor in chief of *Apirion*, is a well-known, middle-aged, North African–born poet. He began with remarks about the difficulties of being a writer and agreeing to take on the editorship of the journal. Then, he switched to the need to distinguish culture from folklore. The Mimuna and the mass pilgrimages mostly of North African and Middle Eastern Jews that take place annually in Israel (cf. Bilu 1987; Weingrod n.d.) are really part of folklore, he argued, and should not be mistaken for culture. And where to place the music of the cassettes sold at the country's bus stations is a difficult question. Socially, Biton carefully stated, they're all important, but shouldn't there be standards of quality in determining what is part of culture?

For Shlomo Elbaz, of Mizrah el Hashalom, the history of the Ashkenazi population's attitude to "Oriental culture" required examination, but so did the problem of defining culture. A former minister of education, he said, came up with a useful answer nicknamed "the three alefs." The key words of the answer all begin with the Hebrew letter *alef*—*emet* (truth), *omanut* (art), and *emuna* (belief). *Emet* refers to the world of knowledge or know-how (*yeda*), technology, and science; *omanut*, to literature and music; and *emuna*, to religion and tradition. The tripartite division, Shlomo proposed, could get them out of the trap of rejecting all of Western civilization for the sake of reasserting the value of Mediterranean culture. "We," he explained, "must continue to get the first from the West since that's where the latest developments are. We need to take some of the second—art—from the West, but there's also a great deal in the [Middle] East that we haven't tapped. The third, *emuna*, has its roots in the [Middle] East." The implication seemed to be that the struggle should concentrate in and on the arts, and not on know-how or science nor on custom or tradition. One was clearly superior; the other, not a valid arena for the contemporary struggle.

Shlomo Ben Ami of Tel Aviv University was concerned about the depiction of the culture of Jewish society before independence as Western, but otherwise agreed with the emphasis on the need to clarify what culture is. We must strive, he kept repeating, for a Western-Eastern cultural synthesis here, but he offered his audience few details of what that meant or how it would come about. He was, however, worried that some Sephardim might want to push too far too quickly. That, he suggested, created a serious problem of inauthenticity.

The most potentially critical remarks came, however, from the one Ashkenazi on the panel—a young woman poet. After reading one of her poems, she explained that she was in full agreement with the spirit of the evening, but that there were some serious problems with the delimitation of their object, i.e., culture. On what, she asked, was the classification of some literature as Oriental Jewish literature based? On the identity cards of the authors of the texts? On the local color used in texts? The latter, she claimed, would be a real mistake since "local color doesn't make literature last," and the former implies giving in to a discriminatory social classification that says nothing about quality.

Several times during her admittedly long talk she was interrupted, and not always politely. At one point, a member of the audience speaking in disagreement referred to her being Ashkenazi. Some smiled and some frowned. It was clearly an awkward moment. But the comment so angered Ben Ami that he threatened to leave the meeting if it turned out that the group assembled there did not really believe in freedom of expression or accept the participation of non-Sephardim in the discussion. The young poet was allowed to continue but, as a result, the meeting which had started just before nine went on till a bit past eleven with little resolution of the basic problem—of what it was they wanted to do with or to culture, how it differed from the promotion of folklore, what standards of quality were to be applied to it, what role it was to play in "Israeli society," and what it had to do with whether one is Sephardic or Ashkenazi. There was, however, general agreement that there is a problem with culture in Israel.

The same combination of critique and affirmative action is evident in the actions and policies of the Center for the Integration of the Heritage of Oriental Jewry. Four years after this center came into operation (in the late seventies), its head, Nissim Yosha, reviewed its role and its impact on the Israeli scene in a speech at a meeting of the Public Council. "Four years of work," he began,

by the Center for the Integration of the Heritage of Oriental Jewry in the Ministry of Education and Culture raised [or made the subject of] the heritage of Oriental Jewry into one of national importance, with the ability to enrich the educational and cultural system of the state of Israel with Jewish content originating in the [Oriental] Jewish communities.

Though he openly refers to *moreshet* (heritage)[5] both in the name of the center and in his description of the object with which his office deals, most of his speech was splattered with references to *tarbut* (culture). "The point of departure for the center's activities," he continued after his opening sentence, "was recognition of the need to arrive at cultural integration in the state of Israel, based on equal appreciation of all the different Jewish traditions. . . ." His remarks about the work done since the mid-1970s pointed to the relative newness of the phenomenon, and his description of the goals of the center implied that Israel had a long way to go to achieve the kind of cultural integration they sought to promote. His frequent references to heritage and culture seemed deliberate, as if to say that worthwhile cultural integration can only be achieved by introducing knowledge of and appreciation for the heritages of non-Ashkenazi Jewish communities.

5. The word *moreshet*, though frequently used in speech, is actually a grammatically specific form of the word *morasha* whose form includes the marker -*et* indicating "of" as in *moreshet yahadut hamizrach* (heritage of Oriental Jewry).

The list of organizations or people fully or partially funded by Yosha's office is long and impressive. It includes established institutions of long standing like the Hebrew University, Tel Aviv University, the Ben Zvi Institute, and the Israel Museum, as well as more narrowly conceived organizations such as the Association of Iranian Jews in Israel, the national organization of Kurdish Jewry, the Council of the Sephardic Community, and Yeda-Am, the Israel Center for Jewish Folklore Research. It also includes individual artists and writers such as Shlomo Habaio, originally from Turkey, and Itamar Siani, a "Yemenite" painter.

In the written materials put out by the center and the speeches I have heard Yosha give since 1981, the explicit emphasis is on education broadly conceived—(1) to provide schools with history books and reference books on Oriental Jewish communities before their immigration to Israel, (2) to encourage creativity on the part of writers and artists of non-Ashkenazi origin and to facilitate publication and dissemination of their work, and (3) to maintain, even enhance, the presence of forms and substance drawn from the heritage of non-Ashkenazi communities in "Israeli culture." Curiously, I have never seen nor read any attempt to define, or even circumscribe, *culture* in the statements Yosha or his deputies have made in public.

The openness with which it leaves culture may provide the center with room to manoeuvre, but it may also be counterproductive. Does the center's mandate include the pushing of "Oriental folklore"? If most of what it supports is considered folklore in contemporary Israel, can one realistically expect Ashkenazim and Sephardim alike to appreciate the contributions of Oriental Jews and Ashkenazim to Israeli culture equally? I have personally heard no Sephardic writer or academic openly criticize the center for its support of museum exhibitions, folklore research, or folklore-based theatrical performances, but I have often read and heard lively discussions in those circles on the subject of culture and folklore.

A MEANINGFUL BATTLE

A hierarchical, value-laden comparison of the spiritual/mental/conceptual characteristics of different peoples underlies Even-Shoshan's description of the semantic parallels and syntactic uses of *tarbut* in his highly acclaimed and preeminent modern Hebrew dictionary. Even-Shoshan itemizes six senses or uses of *tarbut*:

1. *kultura*—the sum of accomplishments in the spiritual/mental developments of an individual or a society in education, science, art, social organization, religion, morality, etc., to be distinguished from *civilizatzia* which refers in

particular to technological accomplishments: peoples with high *tarbut*. primitive *tarbut*. *tarbut* values (language and writing, art, literature, religion, state/government) *toldot* [creations-products] of *tarbut*.

2. (in the restricted sense) education, finish-polish, acquisition of knowledge: the Ministry of Education and *tarbut*. *tarbut* activities in the army. *tarbut* committee.

3. development, advancement, improvement: body/physical *tarbut*. speech *tarbut*.

4. behavior, way of life, manners, *derech eretz* ["way of the land"]: "went toward a bad *tarbut*." "You abandoned a good/modest Persian *tarbut* and took the custom of Romans that is not good/modest . . . ." [two more quotes]. A person of *tarbut*. un-*tarbuti* behavior.

5. multiplication/proliferation and growth, taming, "nursing"-care/special attention: "The time when they (the animals) are tamed [*benei tarbut*]." *tarbut* of beautiful growths/plants. *tarbut* of mushrooms. *tarbut* of germs in a laboratory.

6. multitude, majority: "and here you arose under your fathers/forefathers a *tarbut* of sinners." (Even-Shoshan 1977; my translations)

Common phrases using *tarbut* include, according to Even-Shoshan:

1. *tarbut haguf*—sport, the development of the muscles of the body through exercises and improvement in health. 2. *ben tarbut*—a. intellectual, knowledgeable, developed: "our literature is full and complete with all the fields a people of/with *tarbut* needs for its spiritual/mental nourishment"; a person of/with *tarbut;* b. [in reference to animals] cared for/attended to and raised by man, tamed, domesticated [followed by a quote as in no. 5 above]. 3. *khadar tarbut* —a room in a settlement/town, a kibbutz, resort, etc., opened/created for perusal of books, newspapers and enjoyment from different items of entertainment. 4. *tsimkhei tarbut*—growths/plants people take care of and grow, to be distinguished from "prairie growths" which grow on their own without [special] care: grain, vegetables, different plantation crops—they are *tarbut* growths/plants. 5. *katsin tarbut*—[in the army] appointee in charge of satisfying the artistic and spiritual needs of the soldiers during their free time. 6. *misrad hakhinuch ve hatarbut*—the government ministry appointed/in charge of the network of schools, adult education, institutions of higher education, the arts and the rest of the humanities fields in the country. At the head of the ministry is the minister of education and *tarbut*. 7. *yatza letarbut ra'a*—corrupted his way, deviated from the proper way: "look after R. Meir after he went [astray] en route to a bad *tarbut*," "that [Abraham] would hate Ishmael going off en route to a bad tarbut." (Even-Shoshan 1977; my translations)

Even-Shoshan's entries, like those of any good unabridged dictionary, aim to explain the meanings of the terms by providing the closest semantic glosses based on the substitutability of those glosses in the semantic and syntactic contexts in which the terms appear. The notions of proof and verification rest on the notions of sense, understanding, and feel on the part of a speaker of fluent and multileveled Hebrew. Paradigmatic relations signal "domain" as well as differentiation. Syntagmatic relations signal "domains" of association.

The references to accomplishments, high versus primitive tarbut, development, advancement, and improvement dominate the first three sections of the entry. All contain a sense of trajectory—of something worthwhile emerging along a temporal dimension as a result of human activity. In the seemingly more value-neutral set of semantic glosses contained in Even-Shoshan's fourth section, the inclusion of manners and *derech eretz* reinforces the picture of hierarchy and assessment painted earlier. *Derech eretz,* translated word for word, signifies "the way of the land." The concept is a Judaic one, discussed at length for example in the Talmud and translated by Gilad (1983) as proper conduct. Both manners and *derech eretz* signify propriety—a concept of the desired, valued behavior publically considered normative, an expression of collective ideals for both private and public behavior. The examples given are ipso facto comparative and judgmental.

In number 5, a reference to animals, and in the expression *tsimkhei tarbut,* there is a paradigmatic contrast with flora that remain untouched or unimproved by the actions of man. The references imply the existence of a categorization in the nonhuman world which parallels a categorization alluded to in the human world. In both, the keys are (1) the assumption of improvement and (2) the effect of concerted human action. In fact, it is only in Even-Shoshan's sixth set of semantic glosses that there is no obvious hierarchization of human collective characteristics. And yet as if to relate to the rest of the usages and their implicit hierarchies, the quote he provides is patently evaluative in its intention and message.

Moreover, *tarbut*'s forward-oriented sense of time contrasts with *moreshet*'s backward-looking stance. *Moreshet* appears simpler, from the length of the entry alone. The actual entry is *morasha,* not *moreshet* (see p. 106 n.5). It reads:

inheritance, estate/possession, property: "The/this country was given to us as a *morasha.*" "Moses bequeathed the Tora to us, the *morasha* of Ya'akov's community." "The original creative *moreshet* in Israel multiplied in/was contained [*echad ha'am*] in its literary works." *Moreshet* of the forefathers. (Even-Shoshan 1977)

The reference is to the inherited, the transmitted from the past, a collective "possession" collectively "owned" because it is transmitted generically to descendants. The model is genealogical. One might even say that the now well-rooted social science distinction between achieved and ascribed finds a strong parallel in the ordinary language distinction between *tarbut* and *moreshet*.

Of interest here is the work of the Department of Jewish Ethnography of the Israel Museum.[6] Officially it is separated from the Departments of Jewish Ceremonial Objects, Contemporary Art, and Israeli Art as well as from Archeology. It is supposed to handle *ethnography*, not *art* —whether "secular" or "religious"—and its objects are deemed material culture. Both of its curators over the first two decades of its existence believed their task was to collect and preserve material culture of disappearing Jewish cultures. Neither could possibly be faulted for selectively applying the term *culture* only to Ashkenazim. But both contributed to a kind of folklorization of non-European cultures by having their department of ethnography concentrate on material from non-Ashkenazi Jewish communities in the Diaspora, and stressing that they represent the past.

Let me give a few examples. A pamphlet put out by the Department of Jewish Ethnography (1971:2) described the creation of that department as "one of the first steps towards the systematic study of material culture in Israel." It labels its job that of "urgent ethnology" because so much of the material it exhibits comes from "displaced cultures." In the process, it frequently refers to culture, but the phrases in which it does so are telling. It mentions "displaced cultures," "Arab folk-culture," "material culture," "the infinite variety of the cultures to be dealt with," "indigenous cultures," "remnants of a delicate, almost sophisticated, urban culture" (a reference to items belonging to the Jews of San'a, the capital of Yemen), "the last vestiges of their fascinating culture—a compound of local Berber and Moslem features, but also bearing some mark of black Africa" (a reference to items belonging to the Jews of Morocco), "the cultural patterns and the folk practices of the Jewish civilizations in Moslem lands," "non-

6. The Israel Museum, located on top of one of Jerusalem's hills in West Jerusalem, opened up in 1965 and was intended in many ways to be Israel's national museum. It is made up of several identifiable components. There is the Samuel Bronfman Biblical and Archeological Museum, a Youth Wing, a Sculpture Garden, and the famous Shrine of the Book which houses the Dead Sea Scrolls. The rest of the Israel Museum comes under the institutional heading of the Bezazel National Museum, which includes departments officially called the departments of Jewish Ceremonial Objects, Contemporary Art, Far Eastern Art, Ethnic Art, Prints and Drawings, Design and Israeli Art, and Jewish Ethnography. I take my data for this section from available written texts put out by the Department of Jewish Ethnography and from oral statements given both on tape and at curatorial group meetings by a host of curators and administrators of the museum between 1981 and 1985.

The department does, despite its name, periodically exhibit Arab objects from Israel, especially Beduin embroidery.

Jewish cultures," and "the life and culture of the Jewish community of Morocco." Nowhere in the text is there reference to European culture or the culture of the Jews of Europe.

What kind of image can such a slant transmit? Even when the intention is to try to correct the image that non-Ashkenazi Jews come from less advanced or worthwhile cultures, the slant seems to suggest that those same cultures can make it into a national museum only as ethnography. And the dual classification of cultures is often not far from the surface. In the same 1971 text, for instance, a small section describes "the reactions of those who come from rural settlements and are visiting a museum for the first time." It reads:

Having been told that they could see here objects, discarded by them as obsolete, they come to admire them beautifully displayed *alongside art treasures of the world*. Their pride is great, and there are those who return bringing with them items handed down from their forefathers. Some of these donors represent old, honoured families. Many, however, are humble folk enjoying no privileged position on the social ladder of Israeli society. Another reaction, usually coming from an entirely different social stratum, is the critical inquiry: "and what, after all, is Jewish in all this?" (Department of Jewish Ethnography 1971:7; emphasis added)

Similarly, in the catalog to its first full-fledged exhibition—on the Jews of Bukhara—the staff wrote that that exhibition, like the two exhibitions on Yemenite Jewry that had been mounted in the 1940s and 1950s at Jerusalem's Bezalel School, presented and reconstructed "remnants of cultures that were disappearing and assimilating within the patterns of our *modern life*" (Israel Museum 1967–68:1; emphasis added). The phrase is almost exactly reproduced in a retrospective account on the Kurdish Jewish exhibition—the department's third—submitted to the *Israel Museum Journal* (1983:1) by the then curator: that her department "preserves and freezes for future generations the ways of life of the Jewish communities before their immigration to Israel and *adaptation to modern life* in Israel" (emphasis added).

The hidden message becomes more explicit in the account given by an official of the Ministry of Education with whom the first curator negotiated in her search for funding. According to this official, interviewed in the fall of 1981, the Jewish Ethnography Department's first curator, Aviva Muller-Lancet, got little financial support from the museum at the early stages of mounting a full-scale exhibition on Kurdish Jewry. Thus, she turned to the Art Department at the Ministry of Education. In the interview, the government official admitted that she did not remember why the museum was not willing to fund research on Oriental Jewish communities at the time—1973–74—but she, nonetheless, speculated that it probably regarded such research as superfluous or unnecessary, or at least that it had a different set of priorities (transcription of interview A, p. 1). Her tone was not particularly accusatory, however. She explained that she, too, at the time found the subject very foreign: "that we didn't know what there was to research, who to research." In the end, it was her department's "small section dedicated to *folklore*" that officially funded the initial stages of research on Kurdish Jewry.

OUTLINE OF THE DISCOURSE

Since the recurrent picture this material paints even of "liberal, university-trained Ashkenazim" is one of continued implicit paternalism, I sought a tighter measure of their conceptualization of culture in Israel. My choice of medium for analysis—the weekly news-analysis and feature-story magazine *Koteret Rashit*—was not the only voice of university-trained Israelis, primarily Ashkenazi in background and identification, who regard themselves as politically liberal and secular, but it was unquestionably one of their well-known media of expression. I asked myself a straightforward question: What are the characteristics and attributes of culture mentioned or implied in the whole corpus of references to culture? I went about systematically gathering and analyzing the instances of use of *tarbut* and its derivative linguistic forms, such as *tarbuti/t, meturbat/meturbetet* which appeared in the first 100 issues of *Koteret Rashit* (1982–84).

There are, of course, disadvantages to relying on one public medium as a source of data, but there are also many advantages. The magazine, in this case, was relatively new; it contained both news analysis and non-news-related feature stories, and it came out weekly, so that it was timely and its articles were lengthy enough to develop arguments and present extensive details and quotations. Until December 1988 when it shut down for financial reasons, it had a presence in Israel.

It was in many ways like many others. It included a regular section on theater and the arts in which *tarbut* and the adjective *tarbuti* almost invariably referred to elite culture (*Kultur*). Although I, of course, included these uses of the term in my examination of the data, I chose not to attempt to quantify in any precise manner the frequency with which one kind of usage prevailed over another. It would be deceptive to do so when a regular section of a magazine is dedicated to elite culture. On the other hand, that very fact is also noteworthy, for no section on popular culture, mass culture, or even political culture appeared regularly in the magazine.

That notwithstanding, references to *tarbut* or direct explanations in terms of *tarbut* appear in a fairly wide variety of articles on a number of topics. Appendix 2 lists the articles by name, the issues in which they appear, the authors when the names are given, and basic information about the names, political parties, or events mentioned so as to provide a picture of the nature of the articles and their sociopolitical references.

There are, of course, different levels of deciphering the material. Clearly there is the topical/thematic level—that is, the subject matter in which references to *tarbut* are made and in which they appear as kinds of explanations. Here a "quantitative" measure may be of some use: 30 of the issues contain articles on *adatiut* (ethnicity within Israeli Jewish society), *paar adati* (the ethnic gap), or specific *edot,* and of these, 18 contain references to *tarbut* (i.e., 60 percent). It is interesting both because it points to a tendency to speak of *tarbut* in connection with *adatiut and* because it suggests that that tendency is not as marked as we might perhaps expect. Likewise, of the 43 articles in which I found references to tarbut, 20 deal explicitly with *adatiut, paar adati,* or a specific *eda.* If we were to lump all the articles on Americanization in the ninety-fifth issue together, the figure would then be 20 out of 36 (i.e., 55 percent)—again just over half. But we must note that at the level of theme or topic, there are, in addition to the ethnic theme, strong connections between *tarbut* and theater/visual arts as well as between *tarbut* and religious institutions or values.

The spread is richer, of course, if we examine the actual references syntagmatically (i.e., in the phrases or sentences in which they appear). Table 4.1 gives my translations of the relevant phrases.

In an attempt to understand the nature of the messages communicated in such usages, I asked myself what attributes this thing labeled *tarbut* has in each instance of usage. What are its implicit physical and abstract qualities? What is it thought to do? What can one do with it? What are some of the things done to it? What is it different from and what are the implicit or explicit criteria for claiming or asserting differences? The initial list, reproduced in table 4.2 emerges from examining the list of actual usages carefully.

But are there themes, commonalities, or patterns in all of these qualities of *tarbut* as a semiotic object? A second-level analysis, taking the evoked attributes as the raw material itself to be analyzed, looks for patterns, themes, commonalities in the attributes listed in table 4.2. This second-level analysis outlines the first-order qualities of the *object*—that it exists *concretely,* that it is *changeable,* and that it exists *abstractly.* Actually, two contradictions emerge here as equally true and characteristic of the concept *in use*—that *tarbut* is both concrete and abstract, and that it is identifiable even though it is frequently, if not constantly, in flux.

Table 4.1. Actual References/Usages of *Tarbut* in the First 100 Issues of the Israeli Weekly *Koteret Rashit*, 1982–84

Issue Number	Actual References
10	Ashkenazi culture; cultural contents; the new Israeli culture; Oriental cultural events/developments [*hitrachshuyot*]; Oriental cultural Renaissance; against the oppression of Oriental culture; Ashkenazi cultural dominance; "Ashkezrachit" culture [a made-up term whose first part is taken from the word Ashkenazi and whose second half comes from the Hebrew term for Oriental]; deep cultural roots; Oriental culture and art in Israel; cultural activity; cultural policy; one culture that will/would be detached from country of origin; cultural pluralism; the different cultures; the cultural approach; fascistic culture
12	the political culture and the rhetoric; cultural and psychological/mental/spiritual [*nafshit*] influence
15	peoples, cultures, religions [in reference to the Georgian Jews from the Soviet Union]; about the quarrel of *edot*, the gap between cultures, blacks and whites; cultural room/hall; two cultures?
18	the culture of Jews from North Africa (custom . . . culture . . . heritage)
25	cultural revolution [as a wish or goal—not an obvious reference to *edot* or ethnicity in general]; cultural problems
32	right-wing satire in a hold-out/fortress of the culture of "the left"; open culture; allergic to the culture of the Orient [Middle East and North Africa]
43	culture of governance; the Ashkenazi establishment that unjustly discriminated against Jewry from Islamic countries economically and culturally; the self-exalting relationship/attitude [of Ashkenazim] toward Oriental culture
47	that [I.Q. tests] would be free of cultural implications; cultural bias; in the present cultural conditions; social and cultural environment
49	file on Israeli culture; not one culture; not the English, not the European, not the Israeli; the Czarina of culture; when they get to culture many people say that it's all fat; those who get their nourishment from culture; cultural policy; priorities in culture; cultural services; cultural institutions; the cultural and arts branch in the Ministry of Education; Council for Culture and the Arts; cultural attaché in Boston; the unchallenged first lady of culture and the arts in Israel
50	discriminated-against cultures; fragment of any culture
52	symbols of different cultures in a period of time
57	censure of a cultural creation; you and I don't belong—I don't know why —to the same people, the same culture, the same tradition, the same values, the same norms; the culture of conversation [actually an expression used to indicate manners in dialogues and discussion]
67	the problem was a cultural problem; the things "Iche" lacked—culture, roots, a viable origin; culture of a different kind; the disappearance of a whole culture, the culture of Yiddish
68	the culture war; danger to the superiority of Western culture
69	social and cultural degeneration in development towns
71	the proud side of Oriental culture; Oriental culture is not just Mimuna and *malaveh*, Shalom Shabazi and fancy weddings—there is also cruel rape and

Table 4.1, *continued*

Issue Number	Actual References
	degradation, passivity, and feelings of inferiority; beautiful and noble culture; we/they want to belong to an accomplished culture; Oriental culture flows in the blood of all who suckled on it in their youth; the Oriental heritage has good and bad roots
72	culture of consumption and cultural consumption [or needs]; in half-folkloristic ways unknown to us
77	their culture [a reference to Moroccan Jews who are successful outside Israel]; people of impressive personalities and a developed conversational culture; this cultural-social stratum; the secularization of Western culture; when [it] came up against a different and unfamiliar culture here; it is a cultured and respected/respectable society
78	the public council for the arts and for culture; the coordinators of culture; in art for the people, people think that you have to bring the audiences [the people] to culture; a local student, an instructor working within the framework of the Perakh Project, explains that he brought them "a little bit of culture"
79	[quoting Bar Ilan University anthropologist Menachem Friedman] there is a cultivation/fostering of culture and of tradition [among Hassidim]; [and in reference to a one-woman show] cultural bore
88	[re: puppet theater] it went from the European classical, folklore and musical entertainment to experimental avant-garde that is on the border of representation and integration among the arts
89	on Sabbath mornings there is "Shabbatarbut" ["Sabbathculture"] at the workers' council house [in Petach Tikva]; Oriental culture [from the interview with the cassette music entrepreneur]; ethnic culture [a phrase introduced into the interview by the interviewer]
94	[from a letter] command of the culture of the Land of Israel; their culture [a reference to intellectuals]; "subculture"; the cultural racism of the white American; to appear in the cultural meeting places of those times; the cultural need that led to the growth of Neapolitan songs; this ugly and subcultural [under-cultural] phenomenon, in the general darkening of Israeli cultural situations
95	their people's culture; a different culture; a culture they lived; from the point of view of culture, they came out of Russian culture; your cultural world; Hebrew culture; English culture; German culture; cultural subjects; his cultural and spiritual development; he did not feel the need to demonstrate his culture in society/public; Jewish culture; my father saw the Jewish problem as a cultural and social problem and not as a political problem; re: popular culture —it's all *buba-maises* [Yiddish]; nothing will come out of it; German culture was by then a foreign culture; the culture in which I grew up and in which I spent my most formative years; but there has never been an awakening of any real opposition to the Americanization of [Israeli] society; cultural influence; the system [organization, structure] of the society, the culture, and the economy; the ugly American who disseminates his culture by way of Coca-Cola and jeans; child/product of the culture; English culture; culture of consump-

(*continued on following page*)

Table 4.1, *continued*

Issue Number	Actual References

tion; the culture of Americans; the traditional values of the culture and the governing regime; to invest money in cultural projects; foreign cultures; a cultural perspective; cultural influences; the phenomenon of cultural uprooting/ breaking off; the decision to give up a culture many of whose roots sprouted on foreign landscapes; cultural imitation; applicable to all the components of culture; besides Coca-Cola, the culture of American life embodies the clearest concretization of the modern democratic idea; importer of "what happens there" especially in culture; poses/pretensions of culture; the Americanization of culture in Israel; the institutions of culture; the America-Israel cultural foundation; Soviet culture; the public council for culture and the arts; before there can be an Americanization of culture, there must be culture

Table 4.2. Attributes of *Tarbut*

1. can be the content of something
2. can be created/can emerge over time in new circumstances
3. can be a kind of activity
4. can be oppressed/suppressed
5. can be a form of domination
6. can be a form of rooting (roots)
7. is connected to, but different from, the arts/tradition/values/norms
8. can be directed/regulated by government
9. is bounded
10. can be counted
11. can be identified
12. can coexist peacefully with other *tarbuyot*
13. can be a kind of approach or philosophy (e.g., it can be fascistic)
14. is the "property" of groups of people identified geographically
15. is connected to, but different from, the psychological or spiritual
16. is connected to, but different from, the concept of people
17. is connected to, but different from, the concept of religion
18. occupies space; ergo, we can measure the distance between *tarbuyot*
19. can describe a building
20. can be revolutionized
21. can be a kind of problem
22. can influence stereotypes
23. can influence basic modes of thinking
24. can surface in tests of skill
25. can be considered "fat"/superfluous/a privilege
26. nourishes
27. can be analyzed and its contents "prioritized"
28. can be organized and presented in the public domain
29. can be a kind of service

Table 4.2, *continued*

30. is connected to, but different from, education
31. can be given to someone as his/her charge
32. has supporters, pushers, and backers
33. leaves remnants after it has been taken apart/destroyed
34. has symbols as part of its content and by which it can be identified
35. can be a kind of creativity
36. can be an aspect/property of speech
37. has language as one of its contents
38. can be fought over
39. can be ranked/is often ranked one against another
40. can degenerate
41. has musical celebrations as part of its content
42. can also have crime, cruelty, oppression, passivity, and feelings as part of its content
43. can be pretty or ugly
44. runs in the blood
45. is a need and it has needs
46. has folkloric forms
47. is a slice of life
48. can be known or unknown
49. can be encountered/met (even by force)
50. is connected to, but different from, respect/respectability
51. is something that some societies have; some have less of; some don't have any
52. is something people can be led to
53. can be gotten or received in part or whole
54. can be given special treatment
55. can be boring
56. can be associated with, even delimited by, special days
57. can be ethnic (nonmainstream?)
58. can be the "property" of a group demarcated by level of education and/or occupation
59. can exist, even flourish, underground/subrosa
60. can be the focus of racism
61. is frequently coterminous with nation-state
62. is different from politics
63. changes over time
64. is coterminous with elitism
65. can be familiar or foreign
66. is something people are raised/socialized in
67. can be opposed
68. can be manifest in material items
69. creates people as its "offspring"
70. is something one can resign from
71. has/sheds roots
72. has/sheds roots that blossom/sprout
73. can be copied/imitated
74. has components

Consider then the summary statement on *tarbut* as it emerges from this second-level analysis.

1. *Tarbut* is a thing (content)—it can be counted, occupies space, is "owned," sheds roots, periodically surfaces, is in the blood, nourishes, leaves remnants, has "marks" that identify it, *contains* language, can be fought over, can be ranked, can degenerate, can be pretty or ugly, has needs, has folkloric manifestations, is encountered, may or may not be present, attracts people, can be received or caught, can receive, can flourish, and socializes people *within* it.

2. *Tarbut* is malleable—it emerges, can be oppressed, can be regulated, can be revolutionized, changes over time.

3. *Tarbut* is abstract/conceptual—it can be a problem, a philosophy, or approach, it influences, can be organized and presented, is a service, is an area under one's charge, has supporters and activists, can be a kind of creativity, contains language, can be fought over, includes music and feelings, is a need, is a slice of life, can be known or unknown, can bore, is connected with the arbitrary delimitation of time, is the "property" of certain groups, is coterminous with nation-state and with elitism, can be opposed, abandoned, or resigned from, and can manifest itself materially.

Clustering related themes reveals some of the issues over which there are differences of opinion and on which there is emphasis. To begin with, I find little evidence in all this material of an obsession with the separation of *tarbut* from nature as one might expect from the anthropological literature stressing the nature/culture distinction. What surfaces, instead, is an emphasis on (1) conflict and power relations among *tarbuyot* (cultures), government intervention in *tarbuyot,* and political uses of *tarbut/ tarbuyot;* (2) evaluating, comparing, and judging of *tarbuyot;* (3) positive and negative effects of *tarbut* on individuals; and (4) *tarbut* as a positive contribution to individuals as well as to groups. Consider the following subsets of table 4.2 entries:

Conflict and Power Relations among *Tarbuyot,* Government Intervention in *Tarbuyot,* and Political Uses of *Tarbut, Tarbuyot* (14)

4. can be oppressed/suppressed
5. can be a form of domination
8. can be directed/regulated by government
20. can be revolutionized
25. can be considered "fat"/superfluous/a privilege
31. can be given to someone as his/her charge
32. has supporters, pushers, and backers

33. leaves remnants after it has been taken apart/destroyed
38. can be fought over
49. can be encountered/met (even by force)
54. can be given special treatment
60. can be the focus of racism
64. is coterminous with elitism
67. can be opposed

Evaluating, Comparing, and Judging *Tarbuyot* (11)

13. can be a kind of approach or philosophy (e.g., it can be fascistic)
18. occupies space; ergo, we can measure the distance between *tarbuyot*
27. can be analyzed and its contents "prioritized"
39. can be ranked/is often ranked one against another
40. can degenerate
43. can be pretty or ugly
51. is something that some societies have; some have less of; some don't have any
55. can be boring
57. can be ethnic (nonmainstream?)
58. can be the "property" of a group demarcated by level of education and/or occupation
65. can be familiar or foreign

Positive and Negative Effects of *Tarbut* on Individuals (9)

21. can be a kind of problem
22. can influence stereotypes
23. can influence basic modes of thinking
24. can surface in tests of skill
42. can also have crime, cruelty, oppression, passivity, and feelings as part of its content
45. is a need and it has needs
50. is connected to, but different from, respect/respectability
66. is something people are raised/socialized in
69. creates people as its "offspring"

Tarbut as a Positive Contribution to Individuals as
Well as to Groups (8)

6. can be a form of rooting (roots)
12. can coexist peacefully with other *tarbuyot*

14. is the "property" of groups of people identified geographically
26. nourishes
29. can be a kind of service
35. can be a kind of creativity
59. can exist, even flourish, underground/subrosa
72. has/sheds roots that blossom/sprout

Although the clustering is obviously based on my own judgment, it is still significant that forty-two of the seventy-four attributes identified in the detailed examination of the actual uses of the term cluster so easily into the four sets—especially since all four point to a level of hierarchical orientation both of *tarbuyot* as wholes and of the products of *tarbuyot.* The clear, though unheralded, message seems to be that reference to *tarbut* is at one and the same time reference to the hierarchical placing of individuals and groups in society and to attempts to affirm, change, or create a hierarchical order by which individuals and groups would, then, be judged. One of Sammy Smooha's most persistent arguments over the past ten years seems especially relevant here—that it is precisely because Israeli governments and agencies chose over the years to concentrate on eradicating, correcting, transforming, or recognizing the *tarbuyot* of different immigrant groups that little was done to prevent/correct the structural social, economic, and political inequalities which emerged. What Smooha calls *hagisha hatarbutit* (the cultural approach) embedded within it social, economic, and political inequality. Even in the apparently egalitarian policy of the past decade of recognizing cultural differences as valid, hierarchy was maintained.

We confront here three bodies of discourse on the meaning of *tarbut:* one (e.g., Elbaz and Mizrach el HaShalom members) charges systematic discrimination against non-Ashkenazim in the institutional uses of the term; a second (e.g., Even-Shoshan) makes it easy to see how *tarbut* can serve to establish, legitimate, or push a particular social hierarchy that benefits one group over another; the third (e.g., *Koteret Rashit*) presents a picture of *tarbut* that appears on the surface to depart significantly both from Even-Shoshan's depiction of *tarbut* and from the picture presented by those charging discrimination, but which at a thematic level of analysis also stresses the competitive, conflictual, and judgmental. The intentions are different, the contexts are different, but the analytic results are clearly convergent.

A classic anthropologist analyzing some other native term in a non-industrialized society might jump at the evidence and build an analytic model around the term/concept which he or she would likely label a key cultural concept. A more politicized participant or Marxist scholar might jump at the chance to label this a classic case of ideological domination by the ruling classes. Both, I would argue, would touch on part of the phenomenon but miss the greater picture. The trick, it seems to me, is to entertain the possibility of an ideology of culture being passed on primarily in ordinary language and without the stench of conscious manipulation. Let me explain.

The recent Festschrift (Ben-David and Clark 1977) in honor of Edward Shils reopened the famous 1950s debate on "the end of ideology," with reflective but feisty pieces by two of its major proponents. In Raymond Aron's (1977) "On the Proper Use of Ideologies" and S. M. Lipset's (1977) "The End of Ideology and the Ideology of the Intellectuals," ideology appeared in its multifaceted form as (1) a more or less systematic conception of political and historical reality and a program of action derived from a mixture of facts and values (Ben-David and Clark 1977:1); (2) all the ideas or clusters of ideas tied to a given social group, whose sociohistorical consciousness they reflect and whose claims they justify (a reference to Pareto's "derivations"); (3) the elaboration of false consciousness (Lipset's allusion to Engel's [1972] and Adorno's [1973] works); (4) extreme or revolutionary doctrines (paraphrasing Shils himself); (5) systems of integrated political concepts, of utopian thinking, of class conflict, and their correlates in political positions espoused by the representatives of different classes or other political interest groups (Lipset paraphrasing himself). But time and time again both Aron and Lipset reiterated the position that it is not the set of ideals, ethical standards, general or comprehensive social views whose demise they proclaimed, but rather the existence of passion-provoking, all-encompassing utopian systems of explanation *and* design. A distinction between culture and ideology was both explicitly mentioned and alluded to. Lipset quoted Shils at length:

It is obvious that no society can exist without a cognitive, moral, and expressive culture. Standards of truth, beauty, goodness are inherent in the structure of human action. The culture which is generated from cognitive, moral, and expressive needs and which is transmitted and sustained by tradition is part of the very constitution of society. Thus every society, having a culture, will have a complex set of orientations toward man, society, and the universe in which ethical and metaphysical propositions, aesthetic judgments, scientific knowledge will be present. These will form the outlooks and sublooks of the society. Thus there can never be an "end" of outlooks or sublooks. The contention arose from the failure to distinguish these and ideology in the sense here understood. . . . (Shils 1972:40–41, cited by Lipset 1977)

The problem arises when we allow ourselves to envision the possibility that a given subset of ideas or perceptions might create an ambiance in which it is "natural" to justify the continued superior position of one social group over another. Under such hypothetical circumstances, the academic distinction Shils and Lipset try so neatly to draw loses its meaningfulness. How are we to identify the phenomenon at hand? As a cultural complex legitimating hierarchy in a predetermined way with little or no regard to political or economic conditions and changes? As a political conspiracy so carefully orchestrated that it has none of the smell of propaganda? When there is no elaborate textually encoded platform and no party or framework to push it, are we simply to invoke a cultural principle of hierarchy as adequate explanation? Is this denial of ideology as a relevant explanatory force not possibly the result of the well-known power of ideologies to become second-nature to their proponents?

Antonio Gramsci (1957, 1971) would have called this denial an outcome of the continuous process of ideological struggle ("the war of position") through which social practices are legitimated. This struggle for legitimacy results in the seeming "naturalness" of ideas and practices—ideological hegemony.[7] Recent usages of the concept have tended to equate it with ideological domination and to instrumentalize it by suggesting a simple mirror relation of domination and subordination. As Hall, Lumley, and McLennan (1978) among others argue, though, Gramsci developed the concept in order to analyze relations both within classes and between classes. The idea was that "spontaneous" consent could be won by, for example, the ruling blocs making economic concessions that "yet do not touch its essential interests," combined with other measures that foster forms of consciousness which accept a position of subordination (what Gramsci refers to as sectional and corporate consciousness).

If by *ideology* I mean here not a set of clearly formulated plans, designs, and goals for society but rather a set of concepts, assumptions, and expectations communicated with regularity by ordinary language usage in whose framework a particular power structure is legitimated, corroborated, and pushed, then we retain elements of the sense of ideology without assuming conscious, deliberate, power-hungry manipulators.

7. Gramsci (1971) argues that the process of ideological struggle will have one of two outcomes which will tend to predominate at any given time. In transformist hegemony a dominant group is constituted and transforms, through coercion and rationalization, the contradictions of social relations into legitimated practices in favor of the interests of the dominant group. Expansive hegemony, on the other hand, is characterized by social relations in which legitimated practices continually confront contradictions in an effort to resolve them in favor of a broad range of interests. The potential applicability of these notions to the Israeli setting is either hinted at, or even directly addressed, in the work of some of the members of a more recent generation of scholars with an interest in Israeli "ethnicity." A particularly good example is Arnold Lewis, but I would add here also Deborah Bernstein, Shlomo Swirski, Jonathan Oppenheimer, and Jeff Halper.

The scope of usage presented in the issues of *Koteret Rashit* does not point to a direct bolstering of the socioeconomic or political position of one sector of the population over another, but it does point to the existence of a public discourse—at times a downright debate—about the relative worth of the cultures of Ashkenazim versus Sephardim/Oriental Jews. Since the present-day discussion was triggered by years of formal attempts on the part of agencies and offices of the Israeli government—long effectively under Ashkenazi control—to feed so-called Western culture to Oriental Jews, the argument takes place under conditions of inequality, and the burden of proof remains on the non-Ashkenazi side.

That a certain pluralism has become official policy since the late 1970s both confirms the charge at this level and undermines its visibility. Might the current emphasis on adding the heritage of Oriental Jews to schoolbooks and radio programs not perhaps be a way to appease the nondominant sector of the population without affecting the long-standing interests of the dominant group? It *is* largely the case, in fact, that government agencies created to support musicians, writers, researchers, and artists connected by birth, theme, or style to Oriental Jews use the word *moreshet* (heritage), and not *tarbut* in their formal names. Likewise, the focus on non-Ashkenazi Jewry in the exhibitions and catalogs of the Department of Jewish Ethnography of the Israel Museum actually affirms by its actions the inequality with which the cultures of non-Ashkenazim are viewed and treated.

The differentiation emerges and reemerges in most, if not all, of those areas/domains traditionally seen as cultural in a nonanthropological sense: the arts (ethnic art versus art), theater (folk theater versus theater), dance (folk dance versus dance), and so forth. The previously discriminated-against sector of the population is "bought" by the addition of marked versions of cultural forms. But the hierarchical ordering which has long favored one form of *tarbut* and that sector of the population identified with it remains essentially untouched. One senses that there is *a* culture that is to be pursued and cultures treated as if the best they could do is to go away, and that there is a sameness to be pursued and a pattern of difference treated as if the best it could do is to go away.

5 On the Object of Heritage

ON January 13, 1985, I presented an earlier version of what here appears as chapter 4 to the sociologists and anthropologists at Bar Ilan University. In it I had chosen not to mince words. I was in the process of working out the relationship between *tarbut* and *moreshet* in public discourse, and I saw in the material I had gathered strong evidence of continued Ashkenazi paternalism toward non-Ashkenazim. I spoke about domination, hegemony, inequality, and hierarchy and how they show up in ordinary language that then helps perpetuate them. I wanted to highlight the illusion of cultural equality promoted, on the surface, by the relatively new official policy of legitimating cultural differences. It wasn't that I objected to the acknowledgment of cultural difference; I objected to the illusion it created of equality. I was still stressing differentiation and fragmentation among Jews. The battle over Israeli culture still seemed to me to be about sectoral competition and domination, about Israel's own internal Orientalism (cf. Said 1978) pitting an objectified "Western culture" over an equally objectified "Oriental culture," and about how those representations served the interests of those already in economic and political power. In sum, in looking at "culture" in Israel I was still very much obsessed with "ethnic fragmentation and stratification." I was in for a surprise.

The Israelis in the audience were my professional colleagues. I thought my talk might be provocative, but I didn't want to guess what kind of feedback I would get. That they were social scientists led me to expect that they would pay careful attention to the mode of analysis, the premises, and the theoretical framework in which I presented the argument. That they were also overwhelmingly Ashkenazi led me to expect them to react at least in part as "informants" listening to an outsider's rendition of some phenomenon they take for granted. That many, though not all, were observant Jews led me to wonder if and how Judaism would enter their exegesis of my material.

What interested me in the aftermath of the discussion, however, was the way in which what several of my colleagues said in that forum pointed to a counterstream or theme that seemed almost deliberately, if not consciously, to seek to balance the hierarchy and differentiation which surrounds the concept of *tarbut* in Israel. The atmosphere at the seminar was scholarly, intellectual, polite, and even warm. There was little debate about my claim that the difference between *tarbut* and *moreshet* is substantial in Israel today, but there was, nonetheless, some agitation about my lack of emphasis on Jewishness as a unifying factor.

An advanced middle-aged man volunteered the opinion that the key to the differences between *tarbut* and *moreshet* lies in the Diaspora experience of the Jews. *Moreshet,* he argued, for years referred to the lives of Jews, while *tarbut* appeared in conversations between Jews which referred to non-Jewish life. All Jews had a Jewish heritage whose common core was the basis of their Jewishness. Differences in customs were considered secondary and, therefore, inconsequential. But Jews, he continued, because of the Diaspora lived among a host of different peoples whose strength, value, aesthetic, moral, and technological production could be compared. Some Jews, thus, lived in societies with more advanced cultures than others, and it is to that difference that Israeli Jews refer when they speak of culture. There is, he concluded, no hierarchical evaluation of the *heritages* of Jews from different Diaspora communities, but there is justifiably—he maintained—a hierarchical evaluation of the *cultures* of different non-Jewish peoples.

A middle-aged religious woman known to be a supporter of Jewish settlements on the West Bank complained that *Koteret Rashit* gave a distorted picture of the ordinary language meanings of *tarbut* because it was so secular and so antireligious. The Jewish concept of *tarbut,* she insisted, implied no internal hierarchy within the Jewish people. All I had to do, she suggested, was look in the newspapers and weeklies put out by religious folk for a religious readership—*HaTzofe* (the organ of the National Religious Party); *HaModia* (the organ of the ultra-Orthodox communities in Israel); the newspaper put out by the students at Bar Ilan (even though many nonobservant Israelis attend Bar Ilan); and *HaNekuda* (a paper published by Jewish residents of the West Bank for the Jewish population of the West Bank).

A third established member of the faculty politely but firmly suggested that I not forget that *moreshet* "usually refers to *hamorasha hayehudit*" (the Jewish heritage). I should have asked him exactly what he thought that meant, but I didn't. I had indeed heard it often enough that

I drew my own conclusions and nodded. It may have been a slip in my ethnography, but his comment had made sense. The phrase is a common one in Judaic texts and religious Zionist documents, and I had been doing fieldwork in Israel off and on for almost four years.

Several self-avowed secular friends back in Jerusalem offhandedly dismissed the Jewish theme I reported on as feedback to my talk. That, they remarked with a smile, is Bar Ilan. The university is Jewish and religious by design. All students, regardless of degree of observance or field of study, are required to take courses in Judaica, and the faculty members of at least some departments including the department of sociology and anthropology have ongoing Talmudic study groups whose sessions take place in the departments themselves. Judaism and Jewishness are at least as important there as each department's academic discipline.

But if my female colleague at Bar Ilan seemed to live in a world of her own which denied the legitimacy of nonreligious voices, so my secular Jerusalem friends likewise closed themselves off to much of Israel's public discourse by dismissing the legitimacy of religious voices. The longer I digested the comments I got at Bar Ilan the more I realized that they indexed a common and persistent theme of public discourse intent on affirming and reaffirming the unity of the collectivity it presupposes. Too much emphasis on, or acknowledgment of, fragmentation among Jews threatened the presupposition that there is a collectivity known as the Jewish people. Interpreting references to *moreshet* as references to Jewishness, they implied, would show what keeps Jews together even when so much prejudice and differentiation persists between them. Heritage was pivotal to their sense of peoplehood, because it was in their eyes through and because of heritage that they were *a* people.

I am concerned in this chapter not so much with the validity of their argument, but rather with the extent to which it manifests itself in public discourse and the forms in which it appears. Clearly it is not what actually happened in the past—or how people thought, acted, or lived—that is so consequential here, but rather what is done with and to accounts of the past. Most people think of history as "the things that happened in the past," but every historian knows that what she or he produces is an account, a *story*, about events in the past. The writing of "history" says as much about the people writing the history as it does about the people written about (Carr 1961; Wolf 1982). Much the same is true of tradition —that we tend to think of it as a bounded set of concrete and abstract "things" that have been passed down to us from the past (cf. Handler and Linnekin 1984), when increasingly (e.g., Dominguez 1986b; Handler 1986; Hobsbawm and Ranger 1983) we discover that much of what we take to be "from the past" is a recent invention and how we take what we take from the past is rooted in our lives today and not the events of the past.

The reaction I got from my colleagues at Bar Ilan was couched, because of me, in terms of culture and heritage, but it is the interwoven set of assumptions that produced that reaction that interests me here, rather than references to culture or heritage per se. There are, I believe, five basic propositions contained in the argument that *moreshet* indexes the existence of a collectivity known as the Jewish people. These are (1) that there exists a collectivity known as the Jewish people; (2) that that collectivity is defined not just by arbitrary rules of recruitment but also and necessarily by its "content"—who and what is Jewish; (3) that the Diaspora experience has chipped away at that content in the everyday lives of most Jews, especially in those activities not directly connected with prayer and ritual; (4) that, as a result, much work needs to be done to discover or recreate the Jewish content of the nonreligious side of the lives of Jews; and (5) that it is the duty of every Jew to affirm and even strengthen the unity of the collectivity known as the Jewish people. Heritage (*moreshet*) becomes an object as well as the means.

THE STRUGGLE FOR CONTENT

Who is Jewish matters. I doubt very much that I am the only non-Jew who discovered only while visiting or living in Israel that many internationally known figures like movie stars, artists, writers, scientists, and athletes whose religious or ethnic identification I had never thought about are Jewish. The Israeli media refer to their Jewish identity, with few exceptions, in interviews with them or stories about them. This tendency to point out the Jewishness of such figures jars with the sense outside Israel that a similar reference in a non-Jewish newspaper invites the charge of anti-Semitism. And yet when the references are made by Jews there are few negative repercussions.

Schneider's (1968) "famous ancestor" clause seems clearly applicable, though the unit presupposed in the act is neither a nuclear family nor an extended family in the narrow anthropological sense of the terms. There is a certain readiness to claim internationally famous and respected people as "members of the family" even when they themselves do little to affirm their Jewishness in public. While the Ethiopian immigrants to Israel have to struggle to be recognized as full-fledged Jews in Israel, figures who converted within the framework of Reform Judaism (rather than according to Orthodox Jewish law) as well as those whose fathers or fathers' fathers (but not mothers) were Jewish according to Jewish law—and do not proclaim themselves Jewish at all—do frequently get counted within the fold, at least in references by the media. These include former U.S. senator and presidential candidate Barry Goldwater, entertainer Sammy Davis, Jr., actress Elizabeth Taylor, and swimmer Tiffany Cohen.

The names surface where the person's skill or expertise can be used to claim the success or potential success of Jews in a field accorded international esteem. A good example appeared in commentaries on the quality of the athletic competition at the 1985 Twelfth Maccabiah Games for Jewish youth from around the world. Philip Gillon of the *Jerusalem Post* wrote on July 26, 1985 (p. 3):

> Even allowing for the possibility of this happening, the Games seem to indicate that the standards of the finest Jewish sportsmen in the world fall below those of the non-Jewish superstars.
>
> It must be borne in mind that some leading Jews did not participate in the Maccabiah. Gymnast Mitch Gaylord was not a competitor, and in any case he has retired. Swimmer Tiffany Cohen, whose father is Jewish, did not come to the Games. Jewish tennis players in the top 20, like Elliot Teltscher and Aaron Krikstein, were conspicuous by their absence.

The entries of the *Encyclopedia Judaica* (1971) on many, if not all, subjects from anthropology to literature and theater amount to example after example of the famous ancestor clause.

But while the question of who is to be counted is open to argument and manipulation, it is in a sense easier to deal with than the question of what is to be counted as Jewish. The rule of maternal succession is what makes most Jews Jews. The possibility of conversion to Judaism expands the membership of the collectivity though those who count as converts at any one time form a small percentage of the Jewish population. Even the long-standing attempt by certain sectors of the Orthodox Jewish community in Israel to get the Knesset to enact a law discounting all those who underwent rites of conversion not under the supervision of the Orthodox rabbinate is an issue which can be clearly stated, delineated, and voted on. But if the presupposed collectivity is defined by more than simple rules of recruitment, *what* is to be counted as Jewish?

It is in areas generally referred to under the rubrics of culture, folklore, and heritage that we find the strongest vocalization of what I am calling the struggle for content. Theater is as good an example as any. "In recent years," theater critic Uri Rapp wrote in June 1985, "there has been much talk, and some action concerning 'Jewish theatre.' Throughout Jewish history this phrase would have sounded absurd; but of course Jews have been creating theatre quite intensely for the last five or six generations" (*J. Post Magazine*, June 21, 1985, p. K). Halfway through the three-column article he finally asks, seemingly impatiently,

What does *Jewish* theatre mean, anyway? Is it works *by* Jews (what about Lillian Hellman, *Porgy and Bess* or *Amadeus*)? Is it works *about* Jews (what about *The Merchant of Venice*, or Hebbel's *Herodes and Marianne* or *Ulysses*)? Is it works which carry a Jewish atmosphere and mentality, like, possibly, *Death of a Salesman*, or Woody Allen films? There is no clear answer.

Rapp's approach is at best skeptical, but in denying the validity of something called "Jewish theater" he outlines the elements of the discourse—the unsettled relationship between Hebrew theater and "Jewish theater," the search for roots, religious conservatism, and the promotion of nostalgia. He writes:

Again, there seems to be no need to call Hebrew theatre in Israel "Jewish," although it is made by Jews, for Jews, on Jewish subjects (including, of course, Israeli ones), in a Jewish language.

What is really meant by the term is part of a trend widely disseminated in Israel today, one which to me seems sterile and culturally harmful: a kind of idealization of Eastern European Jewish life and mentality (with some Moroccan spices thrown in), in its most confined and stifling period.

Some of this is a search for "roots"; some of it religious conservatism; some pure nostalgia. Some may come from a feeling of guilt, and a need to atone for the Holocaust. All of it equates the attribute "Jewish" with pre-Emancipation, pre-Enlightenment tradition.

. . . There are almost no theatre plays about this period. . . . So in order to get "Jewish" theatre, narrative tales from a later period have to be adapted, mainly by people who are not playwrights. And adaptations are almost always bad theatre. . . .

For theatre-goers, "Jewish" may come to be associated with boredom, mannerism, conceit, and artistic incompetence. Unless, of course, the weaknesses are covered by playing up to nostalgia and other affectations. . . .

The nostalgia industry puts out literature and drama (and television programmes) of a certain kind. It stimulates (nostalgia instead of sex) and excites by easy means, without demanding any commitment. It may produce a smug, self-satisfied wallowing disguised as reverence for one's grandfathers (ibid.).

What might, however, surprise an unknowing outsider is that Rapp does not then unequivocally dismiss Jewishness as irrelevant or inappropriate. His problem is not with Jewishness per se, but rather with the kind of Jewishness drawn on. He concludes:

Those who wish to make Jewishness the subject-matter of Israeli literature and drama should turn to the rich quarry of activities and personalities, statesmen and wise men, scholars, physicians, leaders and warriors of other eras and countries.

Here they will find sufficient contradiction and conflict, enough drama and analogies with our times. Some were used by earlier Hebrew writers.

What is now happening in some areas of Israeli culture is a distortion of *mainline* Jewishness, and the theatre is only the most obvious example. (ibid.; emphasis added)

It is true that critics have long lamented the plight of the Hebrew-language theater. Mendel Kohansky (1969) certainly did in his book reviewing the first fifty years of the existence of theater in modern Hebrew, and he has since then.[1] The fact is that most plays acted out in Hebrew are translations of North American and West/Central European plays, and a small minority of the performances put on by theater companies in Israel are plays written originally in Hebrew for a Hebrew-language audience or company. In his introduction Kohansky spelled it out:

A perennial problem that has haunted the Hebrew theatre from its inception is the lack of original plays. None of the great Hebrew poets at the beginning of the century seriously tried his hand at writing plays, for it was axiomatic that playwrights and theatres nourish each other, and there was no Hebrew theatre. . . .

The latter years, especially the years following Independence, produced a number of playwrights of a new generation, but it would be vain to expect anything of significant value in a country of such limited human resources, and with a theatre only half a century old. . . . (Kohansky 1969:4)

The problems, he implies, used to be structural and formal: there simply were no Hebrew-speaking companies or, for that matter, audiences. But once both of those obstacles were eliminated, the onus falls once again on the critic who must seek alternative explanations for the scarcity of plays originally written in Hebrew for Hebrew speakers. And, in the search for an explanation, the struggle for content becomes more obvious.

"The origin of the Hebrew theatre," Kohansky (1969:1) writes, "is bound up with the realization of the Zionist ideal; the early Hebrew theatres, whether founded in Europe or on the soil of Palestine, were meant first of all to be vehicles of the Hebrew language—the chief instrument of the *Jewish cultural renaissance,* and their national significance went, therefore, far beyond the purely artistic" (emphasis added). Two pages later he summarized its development:

1. Kohansky's book is largely based on his own extensive columns as theater critic for the *Jerusalem Post* over many years. The *Jerusalem Post* archives have a complete set of his columns in the file under his name. Less formal theater is rarely included in these columns, but it is not impossible to collect information on community theater performances (cf. Dvir 1985).

The Hebrew theatre began on a note of *prophetic pathos,* but this lasted only a few years and was superseded by routine, the same routine which prevails in theatres of other nations. For *theatre reflects life,* sometimes literally as does a newspaper, more often in a much more profound manner, as events of the times are distilled in the alembic of art. The years following World War I were years of great issues for the world at large and for the Jewish people especially. . . . It was against this background that Habimah staged its *biblical, prophetic* plays, and the play *The Dybbuk,* which was permeated with the mystique of *freedom.* Several years later, intoxication with building the Land as a home for free people inspired Ohel, the workers' theatre, to stage plays extolling the *heroism of labour.* And two decades later, the War of Independence was *reflected* on the stages of Israel in plays which echoed the thunder of battles fought in the immediate vicinity of the theatre buildings.

The years following the achievement of Independence and mass immigration were coloured by the people's desire to relax and recover from battle and struggle, and live as other peoples do. There were *no burning issues* to be faced, and minor issues were avoided as much as possible. One symptom of this normality was a great thirst for entertainment. It resulted in both a proliferation of theatres and a prevalence of productions that offered entertainment at the expense of intellectual and emotional effort. (Kohansky 1969:3; emphases added)

There is a hidden and a not-so-hidden message in all this. The obvious point that there are very few original Hebrew plays on the rosters of Israel's theater companies goes along with a carefully couched, but clearly stated, assertion that most of the original Hebrew plays are at best mediocre. But much of what Kohansky says in his book—and continually in his *Jerusalem Post* columns—reads like apologies for the art of writing plays in Hebrew, and the apologies relate to the situational pressures that seem to dictate the content of the plays. Either the playwrights, in his estimation, get carried away with grandiose hopes or emotions they share, or believe they share, with large sectors of the Jewish population —thus limiting the capacity of the play to engage one intellectually as well as emotionally—or they deliberately run away from any potentially significant content.

The critical question, of course, is what criteria are to be used to determine that something carries, or does not carry, a "significant content." Good theater, it has long been said, is theater that appeals to markedly different populations separated by space and time, theater that deals with a genuine issue or problem of enduring universal (or at least widespread) appeal. In complaining about the content of original Hebrew plays, it is clear that Kohansky invokes that criterion of quality. But if instead of asking whether they have a significant content we were to ask for whom is their content significant, both our objective in examining them and our conceptualization of the boundaries of the phenomenon we call theater would have to change substantially.

The growing interest in "Jewish theater" is an outgrowth of one solution to the perceived problem of inadequate content. While Uri Rapp may denigrate the "nostalgia industry" that produces its current incarnation, performers, critics, directors, playwrights, and academics thought it serious enough to organize and attend the First International Conference and Festival of Jewish Theatre in Tel Aviv in July 1982. Sponsors included the Association for the Promotion of Original Jewish Theater, the Museum of the Diaspora, the Department of Cultural and Scientific Exchanges at the Israeli Foreign Ministry, the America-Israel Cultural Foundation, the Tel Aviv Foundation for Literature and the Arts, the Municipality of Tel Aviv, the National Foundation for Jewish Culture, the Kinneret Foundation, and the Emet Foundation. Organizers argued that the event was "the first of its kind in the world to bring together theater people and researchers close to the subject of Jewish theater" and that "the rich fare of [scheduled] lectures and performances testifies to the great interest many have already shown in the convention" (translation from the official brochure and program for the July 3–9, 1982, affair).

The program included performances of twenty-five separate pieces (not all of them stage plays), and twelve panel discussions. Eight of the works performed were dramatic productions put on by Israelis, two were Israeli dance performances, one was a concert, and another a combined concert and dance production. They ranged in theme from a mystical allegory of redemption adapted for the stage from a story told by a well-known rabbi to "experimental theater" with Jewish and Arab actors dealing with "contemporary subjects," "experimental theater" on the annual Jewish cycle, the Yiddish theater, and the possibility of creating an "authentically" new but also authentically Jewish cultural form drawing equally from East and West.[2]

---

2. *Authenticity* appears frequently throughout this chapter, because it appears frequently in discussions concerning *tarbut* and *moreshet* in Israel. Handler (1986:4) is right, at least in terms of Israel, when he writes that "the concept of 'authenticity' is as deeply embedded in anthropological theory as it is in the self-conscious ethnic ideologies of many of the groups that we study." The word most often used in Israel in this context is, in fact, *otentiut,* a Hebraicized form of the English word *authenticity. Amiti* (from the word for truth) and *mekori* (from the word for source or origin) are related choices.

Authenticity is clearly important to those who talk or write about it. It suggests rooting, truth, history, culture, and essence all in one. It also suggests that there is typically too much mixing, too much "impurity," too little regard for the past, and too little clarity in people's sense of themselves (e.g., Shiloah and Cohen 1982). I am not as convinced as Handler seems to be that authenticity is a cultural construct of the modern *Western* world. I think, and in this I agree with Handler, that where there are strong nationalist movements

The panel discussions paralleled the theatrical themes. Three panels concentrated on the potential use of Jewish sources in theatrical productions (e.g., "the theatrical aspects of Jewish ritual," "theatrical basics in Kabbala," "speech, poetry, and movement in the study of the Jewish oral law," and "Yiddish theater"); three explored theatrical perspectives on traditional Jewish storytelling (Hassidic Purimspiel, theater among Jews in Iraq and Morocco, "folk theater" among the Jews of Spain, and the art of storytelling by Jews from Turkey, Morocco, Iran, and Egypt); three discussed the contemporary Jewish theater in England, the United States, Brazil, and Israel; one focused on contemporary Jewish theater dealing specifically with the Holocaust; in another, well-known Hebrew writers discussed their own works "in light of the Jewish experience"; and in the last of the academic panels, participants from different countries speculated on "the future of Jewish theater."

The conference was at times heated, attendance was good but not great, and coverage in the press mixed. The conference attempted both too much and too little. Some of the performances were technically good, but the question of the significance of the content remained. The academic panels seemed to document an interest in *creating* a Jewish theater more than in attesting to its existence. In fact, it was never quite clear just how much was description and analysis and how much was prescription.

Authenticity surfaced with regularity as a theme of discussion throughout the five-day event. HaBreira HaTiv'it (the "natural alternative") musical ensemble was included in the program because it is "an original/authentic [*mekorit*] Israeli musical group that gathers within it a fascinating and exciting blend of East and West" (my translation of the note in the program). "Authentic" storytellers of non-Ashkenazi origin were brought to one of the panels both to perform and to have their stories and performances analyzed on the spot by a panel of folklorists, three of them Ashkenazim. The authenticity of a fifth storyteller, an American of Ashkenazi origin not listed on the official program but brought in at the last minute by the chairman of the panel, was called into question by a number of the panelists as well as members of the audience.

The incident surrounding the American storyteller is telling. A Kurdish Jew from Iran had opened the session with a story which was then commented on by the folklorists on the panel. This had been followed by a Turkish-born Ladino speaker, a Moroccan-born storyteller, and a

there is usually a public discourse concerned with authenticity. But I prefer to reconceptualize it—that where there is a strong sense of peoplehood and of the importance of being a people there is ironically more expressed concern with internal challenges to the collectivity and, thus, more concern with authenticity.

woman of Egyptian origin. The panelists had stressed over and over again "the relationship between text and performance, and the necessity of performance in the telling of, and meaning of, the story." Nothing in the comments had come even close to criticizing the storytellers. Details of their performances were noted, variations compared.

It was at that point that the chairman, well-known folklore specialist Dov Noy, stated that while all of these come from Oriental Jewish communities "the intention is not to associate storytelling only with Oriental Jewish communities and vice versa, that there is also a strong storytelling tradition in Eastern Europe." He announced that he had asked a Lithuanian-born storyteller to participate in the session but that something had come up unexpectedly and he had been unable to attend. But, he said, he was lucky to have thought of someone else—a long-time, serious storyteller of Jewish stories from Eastern Europe in the States—and that he had asked her, therefore, to tell us stories. Noy then introduced her. She approached the podium, apologized for telling her story in English, explained that she was dedicating her story to a friend who was sitting in the audience, then turned to the panel saying "actually the story I am going to tell is not from Eastern Europe—it is from Kurdistan," and moved to face the audience adding "well, it's not a story I heard through the family—I read it but I liked it so much that I like to tell it." At that point, she paused, looked down for a moment and, upon lifting her head, looked almost entranced and began telling her story. After she finished, the younger members of the panel were polite but did not hide their disapproval.

My notes from then on read as follows:

Panel: Aliza said *gently* that there are some interesting differences between Barbara's performance and the others—that she may be more of a professional telling a story, not a story she's heard live; the style is more dramatic, like an actor's.

Galit took the same point, stated it more emphatically—verged on being a real criticism of Barbara (or of Dov for having included her in this)—that one must really ask the question of whether or not Barbara's type of storytelling *belongs* in this group/type/session. It is, after all, a story taken just from a text without the whole context it goes with, the original language; it is then *interpreted* by the storyteller with inflections, tones, suggestions that are not in the original; also that she is more restricted than folk storytellers because she *only* has the *text* and cannot/does not depart from the text.

At this point, Dov tried to ease some of the critical tone of the comments, saying it's a *different* type of storytelling. Galit continued a bit. At that point, an actor/director (mid-30's, Israeli), agitated, from the last row asked to be allowed to say something. Dov gave him the floor, but he said he wanted to do it in the form of storytelling. So he came to the podium/microphone and started imitating Barbara's style (without exaggerating or doing it to the extent *she* does). He was saying, however, that he found the panel's comments insulting, especially these last comments, that storytelling is at the heart of theatre—the fundamental aspect of it—and these storytellers do it without the baggage of modern theatre and the training of actors, that *we* may learn from folk storytellers; that what the panel is doing is separating out the story from the performance or telling of the story (the hands, the pauses, etc.) and that they are *integrally* connected.

Galit, animated, explained that those *are* very much the points they are trying to make and that what he said sounds like what we want students in an introductory course to learn.

Then Simon Litchman [English-born anthropologist/folklorist with a doctorate from the University of Pennsylvania who was sitting in the audience] got agitated and from his seat towards the back of the room on the other side, started saying that the whole *question* being discussed is wrong, that they're talking about authenticity as if any one story-type/teller were more *authentic* than another; that the "folk" storytellers also modify the stories they tell. They're not "original"; in fact, there is no such thing as an original/authentic version.[3]

Dov more or less calmly said that we're getting into the question of edot [Jewish ethnic groups in Israel] and moreshet edot hamizrach [the heritage of Oriental Jewish communities] that is so much in the air these days; that Simon is right about the respect due all storytellers and the fact that part of storytelling is interpreting. But that there is a moreshet yahadut hamizrach [heritage of Oriental Jewry], that part of it at least is alive, and that there is a difference between Barbara's performance and the others'.

3. Here Simon is doing something many Israeli anthropologists do—intervene as academics, rather than as ethnographers, in Israel where they also tend to do their fieldwork. It goes hand in hand with doing fieldwork in one's own backyard. I bring it up not to criticize but to point out how closely tied to the setting the "citizen/ethnographer" is, and how different his or her sociopolitical participation is from those of us who do research far from where we carry out our civic duties. It makes it clear why I conceptualized my initial period of research as including academic social scientists whom I treated for a long time much more like "informants" than like colleagues.

The interesting thing is that anthropological immersion in one's field site can draw a noninsider into similar dual roles, even when she or he is not looking. In reading various parts of my field notes as well as this book, for example, I find myself at times very much an actor and not at all just an observer. I doubt that I am different from other anthropologists in the field, but it is a sobering thought, nonetheless. I did, and do, have an effect on my Israeli friends, colleagues, students, and acquaintances—not always intended and not always the same but still an effect. I know I had an effect on the design of the permanent exhibition mounted by the Department of Jewish Ethnography in 1985, an effect on the way my Israeli students came to view ethnicity in Israel, and an effect on several friends who had never had the opportunity to know up close just how Jewish even "secular" Israeli life could feel to a non-Jew. But this is the kind of realization that makes me wonder how anyone could justify writing about people he or she has studied through fieldwork without making himself or herself one of those people studied, described, and analyzed.

> A woman (ca. 40's) went up to the mike at the podium and began talking about the importance of learning about moreshet yahadut hamizrach—what its elements are, what it is in detail—it is part of our whole moreshet as Jews.

The inclusion of such a panel in the program—and a total of three sessions on non-European Jewish communities—had at first seemed to be little more than a concession to vocal Israelis of non-Ashkenazi origin who, like Nissim Yosha, keep on pushing for integration of the heritage of Oriental Jews in the culture of Israeli society. Without expanding the concept of theater to include verbal and nonverbal performances like storytelling and joking, there would have been few papers to present and relatively little material to counter the feeling that Oriental Jewish communities contributed little, if anything, to the cultural form called theater. But as the discussions ensued, it became clear that the seemingly vulgar political concession could be easily rationalized by Israelis and interpreted in terms of a search for Jewish content.

The American storyteller was problematic because she took a story out of context, unrelated to her own family ancestry, and acted it out so theatrically that it seemed false. Authenticity meant "rootedness," an awareness of and pride in one's personal and collective heritage, and a personal commitment to the perpetuation and dissemination of products of that heritage. Barbara had no personal tie to Kurdistan and, thus, told "someone else's story." In the context of a widespread emphasis on the search for significant content for the Jewish collectivity, telling "someone else's story" smacked of appropriating someone else's content.

The juxtaposition between the HaBreira HaTiv'it musical ensemble and the incident surrounding the American storyteller highlights important analytic dimensions of the struggle for content. Inclusion of HaBreira HaTiv'it in the conference's program made sense not in terms of the form of their performances—which was not theater in anything but the broadest possible conception of theater—but rather in terms of their explicit goals. The ensemble was founded by a Moroccan-born, professionally trained social worker who gathered around him a mixed crew—an Israeli-born bass player of Eastern European origin, a guitar and banjo player originally from New Mexico, an Indian sitar player, and from time to time additional musicians. Both the group's Hebrew name—meaning the "natural alternative"—and its self-accorded English name—the Natural Gathering—hint at the group's image of itself and what it seeks to accomplish. The idea is that what they do is and should be natural, that what they produce comes out naturally, that their getting together to play makes sense, and that the music they produce is and should be a good alternative to the rock, classical European, classical Middle Eastern, Brazilian samba, and Europop that still dominate Israeli music. The result is a sound that is uniquely its own, easily identifiable from a distance, penetrating, and to my ears, eerie and strange. It is deliberately neither Western nor Eastern, but rather a creation of the group's own, drawing consciously and actively from Ashkenazi as well as North African, Middle Eastern, and South Asian music. The goal is to produce more *authentically Jewish* music. I quote from an interview with the group published in *Ma'ariv* in December 1981.

Shlomo Bar (founder, singer, and percussionist): In the conception [worldview] of Oriental art, there has to be a continuity between past and present. There has to be a tie between what I do today and what I have belonged to for 2000 years. I try to create that tie in my music.

Tzeruya Lahav (Ashkenazi, kibbutz-bred and, at the time, violist and singer): Judaism has to return to the Orient [Middle East]. Not by force or aggressiveness. . . . What is important to us is our autonomy. We run after America and don't find ourselves. The solution is Judaism. Not fanatic and closed Judaism, but rather Jewish values with openness . . .

Miguel Hershtein (American-born guitarist): Everyone changes here. It's a process whose results we'll see only in a few generations. In the end, there will be one people here. We have to come closer, to open doors.

Sami Bat-Ayin (bass player): Our group is not just "show," like many pop groups. When we play something we point the way. Pop artists don't think about what comes next. Tomorrow there'll be something new. HaBreira HaTiv'it is not pop. The Tora never changes. They didn't make a poster out of Moses in the "Lehiton." "Know where you come from and where you're going." (*Ma'ariv*, December 12, 1981, entertainment section, pp. 2–3)

One of the ironies of HaBreira HaTiv'it, however, is that in the attempt to create music that presupposes and simultaneously accentuates the oneness of the Jewish people, they produce music that is neither here nor there and, thus, often appeals more to highbrow writers, critics, and intellectuals who are overwhelmingly Ashkenazim rather than to the majority. The LP "Waiting for Samson," for example, is sold with a copy of a *Ha'aretz* review of one of their performances which starts out by commenting on the predominance of "Western" Israelis in the audience. The appeal is at once emotional and intellectual. On April 18, 1982, for instance, an article commenting on Israel's participation in the annual Eurovision song contest was given the title "HaBreira HaTiv'it" (the "natural alternative"). It read:

We don't always have to learn from others but—it's possible. It's possible, for example, to learn from the French broadcasting authority that decided not to participate this year in the Eurovision contest because the tunes were at such a low level [that] it was better to invest the budgeted money into developing creative programs than to help commercial record companies increase their sales.

It is so simple and logical. . . . Here we justify everything by mentioning [the need for an Israeli] "presence" in the international media. True, but we don't have to forfeit that. We can follow the artist-musicians throughout the year, turn to the one who stands out and enable him to compete in the contest as he sees fit. . . . That's [what came to mind], for example, when I was sitting at a performance of HaBreira HaTiv'it—I thought to myself how nice it would be to send them to the European song contest and to allow them to represent us with the Hassidic-Oriental composition and the combination of their unique flavor . . . with a lot of melody. Strength. And emotion. (*Ma'ariv*, April 18, 1982, p. 21; my translation).

The message was repeated by Tzeruya Lahav, even after she had left the group, in an interview she gave the local Jerusalem newspaper *Kol Ha'Ir* in September 1984.

Q: What exactly happened with HaBreira HaTiv'it?
A: The first time I heard HaBreira HaTiv'it I actually cried. I loved the material so much. I simply loved it in my soul. Also Shlomo's poetry [singing, chanting]. Already then I was dying to be in HaBreira.
Q: Even though it was Oriental music?
A: For me it was Jewish. It brought my father and my grandfather and the Jewish objective/hope [*kavana*] back to me. The Hassidic and Oriental melodies come together a lot. I wasn't aware then of the more practical side of the whole thing—the fact that I am a woman, an Ashkenazi, and a kibbutz member. I still didn't understand what it could do to this whole band. Suddenly something totally different entered the group. For good and for bad. . . . (*Kol Ha'Ir*, September 9, 1984, p. 37)[4]

The "authenticity" of HaBreira gets juxtaposed to the "inauthenticity" of the American storyteller theatrically telling someone else's story. But from a distance both claims warrant explanation. HaBreira is, after all, creating new pieces and inventing its own style of music, not hunting

---

4. The two major kibbutz movements—HaKibbutz HaArtzi and the United Kibbutz Movement—which together comprise over 90 percent of the population in Israeli kibbutzim are secular by self-representation, though there is some range among them in their tolerance of Jewish ritual, custom, or tradition. As Bowes (1982:45), for example, puts it, the Artzi "is, and always has been the most left-wing of the kibbutz movements. It is officially atheist, whereas others are agnostic, and one is religious." Of the others she labels as "mainly agnostic," she adds that "some tolerated religious members, and even built small synagogues for them (ibid., p. 46). The point is that *kibbutznikim* (i.e., people from kibbutzim) are expected to be at least unreligious, if not antireligious outright.

down ancient scores and playing them on specially made reproductions of ancient instruments. Barbara the storyteller was indeed telling a story that had been handed down over at least some generations from Jew to Jew, albeit not to her immediate family. The keys to understanding the very different receptions they get are twofold: (1) HaBreira is itself a group of ethnically heterogeneous Jews coming together to try to tease out of the diverse Diaspora cultures of the Jews a single, unified, and unique cultural form. It is a collective effort toward a collective goal. Barbara was a single American with no known ties to Kurdistan, and she seemed much more interested in dramatization than in unification of the Jewish people. The result is a feeling of illegitimate appropriation of something that belongs to another. (2) HaBreira HaTiv'it produces new music and is explicitly creative. It is not considered folklore. Folklore is expected to be inherited and, thus, to serve as a tie with the past. Barbara's performance was an attempt to reproduce the telling of a folk story and not to create a new one. It does not count as creative arts and does not, therefore, get accorded the license awarded to "creative artists." However, it does not meet the criterion of serving as a tie with one's past: her Kurdish story was part of other people's past, not her own. Her effort simply did not follow the "rules" of the contemporary Israeli struggle for content: it drew on an inappropriate past and thus broke the "rule" of authenticity, and created nothing synthetic that could be used as content for the future.

THE PREVALENCE OF STORYTELLING

That the struggle for content is not simply an elite preoccupation is evident in the prevalence of what I call collective storytelling. A group or community, village, or even city neighborhood researches, writes, acts out, exhibits, and/or tells others about its past. Much of what results is labeled folklore, community theater, or ethnic history, but its main purpose is rarely the simple celebration of folklore or of historical facts. The simplest explanation is that these activities are all politically motivated —an attack on the dominant position of Ashkenazim in Israeli society and culture—but I find in them a much more genuine, less manipulative side which transcends the ethnic divide. Presupposition and prescription shape most of these activities—the presupposition that content exists and must simply be found and exhibited, and the conviction that only by being familiar with the content of all preexisting Jewish communities can an appropriate content be given to the single collectivity of Jewish people that those who participate in collective storytelling hope is in the process of emerging.

On June 2, 1982, for example, at the First International Meeting on

Folklore Research in Israel which was held at the Hebrew University, I
was introduced to a man I shall dub "Yehuda" who claimed to have put
his academic training in folklore to use in business. In business since 1977
and with at least three part-time employees, Yehuda interviews residents
of small and medium-sized towns in Israel, makes films and videos of
the towns, writes local histories for them, and sells them to the towns'
residents. He claims "it just took knowing how to sell ideas to people,"
that he "just sensed and believed that people were just ready, interested
in these things, but [that] someone had to come to them and show them
what can be done and how."

That the interest in what I dub storytelling is not restricted to Israelis
of North African and Middle Eastern Jewish origin was driven home in
learning about his work. He works mostly with towns he describes as "the
old established communities" in which the vast majority of the population
is Ashkenazi. In fact, he admitted that he has had a hard time "breaking
into" Sephardic communities, trying for about four years to sell a project
to the predominantly Yemenite town of Rosh Ha'Ayin and for about five
years to start something in the largely Moroccan development town of
Dimona. On the other hand, he claimed that "some people at Kfar Cana"
(an Arab village) had approached him "to do some things for them." The
problem in Oriental Jewish communities, he hypothesized, is not lack
of interest in their heritage but rather "that the look of the places—the
buildings—they live in now doesn't exactly get them to feel pride in their
[current] neighborhoods and towns."[5]

The matter was scarcely that simple, however. For months, I had been
closely following "storytelling" events throughout Israel. I knew that a
small- to medium-sized museum on Moroccan Jewry was in the works
in Dimona, that conferences had been held and exhibitions mounted during the previous half-year celebrating the one hundredth anniversary of
the arrival in what is now Israel of the first documented Yemenite Jewish
immigrants (in modern times), and that one of the oldest and most suc-

5. The publication of *Pe'amim*, beginning in the spring of 1979, comes in the wake of
this concern and the funding possibilities created by the existence of Nissim Yosha's Center
for the Integration of the Heritage of Oriental Jewry. The journal is appropriately subtitled
Studies in the Cultural Heritage of Oriental Jewry. To the point was the inclusion in its very
first issue of two articles on the very conceptualization of the cultural heritage of Oriental
Jewry that the editors saw as "a topic for debate"—one by Shaul Shaked (1979), concerning
research and the academic teaching of the "cultural heritage of Oriental Jewish communities," the other by the late Haim Hillel Ben-Sasson (1979), rejecting "the validity of the term
'Oriental Jewry Heritage.'" That these thinkers, writers, and entrepreneurs find it necessary to discuss the whole concept of Oriental Jewry is an interesting indication that Arnold
Lewis has been on the right track in talking about "phantom ethnicity," and exploring what
political functions the creation of the term *Oriental Jewry* may have.

cessful dance companies in Israel, Inbal, had been founded by an Israeli of Yemenite origin back in the early 1950s to work with Yemenite Jewish "folklore," its rituals, dances, songs, and decorative arts and produce "theater that would be truly national" (Kohansky 1969:190). Yehuda and I concluded that what was interesting about his work was not so much what it might say about Oriental Jewry but rather what it says about the current interest in heritage and folklore in the public at large. He earned an income without working on Oriental Jewish folklore.

In fact, at the national level, this kind of storytelling is so common that an alert observer could be kept quite busy going from exhibition opening to exhibition opening, community theater to documentary film, radio program to television program, historical conference to "ethnic happening." I at least was kept on the run. From mid-August 1981 through mid-August 1982—just to give an idea of their frequency—either I or one of my research assistants attended, observed, and/or obtained information about over fifty events of this sort (see appendix 3).

I offer a list of events as a glimpse of what was available nationally, and not as a comprehensive listing of storytelling events. A more complete picture would have to include the numerous radio and television programs that told the story of one or another community on the national media, and the myriad articles of the same genre in the national and local newspapers. It would have to include, for example, references to the weekly radio programs of "Hassidic songs and melodies," "Sephardic folksongs," "folk dances," "folk songs," "Jewish traditions," "the Jewish people," "Oriental songs," "Folklore magazine," "Roots—folklore magazine," and "Yiddish songs." And it would, of course, be incomplete without reference to the special programs and series that have been aired in the same genre.

Of the latter, I shall give two examples. In early February 1982, Israel's generally popular army radio broadcast a series telling the story of different Jewish communities before their immigration to Israel, their immigration to Israel, and their contributions to Israeli society. The series discussed Ashkenazi as well as Sephardi communities, was given the name "Shorashim" (roots), and aired for eight straight hours.

Meanwhile, much of that storytelling had been going on on television in a series entitled "Eretz Ahavati" (the land of my love). Originally started in January 1981 as a television magazine for youth with the express purpose of exploring aspects of the geography and history of "the land of Israel," it had by fall 1981 expanded its viewing audience and changed its focus. In an interview with one of my research assistants on June 10, 1982, an assistant producer of the series admitted that it had been dedicated from the start to looking at places (sites) in Israel but that "there have been developments since then and more and more it's dealing with *edot* [Jewish ethnic communities]."

The subject matter of the actual programs confirms that assessment. Between September 13 and May 30, 1982 (when the program went off the air for the summer), fourteen of the programs aired fell into the storytelling genre. These included programs on Kurdish Jewry broadcast directly from the Israel Museum, on Nahalal (Israel's oldest *moshav*—an Ashkenazi community famous for being among other things Moshe Dayan's home), on the kibbutz community of Sde Boker in the Negev (to which Israel's first prime minister retired after leaving office—also an Ashkenazi population), on Moroccans in a neighborhood in Jerusalem, on "Poles in a Polish cafe in Tel Aviv," on the Georgians of the port city of Ashdod, on Americans in Israel (broadcast from an "American" *moshav*), and on the oldest urban settlements founded by Jews since the beginning of Zionism and their (largely) Eastern European legacy. Almost without exception, the programs avoided any and all mention of social inequalities, the political economy of the "ethnic gap" between Sephardim and Ashkenazim, and national party politics. Folklore, music, dance, material culture, and stories about the old days dominated nearly all of the programs.

The storytelling genre I am associating with the search for content is, in fact, for the most part celebratory in tone and far from critical of the section of the Jewish people whose history or lifestyle it depicts. That goes for Eastern European storytelling events as well as non-European ones, events initiated by government institutions as well as those initiated more informally at the local level, exhibitions and amateur musicals, national convocations of former residents of one country or another as well as kibbutzim. That is not to say that there is no criticism of Israeli government policies in the 1950s or 1960s or no established avenue for criticism, but it rarely takes the form of staged and public storytelling. The emphasis in all these events is the worth and value of the community's past, and the need for the collectivity known as Israeli society both to recognize that worth and incorporate its contents. I shall document the variants of the genre with selected examples drawn from different sectors of the population.

Yiddishkeit

Yiddishists have always existed in Israel, but not until recently have they been accorded legitimacy. The May 5, 1982, meeting at the Museum of the Diaspora, so packed that there was little but standing room, and the screening of the documentary film *Image before My Eyes* at the Jerusalem Cinematheque on February 3, 1982, are two good examples of the publicness of the celebration of Yiddishkeit.

Image before My Eyes, made in New York by YIVO (the Yiddish language and culture research institute) with funding from the U.S. National Endowment for the Humanities, depicted the Jewish community in Poland up to World War II. That night it drew a full house—mostly over the age of forty but not exclusively, many English speakers, many university academics, and by all my informants' assessments almost all middle class to elite Ashkenazim. Part of the audience was there by invitation. An American woman appearing to be in her thirties introduced the film saying—in English—that it was the first in a series to be shown at the Cinematheque on "Jewish topics, our history, our heritage, movies in effect about our Jewish ethnic identity." At the end of her remarks, a woman in her early sixties yelled out, "Ivrit! ivrit!" (Hebrew! Hebrew!), and was echoed by a young couple—twenty-eight to thirty-five years old—sitting to my right.

Something was definitely changing in Israel. An Israeli colleague closely connected to YIVO claims that Israeli television had had a copy of the film for half a year and had not put it on the air, and that "apparently the television people had told the filmmakers that it wasn't interesting enough [as a film] but that its main problem was that it wasn't Zionist enough—didn't present Zionism strongly enough." The television authorities denied both allegations, but still did not air the film. I had heard the story before February 3, but heard it again from the same colleague as she proudly but somewhat resentfully left the Cinematheque when the film ended. That the movie theater was packed showed her that there was an audience "out there." The celebration of heritage was not a contradiction of Zionism, at least to these people. But they were aware that it had long been seen as contradictory, and they reacted with a quiet sense of defiance toward a previous generation of policy makers they now identify with such a view.

Turn taking

I include in this storytelling form exhibitions taking place in the country's major museums and "cultural centers," especially the Museum of the Diaspora, and events planned around such exhibitions. The events are initiated by and housed in well-known public institutions, and different heritages are celebrated in succession. The Museum of the Diaspora in a suburb of Tel Aviv and the International Cultural Center for Youth in Jerusalem are both good examples.[6]

6. These institutions mount exhibitions and put on, or invite, musical or theatrical performances to accompany some of their themes. They also publish catalogs, pamphlets,

Built with funds donated primarily by Diaspora Jewry and officially open only since 1980, the Museum of the Diaspora caters both to tourists from Diaspora Jewish communities and to Israel's educational institutions. Its exhibitions are mostly photographic, audiovisual, and reconstructive. It does not display actual material culture, but it does have numerous screens and monitors where visitors can watch documentary films on scores of Diaspora Jewish communities. In addition, it periodically mounts special exhibitions on particular communities—from the little known Jewish communities of the Caribbean to the pioneering agricultural settlements of Eastern European Jews in nineteenth-century Argentina, the varied Jewish communities of India, and the "now extinct" Jewish community of Libyan Tripolitania—and sells thin catalogs with photographs and explanatory texts on the community in question. Each week the newspapers publish a list of the activities, lectures, and special events that accompany both the special exhibitions and their permanent displays.

The opening of the exhibition on modern Rumanian Jewry on June 7, 1982, allows us to see some of the main features of this kind of storytelling celebration. To begin with, the opening was both a gathering and a ritual of celebration. The opening was open to the public, but many of those present were there by special invitation. Public figures graced the museum and Rumanian Jewry with their presence, thus legitimating the celebration of heritage. There were frequent references to the importance of, and the interest in, the heritages of all the sectors of the Jewish community.

The celebrants were, however, primarily older and still spoke Rumanian freely. About three hundred people attended. No more than twenty-five people looked under forty. Modal age, I estimated, was between sixty-five and seventy. About twenty men wore suits—actually a high figure in Israel. I estimated about equal numbers of men and women. No more than about 20 percent of the conversations around me before and after the official ritual of greetings were in Hebrew. I estimated that at least two-thirds of what I heard was Rumanian with some Yiddish thrown in.

There was no reference anywhere in the exhibition to "the ethnic gap" or to Oriental Jews, although the word *Sephardi* (in both Hebrew and English) appeared eight times in the captions accompanying the photo-

brochures, even journals. The Israel Museum publishes the *Israel Museum Journal* as well as, in ethnography, an occasional paper series entitled *Edot: Studies in Ethnography* that began in 1984. Companion booklets/catalogs get printed for every exhibition of note. A book-length volume about the Museum of the Diaspora entitled *The Diaspora Story: The Epic of the Jewish People among the Nations* came out in 1981. It was authored by Joan Comay "in association with Beth Hatefutsoth–The Nahum Goldmann Museum of the Jewish Diaspora, Tel Aviv."

graphs on display. No section of the exhibit dealt with Rumanians in Israel today. Shlomo Lahat, mayor of Tel Aviv, and Yitzhak Arzi, Rumanian-born deputy mayor of Tel Aviv, both gave short congratulatory speeches —stressing that Rumanian immigrants to Israel had contributed to Israeli society in many fields (in, for example, founding the towns of Rosh Pinna and Zichron Yaakov, serving in the army, working in education, and participating actively in politics), that the work of the Museum of the Diaspora was important because of the general interest in "morashot yehudiot [Jewish heritages] from the West as well as from the East," and that the importance of such an exhibition is "to pass on information [about roots and heritage] to future generations."

The International Cultural Center for Youth, located in Jerusalem, is an example of a slightly different type of institution participating today in what I call "turn taking." Long in existence, it is only in recent years that it has taken on the task of contributing to the celebration of heritage. In 1980, upon returning from a year in the United States, a well-known folk dancer, folk dance teacher, and organizer of "folklore" events developed the idea of fostering "the folklore of ethnic groups in Jerusalem and environs." She admits to having been influenced by the contemporary North American interest in roots and ethnic differences while in the States, but points out that her project would have gone by the wayside if the atmosphere had not also been favorable in Israel. She wrote a "project proposal" for the top administrators at the center and began, with their agreement, to execute the plan. It was to be a five-pronged approach: (1) song and/or dance troupes, (2) exhibits, (3) shows, festivals, conferences, and events, (4) days or weeks set aside for certain ethnic groups organized as "happenings," and (5) visual material.

A mimeographed announcement put out by the center dated November 22, 1981, explained that the center had already prepared four exhibitions—of photographs and accompanying texts—that it was willing to mount in schools, community centers, clubs, or other institutions anywhere in the country that showed interest. These told the stories of (1) North African Jewry ("their places of residence in North Africa, lifestyle, customs, material culture, their links to Zion, and their immigration to Israel"), (2) Iraqi Jewry ("their customs, lifestyle, material culture, and links to Zion"), (3) North African Jewry—Zionism, immigration, and settlement ("in detail on the links to Zion among Jews from the Maghreb, the different waves of immigration to Israel, Zionist activity, illegal immigration [just before the establishment of the state], absorption lines, and settlement in Israel"), and (4) Georgian Jewry ("the history of the ethnic group, its links to Zion, the settlement of Georgians in Jerusalem, material culture, and lifestyle"). In addition, the November 22 mimeo mentioned that a similar traveling exhibition on Yemenite Jewry—"the history of the ethnic group, its different waves of immigration, and its contribution to Israeli Jewish society"—was in preparation.

An exhibition commemorating the one-hundredth anniversary of the first Yemenite wave of immigration to Israel in modern times did, in fact, open on December 27, 1981, accompanied on December 30 by an evening of Yemenite song and dance, and on December 31 by the staging of a musical production, *1882*, "that reflects in acting and singing parts of [the story] of the immigration of Yemenite Jews to Zion." Iranian Jewry had their turn a year later, on December 29, 1983, when the Center opened its new exhibit entitled "Iranian Jewry—The Story of the Ethnic Group." And Ethiopian Jewry joined the fold with the opening of an exhibition about them on June 10, 1985.

Much of the ethos of this project at the International Cultural Center for Youth can be gleaned from remarks made by the coordinator of the project in an interview in February 1982. She spoke of her mother, a well-known ethnomusicologist of German Jewish birth and parentage, as a key figure in her professional development. As a young woman in Germany, she had begun to collect "the folk dances of the Jewish people from all over the world. It was part of her Zionism and it was fueled even more when she met [her future] husband. He was an ardent Zionist." In the beginning, her mother's task "was very difficult." "There was," Ayala explained, "*very*, very little folklore that was *Jewish*." Her mother's life project and, by extension, my informant's increasingly concentrated on discovering and exhibiting Jewish folklore so as to provide a unified folklore for the Zionist collectivity. Rather than try to forget the characteristics on which different Jewish communities in the Diaspora differed (which was the documented public emphasis during the early years of the state), they try—now with institutional support—to use those differences as the raw material from which to create a single collective and appropriate content for the collectivity. Storytelling is paradoxically what strives for unification of content in the very act of detailing the differences between Jewish populations in Israel and the Diaspora.

Attempts at self-objectification

This third variant of collective storytelling consists of national, even international, convocations of members of particular ethnic groups as well as semiamateur musicals staged for members of the groups whose story they tell. I include here the "celebratory assembly" of Libyan Jewry that took place in Tel Aviv's main cultural center on November 24, 1981, the staging of the musical *1882* by youths of Yemenite origin in 1981–82, the performance of the musical *Casablan* in the winter of 1981–82 by youths of Moroccan origin, the development of the musical *Yaldei HaKrakh* and its successful performances in the summer of 1982, the staging of the musical *Ana Kurdi* in the summer of 1983 by Kurdish Israelis of varying ages, the convocation of North African Jewry ("their history and heritage") the first week of August 1983 in the main exhibition grounds of Tel Aviv, the mass gathering of Cochin (South Indian) Jews in the southern *moshav* of Nevatim on August 29, 1984, marking the thirtieth anniversary of their mass immigration to Israel, and the festive gathering dubbed Habbani Jewry Day in Bareket, a *moshav* in the coastal plain, on May 12, 1985.

In organization and structure, these events have a number of characteristics in common: (1) they cater to "native sons" of the ethnic group whose story is being told and not to the general public; (2) organizers expect and get visits and speeches from members of the Knesset, the chief rabbis, regional and local politicians, and government ministers; (3) the auditoriums and halls in which they take place are almost always filled to capacity, at times forcing some people to be turned away; (4) the performers are members of the group celebrating its heritage, but there is always, almost without exception, an outsider—anthropologist, entrepreneur, folklorist—who has planted the seed and/or provided the encouragement or the know-how; (5) music provides the local color; (6) all of these events are held in Hebrew though non-Hebrew words are always thrown in and at least part of the audience speaks in its native tongue; (7) the aim is to stress the overall success of the group in question while pointing out all its troubles and difficulties both before arrival in Israel and in the first two decades of settlement there.

Particularly interesting, however, is the similarity in content. Represented on stage in each and every case is a collectivized story. Individual characters embody stereotypes of the men and women of that community in the different age groups and generations. The collectivized story is, moreover, a statement about the relationship between past, present, and future in which the theme of progress dominates throughout. Each story is presented chronologically. Each opens the performance with a scene about life in rather primitive surroundings before immigration to Israel. Each shows the newly arrived immigrants in ecstasy upon first arriving in Israel. Each develops characters representing three generations, and showing the increasing Israelization of the more recent generations. Each cracks jokes about *kibbutznikim*, Ashkenazi accents, unyielding clerks of the government bureaucracy, and Ashkenazi self-importance. In nearly all, a second generation male gets involved with a stereotypically Ashkenazi female, who is initially met with suspicion especially by the older family members but who is eventually accepted by the young man's family. All, without exception, include a life cycle ritual—a wedding, a *bar mitzva* (a thirteen-year-old boy's rite of passage to ritual manhood), a *brit mila* (ritual circumcision). All end on a positive note—that "like it or not we are one people, we will soon so intermarry that we will really be indistinguishable";[7] "we are socially and economically integrated and we will soon be even more integrated"; "we have come a long way from what we used to be, much of it is positive, some of it is negative, we must now turn toward our past selectively and retrieve that which was uniquely ours." All proclaim the success of the group in achieving upward mobility despite nearly impossible odds.

I have explored and dismissed three possible explanations for the uncanny similarity among the performances—that this is the true story of each of these populations, that they all use the same written script, and that they are all organized, directed, and controlled from above by a particular government office or private company. The first is naively simplistic. Like the writing of history, the telling of a story involves the careful selection of moments, anecdotes, themes, and periods rather than the telling of all that ever happened. Why do these representations all depict Jewish life before immigration as backward and unchanging? Did all come from rural, almost bucolic, but primitive surroundings? Did they all walk around in ecstasy in Israel for months after immigrating? Did all, or even most, really outsmart the Ashkenazi work recruiters who came to boss them around? The homogeneity they depict finds little support in the historical record.

Second, there is simply no common written script. Indeed for many of them there is no available written script at all. The performance is put together by working with those members of the community who wish to participate. Frequently, the participants envision only one performance

7. Intermarriage has long been talked about in government and academic settings in Israel as a measure of social integration. The Central Bureau of Statistics even calculates the percentage of marriages between grooms and brides from the same continent of birth, and has done so for many years (see *Statistical Abstract of Israel*, table III/7). The special 1984 issue of *Megamot* on "The Ethnic Problem in Israel—Continuity and Change" not surprisingly included an article on intermarriage, specifically on whether the offspring of Ashkenazi-Oriental couples are socially marginal in Israeli schools (Yogev and Jamshy 1984). The authors argue, based on a sample of junior high school students (218 "of Ashkenazi-Oriental origin, 247 Ashkenazim and 387 Orientals"), that students of "mixed ethnic origin are less marginal than Orientals." Interestingly, since I believe it reveals the authors' own perceptions of hierarchy in Israel, they also talk about the marriage of Oriental Jewish women to Ashkenazi men as hypergamous, i.e., the woman marrying up, and the tendency of the children of these "hypergamous" marriages to "be closer to Ashkenazi students in their social attitudes and behaviours than children of hypogamous couples."

of the story ever, though they often find that success at that one performance pressures them to "carry the show" to other towns and cities. A reproducible written script tends to emerge the longer the show is put on, especially when substitutes take over the acting done by the original cast.

Third, there is no one organization or agency that provides the professional know-how or expertise. The Ministry of Education's Center for the Integration of the Heritage of Oriental Jewry frequently helps with some funding, but the "ethnic community" itself typically defrays the bulk of the expenses. Typically, the organizing committee hires or recruits a young theater professional to help structure the event and direct the show. Typically, the outsider is Ashkenazi, frequently socially liberal, and not fully established in theatrical circles in Israel. Nobody works under threat of censorship. Thus, the question remains, why the similarities, especially when such evidence of similarity seems to call into question the popular claim to the authenticity of these "celebrations"?

The concept of a script, derived from cognitive scientists, psychotherapists, and artificial intelligence experts, but freed of many of its contextual restrictions, I believe, goes a long way toward providing an answer. Outside their purely theatrical setting, scripts are common. Eric Berne (1961) "discovered" them in the way people live, interact, and perpetuate their trouble with others. "Games," he wrote, "appear to be segments of larger, more complex sets of transactions called scripts. . . . A script [was for him] a complex set of transactions, by nature recurrent, but not necessarily recurring since a complete performance may require a whole lifetime" (quoted by Steiner 1975:16). Among those the transactionalists have identified, we find what Steiner calls the Mother Hubbard script, the Big Daddy script, the Woman behind the Man script, and the Poor Little Me script.

For the cognitivist, "a script is basically an ordered sequence of actions appropriate to a particular spatial/temporal setting, organized around a goal. . . . The script is made up of slots and requirements on what can fill those slots . . . the script specifies roles and props and defines obligatory and optional actions" (Nelson 1979:1). Often mentioned by Schank and Abelson (1977) is the typical restaurant script, knowledge of which all functioning members of American society have and according to which they proceed to enter a restaurant, order their food, eat, and pay for their meal. But the range of contexts in which people "act out scripts" is extensive. Getting dressed, carrying on a phone conversation, going to confession, having dinner at home with the family, going for a job interview, and giving a scholarly paper all consist of sequences of actions appropriate to particular spatiotemporal settings organized around particular goals.

Once freed from the narrow theatrical concept of script, we can then begin to see both what a professional theatrical script is and what these celebratory performances among non-Ashkenazi Israeli Jewry are in the context of the larger society. Scripts, in the broader sense of the concept, vary along three lines: (1) the extent to which they assume or require the presence of others; (2) the manner of their reproduction; and (3) the extent to which one can assign authorship to them. Thus, scripts can be personal (private), interpersonal, multipersonal, or even impersonal; they can be reproduced primarily through socialization or reproduced through explicit rules or laws; and they can be formally authored or unauthored. Most of the scripts of interest to Schank and Abelson (1977) would fall into the unauthored category. But a careful classification shows how easy it is to relate the authored type of script to the unauthored types. Consider table 5.1.

It would be difficult, if not impossible, to assign authorship to any of the scripted actions in column A. Ownership of each of these scripts is rarely, if ever, an issue. It is less difficult to assign authorship to the scripted actions listed in column B. A careful historian might well uncover specific texts in which the rules for the scripted action were first explicitly articulated. Indeed it is here that we find professional stage performances in which authorship is both highly coveted and respected. Most professionally staged plays would be multipersonal in terms of relations within the cast, and impersonal in relation to the audience.

These celebratory Israeli ethnic performances have several contradictory qualities that tend to affect the way they are perceived by locals and anthropologists alike: (1) they are offered as theater but appear to be unauthored; (2) they are offered as theater but do not appear to be ruled or scripted; (3) they appear as theater but tend to have a multipersonal orientation not just within the cast but also with the audience; and (4) they appear as theater but not as High Culture.

When we see professional stage performances, we assume the actors are acting out a written script. When the object of the performance is to

Table 5.1. Examples of "Scripts," Their Mode of Reproduction, and Their Differential Involvement of Others

	A Reproduced through Socialization	B Reproduced through Explicit Rules
Personal/private	Getting dressed	Driving a car
Interpersonal	Phone conversation	Catholic confession
Multipersonal	Family dinner at home	Football game
Impersonal	Traveling by bus	One-person stage performance

represent "one's own" collective story on stage, we assume that amateurs can do the job because they are simply reliving their own experiences. That the latter may be scripted appears as a contradiction in terms because, as both therapy and studies of cognition show, most people have little awareness of the existence of scripts guiding their lives or their situational behavior. This results in large part from the extent to which we live according to scripts so that they no longer stand out, and in part from a common desire for "authenticity," for "rooting."

Consider these celebratory ethnic stage performances once again. The stories they act out are thematically so similar to each other that it is, in fact, hard not to speak of an unwritten script on which all these plays and performances are based. They overwhelmingly proclaim the success of the *group* in achieving upward mobility despite nearly impossible odds, they seek to impart to their younger generations both a sense of pride and a glimpse of their heritage, and they present their stories chronologically. But the thirst for "authenticity" leads participants to deny the possibility that they may just be acting out a nationwide script. It is more than vaguely reminiscent of the American Horatio Alger story in the role it plays in promoting a vision of a society committed to equal opportunity and social justice, and in the way in which it is passed on from generation to generation.

In the Israeli case, however, it is the group, rather than the individual, that must be shown to have been upwardly mobile through hard work and perseverance. The stage performances must, in principle, celebrate the heritage and history of each group *for the sake* of announcing to fellow Jews the group's own worth and value as contributors to the collectivity known as Israeli Jewish society. Celebration, then, is like dressing for success. The attempt by the actors and spectators in these events to control their own objectification indexes their experiences of past inequalities, presupposes their right to full partnership in the Jewish collectivity, uses heritage (*moreshet*) as its raw material, and strives to create the feeling that with their social, educational, political, and/or economic success they have acquired the right to have their content taken seriously and used in the struggle to decipher or develop the content of Israel's Jewishness. The goal is not revolution or segregation. It is integration. The values of those at the top are only mildly questioned. Culturally they seek to add rather than to supersede.

Behind the scenes, then, a classic social script generates similarities in performances presumed to celebrate *one* community's history, culture, and uniqueness. The script is unseen because, like those in column A, it is reproduced through generalized socialization rather than through explicitly articulated rules, and it in turn participates in its own reproduction.

Of greater potential import, of course, is the way in which this unwritten
script gets the underprivileged to participate unconsciously in the legiti-
mation of the structure of the society they live in, regardless of their own
relatively powerless and underprivileged position.

Israeli academia much resembles its English-speaking North Atlan-
tic counterparts. A consensus model of society long dominated analysis.
Common values were assumed. The term *absorption* was used to refer to
the goal of getting Israel's recent immigrants to share the values of its veteran citizens. Innumerable studies of schools and schoolchildren have over
the years monitored the road to absorption. Opponents have argued that
the picture is utopian, and that reality is conflict ridden, but in the process
they have had to make sense of cases and circumstances in which there
is undeniable evidence of "normative" sharing among people otherwise
divided by sociopolitical conflict.

The identification of scripts of the A type functioning in Israeli society ironically salvages a consensus model of Israeli society while adopting
the terms of conflict analysis. When we assume conflict and hierarchical domination, we look for the ways in which those in power seek to
keep themselves in power. In the process, we discover instruments of collective socialization and the organization of different avenues of social
control. In scripts we find what I call subliminal instruments of social
control and vehicles of its perpetuation. These scripts are, in fact, widely
shared, operate without explicitly articulated rules, and are almost always
"unauthored." On the other hand, they clearly serve as the mechanism
through which "the system" is continually reproduced, through which resources are allocated, status is differentiated, and power is distributed. To
continue to depict socially scripted performances as reflexive representations of experience would, under these circumstances, be to fall for the
illusion of self-objectification and authenticity that they create for their
participants. Heritage is presupposed, people turn to it in their search
for raw material for "Israeli society," and yet whitewash enough of their
differences so that all that's left are differences in local color.

6 On Authorship and Otherness

Apicture emerges of an Israeli Jewish population so involved in its struggles to figure itself out that it looks self-absorbed, uninterested in others, except when it perceives it must be interested in them—for reasons of security, international relations, trade, or finance. In the spirit in which I have tried to write this book, I pondered how much of that picture was my own construction of them and whether it could be useful in exploring their construction of otherness and its relations to the collective self. It was clear that the simple dichotomizing of self and other would say little about how Israeli Jews relate to their sense of peoplehood. It was also clear that the image of Israeli Jews as self-absorbed did not, at least on the surface, match the general impression many people have outside Israel that life in Israel is dominated by the constant fear of war and a constant potential for confrontation with "Arabs." Clearly, otherness matters. The question is *how*.

AUTHORING WHAT? AUTHORING WHOM?

I went to Israel in the summer of 1983 with two professional goals in mind—to keep abreast of issues and problems I had followed during the 1981–82 period of initial research, and to try out living in Israel outside the boundaries of structured anthropological fieldwork. I contemplated moving to Israel, but wondered if it would ever be possible for me to be scholar, writer, and academic in Israel, rather than its ethnographer. To try it out, I chose to spend the bulk of my working hours writing and revising my book *White by Definition: Social Classification in Creole Louisiana*, based on research I did prior to my research involvement in Israel.

I succeeded in the narrow sense. I got quite far with the draft of what eventually became *White by Definition*. But I could not shed the role of ethnographer.[1] I had established a pattern of daily life in 1981–82 that created a framework through which my many Israeli contacts, acquaintances, and colleagues saw me. They knew I wanted to know everything that was going on, and probably attend every possible public, cultural, potentially reflexive event. By August 1982 I had selected out certain activities, certain "phenomena" to follow. The following summer I turned down some invitations so that I could work on *White by Definition* but, still, my pocket diary for those three months of 1983 looks very much like the one I used in 1982. It is full of references to meetings with "informants," "cultural" events I attended because of their sociopolitical themes, exhibitions and mass gatherings I checked out, academic seminars and discussions on "Israeli society," and scheduled interviews with individuals in institutional positions of potential power and influence. Israel was so active a part of my thinking that it was Israel from which I drew the material for the first three paragraphs of the preface to *White by Definition*.

But what I drew from Israel is here at least as revealing as the fact that I drew anything from Israel in a book that would never explicitly deal with Israel. Without any real awareness I obviously took what I saw as linking not just Israel and Louisiana but also my conceptualizations of the analytic problems I studied in the two places. A census was being taken in Israel. It had been over a decade since the previous one. Not only did I realize then that I had never dwelt on census taking in Israel in earlier periods of research—the politics of when and how they take place or what gets asked and how—but I also realized that some of the rumbling concerning its details fit in well with the thrust of much of the argument in *White by Definition*. They raised issues surrounding government actions limiting the abilities of individuals or groups to decide for themselves who and what they are. I wrote with conviction:

I write this preface sitting in Jerusalem, a non-Jew in a Jewish state. The country's fourth national census is nearing completion. Of the ten questions on the short form, one catches my eye. "Are you," it asks, "(1) Jewish, (2) Moslem, (3) Greek Orthodox, (4) Greek Catholic, (5) Latin (Catholic), (6) Christian—other (specify), (7) Druze, (8) other (specify)?" There is no parallel question: "Are you (1) Jewish, (2) Arab, (3) Semitic (other), (4) Indo-European, (5) Negroid, (6) Mongoloid, (7) Oceanic, (8) other (specify)?" Nor is there a question, "How many of your great-grandparents were born Jewish?"

1. I am reminded here of some of the problems and dilemmas Jim Boon discusses in *Other Tribes, Other Scribes* (1982).

I went on:

> I am intrigued by the alternatives it offers to Jewish identity. Four are Chris-
> tian denominations. One is a general term for followers of Mohammed. A sixth
> identifies a sociopolitical enclave of followers of a medieval leader who broke off
> from mainstream Islam.

The semantic and the informative at this point become the questioning. "An Israeli Arab friend," I add, "says it is a bureaucratic ploy to
undermine Arab nationalism. The vast majority of non-Jews in Israel, he
is convinced, if given the choice, would identify themselves as Arabs and
not as followers of one or another religious leader." But I try to make it
balanced. I quote an Israeli Jewish friend who

> says it is a bureaucratic ploy to undermine Jewish secularism. The question, he
> is convinced, plays upon different interpretations of what it means to be Jewish.
> The question is simply put: Are you or are you not Jewish? The secular Jew,
> Jewish by ancestry, finds it difficult not to check off the box identifying him as
> Jewish. But in the formulation of the question, Jewish is juxtaposed to Greek
> Orthodox and Latin Catholic, making it therefore a religious identification, to
> be used as such by religious interest groups against the wishes of the secular.

Knowing that this is not an isolated bit of data I end my vignette on
Israel with references to the Law of Return and "the perennially debated
proposal to establish by law once and for all who is a Jew." I explain:

> Under the former, anyone born to a Jewish mother who has not taken formal
> steps to adopt a different religion has the right to become a citizen of Israel the
> moment he or she arrives in the country as an immigrant. Under the latter, only
> those who convert to Judaism according to Orthodox interpretation of Jewish
> law will be accepted in Israel legally as Jews.

A highly educated middle-aged *sabra* and friend upon reading the
typescript of this preface urged me not to print it. Taken aback I asked
why. "I don't know, Virginia," he said. "Something about it sounds anti-
Semitic." I was, needless to say, *very* discouraged. I pleaded for clarification. He turned to his wife in search of confirmation. "Don't you sense
what I mean?" he asked. Either to avoid conflict for the sake of friendship or because she didn't quite feel what he did, she gave an unengaged
and noncommittal answer. He thought about it for a few more seconds.
Then looking satisfied to have found what he thought was the cause of
his discomfort, he began to explain that I "make it sound like there is a
bureaucratic ploy to undermine Arab nationalism" and that the divisions
along religious lines are indeed *theirs,* not *ours.* I protested: "I don't say
that there is such a ploy, rather that that was what one Israeli Arab friend

said in response to having to answer that question on the latest census."
"But you only cite one Arab reaction!" he exclaimed, "and in so doing
you privilege this guy's views." Part of me marveled at his sensitivity to
writing techniques that deliberately or not displace authorship of ideas,
while proclaiming them to the world, nonetheless.[2] He was not a literary
theorist. I could see his point, in part, but I was too attached to the overall
message I wanted to convey with those paragraphs to yield very easily. I
brooded over it.

I doubt he was aware of doing anything other than pointing out
where, in his view, I simplified the relationship between Jews and Arabs
in Israel and, in making Jews appear controlling and insensitive to Arabs,
I added fuel to the fire of anti-Semitism. I, as far as I can recall, was
taken aback because I had *to my knowledge* simply reported what various
Israelis had said and written about these labels of categorization formal-
ized in the Israeli census. Moreover, I had consciously chosen to refer to
criticism I had heard from Jews as well as Arabs in order to make sure
that my overall point about the issue of control over principles of social
classification not be interpreted as something that happens only between
conqueror and conquered.

But clearly Arye and I were doing other things in our respective
"texts." He honed in on my reference to Arabs; in fact, he had nothing to say about the rest of it—not on the suggestion that there might
be a secular objection to the bureaucratic options given individuals for
self-classification, not on the implicit suggestion that one could conceiv-
ably perceive Jewish to be a racial identity (though the categories actually
offered on the census form suggest otherwise), not on the suggestion that
the census, the Law of Return, and the long-debated bills nowadays referred to in shorthand as the "Who is a Jew? question" are part and parcel
of the same phenomenon. No, he was concerned with my representation
of what Israeli Jews do or don't do to Arabs.

The reason may be simple—the special sensitivity of many Jews given
centuries of experience with anti-Semitism. But I think there is more to it
than that. He had known me for about two years when that incident occurred. We had discussed numerous social, cultural, economic, and political issues affecting and concerning Israel—many of them critical—at his
initiative as well as mine. Never before had there been any hint of an accusation of anti-Semitism. Moreover, there was little on the military-political
front at the time of this conversation to mark it as a particularly nervous

2. Paul Rabinow's "Discourse and Power: On the Limits of Ethnographic Texts"
(1985) contains, in my opinion, some of the best descriptions of devices differentiating
authors from writers and the assumptions they support.

or sensitive period. No, I think, as I examine my discourse, that there was a foreignness about my exposition that highlighted my foreignness, and that both were heightened by the fact that much of the text of those three paragraphs dealt with non-Jews in the state of Israel and not just with categories of Jews. Two things were different that day: (1) the book had been accepted for publication, so the words were going into print, and (2) for a change, at least explicitly, I was not talking about Sephardim and Ashkenazim but rather about Jews and non-Jews. I saw all of these as categories in a system of classification constituted and promoted by a dominant population and its institutions and sometimes contested by some members of some of its categories. I made the cultural "mistake" of not separating the "external" problem of Jewish-Arab relations from the "internal" problem of disunity and differentiation among Jews in Israel. In my terms, I made the mistake of linking otherness to selfhood.

Realizing that felt like a great discovery, but it also opened up a can of worms. If, in strictly theoretical treatises, one might be tempted to let one's persuasive rhetoric take the place of careful contextualized analysis, the opposite was the case with Israel. I asked myself questions I could "hear" my Israeli friends asking. Am I not unduly generalizing from one dialogue with one Israeli? And how could I imply that there is such a clear perceived distinction between the "internal" and the "external" when there have always been Arabs in Israel and Arabs have been foremost on the minds of so many Israelis for so long when they worry about the survival—and even the character—of the state of Israel? Otherness, I came to realize fully, is as complex and ever present a semiotic problem in Israel as the presupposition of the collective self. The fact that it appears more matter-of-fact on the surface—Arabs as others—is not only deceptive; it is a direct product of the phenomenon of otherness itself that is so integral a part of the ontological and epistemological problem of peoplehood.

In the exchange with Arye, I saw semantic as well as pragmatic components of the constitution of otherness and its relation to the collective self. My mistake may have been cultural and epistemological, but his concern was not simply that I had made a mistake. Representation and control were his subtext. He sought some control over my representation of him and his "people," though he acknowledged he had no recourse other than persuasion. My otherness was indexed in his objection. It was not just that I *linked* otherness to selfhood in a way foreign, even offensive, to Arye. It is also that *I* did so. Suddenly my non-Jewishness became relevant. I sensed the need to return to an exploration of the issue of right and authority that I raised in the introduction to this book. I sensed that the exchange with Arye was yet another manifestation of the struggle to shape the collectivity commonly referred to as Israeli society, that the constitution of the other is part of the constitution of the self, and that, therefore, control over the constitution of the other is explicitly or implicitly always part of the struggle over the constitution of the collective self. That I was not Jewish mattered. In appropriating their constitution of their other, I was "otherizing" their other—"liberating" the other from its author(s). It wasn't quite clear what I was, thereby, doing to the self.

The right to represent

I, of course, am basically inconsequential in the overall picture of Israeli society, but my experience is neither unique nor inconsequential. A writer's identity *is* taken into account in reacting to his or her representation of Israeli society by itself or in relation to others. That same dynamic paradox of simultaneously presupposing and creating the collectivity known as the Jewish people, which we have seen at work in other aspects of life in Israel so far, is indexed in these reactions. At issue I will argue is the right to participate in the struggles to shape Israel's collective self.

As should be evident from the preceding chapters, Israelis are not exactly passive, complacent citizens. There is a lively press, an outspoken cadre of writers, a parliamentary system that permits—even fosters— heated discussion, and numerous versions of self-referential jokes alluding to the prevalence of differences of opinions and argumentation among Jews (cf. Galnoor 1985).[3] Criticism is alive and well in contemporary Israel; that is neither a problem nor my point.

But when there is a question about the otherness of an author there is usually a question—explicit or implicit—about the authorship of his or her representation/objectification of Israeli society and its others. The dismissal of obviously critical anti-Zionist or anti-Semitic texts produced by non-Israelis and non-Jews is so generalized and for many so habitual that it often goes by unnoticed. Unless such a text is getting wide publicity outside Israel or is gaining a receptive audience among people of power and influence outside Israel, it is likely never to even enter Israel's public discourse.[4] VanTeeffelen's critique of Israeli anthropology is a good example.

3. Preeminent among these comedians are the Gashash HaKhiver—very popular, at times even acerbic in their humor, and able to say things people normally find offensive or delicate without being thought offensive.

4. I hold this to be true for a large majority but, of course, not for all. Raymonda Tawil's *My Home, My Prison* (1983) clearly has a Hebrew-reading audience. It was published in Hebrew by Adam Publishers in Jerusalem at the same time an English-language edition was published by Holt, Rinehart, and Winston. I saw the Hebrew-language version,

If, however, otherness is less extreme—as when the author is Israeli, Hebrew speaking, and Israeli educated but not Jewish, or when the author is Jewish but not Hebrew speaking, a very new immigrant or not even a resident—their texts are not automatically dismissed but their credentials enter the discourse at least as much as the substance of their argument. Examples of this include television correspondent Rafik Halabi, former newspaper editor Jacobo Timerman, writer and poet Anton Shammas, and writer and journalist Atallah Mansour. The first is an Israeli Druze, the second a recent though prominent Argentinian Jewish immigrant, the third and the fourth Israeli Arabs.

Halabi, Shammas, and Mansour all write directly or indirectly about it. Halabi opens his 1982 book on the West Bank, translated from the original Hebrew, with the line: "I am an Israeli patriot, though I am not a Jew." Two sentences later he details his bottom line on Zionism. "Arabs," he writes, "consider me a Palestinian, though I have no desire to become a citizen of an independent Palestinian state—if and when such an entity comes into being." In the ensuing page and a half, he describes the frequency with which when addressing kibbutz audiences throughout the country "the one question that inevitably comes up is: 'Who are you, Rafik Halabi? A Druse? An Israeli? A Palestinian? An Arab? Or perhaps a Zionist?" (Halabi 1982:3–4). The chapter is entitled simply "Credentials."

Shammas—whose most recent novel *Arabeskut* (1986) made such a big splash in Hebrew literary circles that it is being hailed as the first great work of Hebrew literature written by a non-Jew (cf. *Koteret Rashit* reviews and discussions)—entitled his contribution to *Every Sixth Israeli: Relations between the Jewish Majority and the Arab Minority in Israel* "Diary" (1983), and devoted its first few paragraphs to how he is like and unlike other Arabs and how he must, therefore, be taken as representing only himself. "For a number of reasons," he began, "I have chosen to give this talk the title of Diary." He goes on:

In the first place, I cannot maintain, at least in a fairly well-defined early stage, that the Jewish majority regards me as it regards someone like myself who has never left his childhood home, in my case, the village of Fassuta in the north. I cannot maintain this, because in 1968, at the age of 18, I chose what I had no choice but to choose, namely to regard Hebrew as my stepmother tongue. Sometimes I feel that this was an act of cultural trespass, and that the day may come when I shall have to account for it. Sometimes, when I think about the things I see and hear and read. (Shammas 1983:29)

---

for example, for the first time at the home of a *sabra* friend my age who at the time was a social worker in Jerusalem and who, though liberal and concerned, would never describe herself as particularly political.

Mansour, the only Arab correspondent on the staff of *Ha'aretz* for years, tends to be cautious. In a long conversation in Durham on a visit to Duke in 1986, we talked extensively about his strategy toward his work, and how he prefers being regarded as a journalist for *Ha'aretz* who is also an Arab rather than as its Arab journalist. His contribution to *Every Sixth Israeli*, "On Integration, Equality and Coexistence" (1983), had an objectivist academic or journalistic tone to it as if he felt that the facts spoke for themselves, regardless of his being an Arab. But he ends, nonetheless, with what the others began with. "This perhaps," he writes, "is the place to inform the readers that I do not challenge the right of the Jews to have a state of their own, just as the French and the English have a state of their own—but the Jews' state is not entitled to ignore the rights of the minority living within its midst, either on the symbolic-emotional level or on the practical level." In this, Mansour is not just casually explaining his views on Zionism; he prefaces his most forthright criticism of the state of Israel in that text with the assertion that he does "not challenge the right of the Jews to have a state of their own"—suggesting that he anticipates the question from a Jewish readership or audience because he is not Jewish.

I have asked myself what I imagine readers will ask: Are these writers just overly sensitive? That perhaps it is all paranoia based on their membership in, and identification with, demographic minority populations that are also politically subordinate? No doubt years of belonging to an underempowered section of the population, and carrying that experience with them as they created successful individual careers in overwhelmingly Jewish sections of the society, could not have gone by without developing special sensitivities and finely tuned "antennas." But the temptation to interpret these writers' express need to present credentials as *their* problem is little more than begging the question.

Halabi would have too much to lose professionally if he even exaggerated about the relevance of credentials in his work experience throughout much of Israel. Yet he writes,

The demand that I come forth with clear-cut positions and definitive answers and the disregard of—or perhaps obliviousness to—the personal dilemma I face in attempting to confirm my own national identity are challenges I have faced every hour of every day since I began confronting the citizens of Israel with the hard truth about the national struggle in this region. (Halabi 1982:4)

And he precedes that comment with a description of his visit to Kibbutz Givat Chaim in July of 1979—included in the book to illustrate the demands on him, not because it was in any way exceptional.

Halabi writes that he was invited to speak at this established and generally prosperous kibbutz located between Tel Aviv and Haifa. He accepted and delivered a formal presentation. Then, he writes that, in the question and answer period, he recognized the first questioner as a former member of the Knesset and veteran of Mapai (the center and heart of the Labor Party in Israel) who "studied [him] closely, as if trying to measure the sincerity of [his] words, and challenged, 'Why can't you speak in terms of clear-cut positions? How would you act if you were a military governor in the occupied territories?'" (Halabi 1982)

The reported challenges continued. "Another member," Halabi goes on,

capitalizing on the tension generated by the first question, pressed further. "We differ on basic issues," he declared, "and my Israeliness bears no resemblance to yours. I came to Givat Chaim after the Holocaust, at a time when the Arabs in this area were busy massacring Jews. *You* don't begin to understand the meaning of the Holocaust to *the Jewish people*. *You* don't begin to understand the significance of the Ingathering of the Exiles."

This kibbutz member may have invoked the Holocaust where other Israelis —non-Holocaust survivors and native-born Israelis—might not have, but the spirit of the challenge was similar even when these others spoke. "And," Halabi explains,

as if they were trying to make the point that I, in particular was shamefully ungrateful to the country in which I lived, argued that "in Egypt *you* wouldn't be allowed to speak freely, or in Syria or Iraq. But *here*, in this kibbutz, *you* can stand up and imply that you don't reject the notion of self-determination for the Palestinians, and *no one* has even attacked *you*!" (Halabi 1982; emphases added)

Rafik Halabi's account is obviously personal, but it fits in well with how Alouph Hareven, an Israeli Jewish scholar who edited *Every Sixth Israeli* (1983), interprets the results of a survey conducted in July 1980 by Sammy Smooha, probably the most prominent non-Ashkenazi Jewish social scientist in Israel.[5] Smooha took a representative sample of 1185

5. It is no accident that such a survey was conducted by Sammy Smooha. His analyses of Israeli society are always tripartite—borrowing a "plural society" model from the social science literature and applying it to Israel. In that depiction, Arabs are given a more integral role in Israeli society (along with Sephardim and Ashkenazim) than elsewhere.

What is the more typical depiction of the role or place of Arabs in Israeli society? First, I would say, is that they are relatively absent. The introductory course on Israeli society required of sociology majors at the Hebrew University is a good example. It includes a

Israeli Arabs and, at the request of the Van Leer Jerusalem Foundation, also included several questions parallel to those in a survey carried out among Jews in 1980 by Mina Tsemach. Of the Jews surveyed, 47.6 percent said they believe that all or at least most Arabs in Israel hate Jews, whereas only 29.1 percent of the Arabs surveyed said so. Likewise, only 29.2 percent of the Jews in the sample said they believed Israeli Arabs had reconciled themselves to the existence of Israel, in contrast to 67.7 percent of Arab respondents. Hareven suggests that these divergent responses reveal "that Jews tend to attribute to Israeli Arabs positions far more ex-

---

short section on Arabs, but is structured to highlight the Zionist project and the problems of building a new nation-state for Jews. Arab students at the Hebrew University frequently find themselves taking this course and feeling quite marginalized by it (cf. Szudarek 1985, 1988). Ironically, the more the intifada leads Jews to talk about Arabs the more it "otherizes" them (cf. Ben-Ari 1989; Green 1989; Valentin 1989).

Quite a few Arabs, however, form part of the Israeli labor force, and there *is* talk of that often within Israeli Jewish circles (cf. Ben-Porath 1966; Benvenisti 1983; Oz 1983; Romann 1984; Rosenfeld 1978). Most Israeli Jews regularly and knowingly employ the services of Arabs who work as gas station attendants, construction workers, and cleaning women. (cf. Bernstein 1987; Lewin-Epstein and Semyonov 1987). Many also come in contact with Arabs in less stereotypically unskilled jobs, but do not always know it.

But are the Arabs seen as relevant to "Israeli society"? Gideon Kressel (1984) tries to argue, convincingly I think, that there is a strong tendency in Israel today (as much as there was twenty, thirty, or forty years ago) to ignore "the specificities of the impact made by Arab culture on the community gap and on inter-ethnic encounter in Israel" (p. 66). More specifically, he argues that "according to unwritten conventions, the linguistic combination 'Arab-Jews' or 'Arabs of the Mosaic persuasion' is prohibited . . . lest the Jews of the Arab world be identified, unintentionally, with the enemy (cf. Michael 1974:22)" (Kressel 1984:71). He explains that the problem "originates in the view that the '*urubah* [Arabism] is inferior, a view that has become part of the public convention in the country, and in a projection of this attitude onto those who immigrated from the Arab countries, who are, supposedly, ashamed of their origins" (ibid.). Kressel calls it Arabism; I'd call it what Edward Said calls it—Orientalism—turned inward as well as outward. See also Albert Memmi's *Who Is an Arab Jew?* (1975b) and *Jews and Arabs* (1975a).

On the whole, up to the mid-1970s, anthropological work on Arabs in Israel focused on their internal social organization and how it was being *affected* by life in modern Israel. Handelman and Deshen's (1975) section on non-Jews in Israel, for example, was entitled "Traditional Villages and Nomadic Groupings." Abner Cohen's, Emanuel Marx's, and Henry Rosenfeld's earlier work all fit this general description. Sociological work focused on the structures of encounters between Jews and Arabs, the phenomenon of stereotyping, the degree of conflict and accommodation found "among Arabs" in Israel, Arab participation in the labor force, and the mode and extent of political participation among Israel's Arab citizens (e.g., Kahane, Herdan, and Rosenfeld 1982; Landau 1969; Peres 1970; Peres and Levi 1969). Some recent work focuses on change, politicization, and national aspirations. Most prominent among these are the works of sociologists and anthropologists associated with Haifa University and the academic (but low-circulation) social science journal published in Haifa, entitled *Makhberot leMekhkar u leBikoret* (Notebooks for Research and Criticism) (e.g., Oppenheimer 1978; Rosenfeld 1978; Smooha 1980).

treme than Israeli Arabs tend to attribute to themselves (even when we assume that a certain part of the Arab respondents distorted their answers deliberately so as to hide their negative feelings)" (Hareven 1983:9–11). Hareven points, further, to Arab respondents' answers to questions about their attitudes toward Israeli leaders and institutions, and to the knowledge and differentiation evinced by the heterogeneity of their responses —that 55.1 percent were satisfied with then President Navon, that 65.6 percent were dissatisfied with then Prime Minister Menachem Begin, that 36.7 percent were satisfied with the Knesset, 37.2 percent with democracy in Israel and 33 percent with freedom of speech, that 58.2 percent were satisfied with Israel's legal system and 90.1 percent with its medical services (Hareven 1983:11). These are clearly not responses anticipated by all those Jews surveyed who assume that Israeli Arabs—all or at least most—hate Israel.

The figures are useful, but Hareven's analysis of them is even more suggestive. "The Jews' idea of what Israeli Arabs think of them," he writes,

is based largely on our own attitude to the Arab minority. The more we reinforce negative stereotypes ("dirty," "spies") the more we strengthen negative elements in their attitude to us. And the more we strengthen existing positive elements in the attitude of parts of the Jewish majority, the more we increase the Israeli Arabs' consciousness of being equal citizens of Israel. (Hareven 1983:9)

I like the intended liberalism and inclusiveness of Hareven's remarks, but I find both descriptive and prescriptive assertions in them that do much more than simply call for tolerance. Note the explicit and implicit use of pronouns. "We" are the Jews; "they" are the Israeli Arabs. "We" are the doers, the agents; "they" are the done to, the ones whose attitudes, consciousness, and (implicitly) actions respond to what "we" do to "them." "We" should take responsibility for what "they" think of "us," for what "they" think of "us" is largely, if not exclusively, an extension of how "we" see "them." In fact, the statement is even stronger in the last two lines. I doubt it was Hareven's conscious intention, but does it not read as if he is saying that "we" should also take responsibility for what "they" think of "themselves," for what "they" think of "themselves" is largely, if not exclusively, an extension of how "we" see "them"?

Hareven sticks his neck out here. What he has to say is not mainstream opinion among Israeli Jews. He is pinning an enormous amount of responsibility for Jewish-Arab relations within Israel on the Jews. It is an attempt to facilitate better relations by making Israeli Arabs look less like dangerous enemies to Israeli Jews. But what he does has its own cost. There is little room left in his analysis of the situation for self-objectification among Israeli Arabs. Control, representation, manipulation, even authorship appear to be overwhelmingly in the hands of the Jews. So in Hareven's well-intentioned liberal position we see the heavy hand of that pervasive long-time struggle among Israeli Jews to affirm, shape, and control their self-objectification—in this case by acknowledging that otherness is linked to selfhood but also, in at least periodically suggesting that "their" otherness (in the eyes of the Jews) is a (perhaps the) dominant force in shaping Israeli Arabs' representation of themselves, by describing and I would say, therefore, affirming the representation of Jews as being in control both of their own self-representation and of the self-representation of those they regard as their others. Semiotically, it is a plea for change in Israeli Jews' view of Israeli Arabs as well as themselves, but not as great as it might have appeared on the surface. It is an argument for regarding Israeli Arabs as internal rather than external others; it is not an argument for making them part of the self. In this case, the signified self is the collectivity known as the Jewish people. It is unclear to what extent that is to be equated with the collectivity referred to as "Israeli society."

But where does all this leave non-Jews in Israel who speak or write about Israel, Israelis, even Israeli society? They can, and are, treated on an individual basis, as Halabi, Shammas, and Mansour all report, but from an Israeli Jewish point of view it is hard to know what to do with them. In speaking and writing about Israel, they do not appear to be simply passive actors. Their Hebrew is impeccable; their knowledge of Israel far greater than that of many Israeli Jews not born or raised in Israel. But is their participation in the discursive construction of Israeli society kosher? If they are perceived as external others, their participation goes against the Jews' struggle for *self*-objectification. If they are perceived as encompassed (internal) others, then their participation may itself be an artifact of the paradoxes of Jewishness. If the cultural content of Israeli society does not count Judaism as one of its necessary components, then there is no reason to necessarily deny these writers the right to represent Israeli society. If culture and language are to be subordinated to genealogy in the constitution of the collective self—and Jewishness is to be a synonym for Israeli society even if non-Jews live in Israel—then there is no way in which these others could write about Israel without threatening Israeli Jews' striving for control over their own self-objectification. Herein lies the reason highly "acculturated" Israeli non-Jews must so frequently pronounce their credentials, and the reason they frequently still remain suspect. How Israeli Jews view Israeli Arabs indexes how they view themselves—not just in terms of the limits of their individual tolerance or what they individually perceive their culture to be, but even more importantly in terms of how uncertain they are about who they are as a "people."

Enter Jacobo Timerman—Jew, Ashkenazi in origin, Ukrainian by birth, Argentinian by previous citizenship, editor and publisher of the newspaper *La Opinión* in Buenos Aires, and one of Israel's more famous immigrants of the past decade. On April 15, 1977, he was arrested by Argentinian military authorities; in 1979 he moved to Israel entering as an immigrant with full-fledged rights to citizenship under the Law of Return. When Israel invaded Lebanon in June 1982, he found himself having strong—even impassioned—reactions. He kept a journal. By fall it had been translated from the Spanish and published in English by Alfred Knopf in New York and Random House of Canada in Toronto. It was entitled *The Longest War: Israel in Lebanon* (Timerman 1982). He was not a supporter of the invasion of Lebanon.

The Longest War was not well-received in Israel. When in mid-December I went to Israel for three and a half weeks, I found that even most of my dovish friends and contacts were troubled by the book. They who had gone to many antiwar demonstrations during the summer and early fall, they who shared Timerman's basic opposition to the invasion, they who felt themselves turning more and more "to the left" because of the invasion of Lebanon almost without exception told me they felt Timerman had gone too far. Most mentioned that the book was full of mistaken details, that it followed from the fact that he still "didn't know much about Israel." Many mentioned what they had heard as hearsay or actually read in the book (Timerman 1982:161)—that Timerman could barely speak Hebrew. He was thought premature not just in writing about Israel's war in Lebanon but in writing about Israel at all. His Jewishness was not in question, but his *Israeliut* was.

He was at least in part a mirror image of Halabi, Shammas, and Mansour. They had extensive linguistic and cultural familiarity with Israel, but were not Jews; he was Jewish but did not have extensive linguistic and cultural familiarity with Israel. But while they saw their own problem with credentials in representing Israel and addressing Israeli Jews, he seems to have taken the Law of Return to heart and did not see fit to document, or argue for, his credentials in *The Longest War*. Much of the book is written in the first person plural—we, our, ours, us—when it is not simply Timerman talking about himself. "And I'm angry, too, with us," he writes on page 44, "with the Israelis, who by exploiting, oppressing, and victimizing the Palestinians have made the Jewish people lose their moral tradition, their proper place in history. The Israelis . . . but who are we?" On page 66, he writes that he "would have preferred that [a visiting Argentinian Jewish friend] had stayed in Buenos Aires, but [that] at one time

or another the Diaspora descends upon us Israelis." And toward the end
of the book he seems even more identified. His last full chapter entitled
"Rage and Hope" is full of first person plural pronouns: "yes, we have
killed our moral integrity. I feel that quite soon the Diaspora Jews will
begin to experience the consequences of the process started by Menachem
Begin" (p. 156); "we Israelis will do the same [as the Palestinians]. We
will defend our democracy. We will try to recover our dignity" (p. 158);
"we Israelis will have to overcome our hallucinations through an effort
of imagination, through an audacious ideological conception, through a
total commitment to the struggle for democracy" (p. 160).

But who is Jacobo Timerman? He does not always write in one voice.
At times, in writing about Israelis in the third person, he seems distant. It
seems true especially at the outset. "Israelis," he writes on the very first
page,

are proud of their coolness in hard times. They are mistaken. They inflict on
themselves an unnecessary burden that weighs heavily on their psyche, on their
spiritual conflicts, on their morale. . . . Only when enraptured by their songs,
drunk with them, only then can you see Israelis relaxed, outgoing, sentimental,
dreamers all. I would not, however, go so far as to say they are happy. (Timerman 1982:1–3)

He is, or at least used to be, a Zionist (p. 161); he frequently distinguishes
between Israelis and Diaspora Jews and identifies himself as Israeli; he
almost never writes about "the Palestinians" without juxtaposing them
to "we the Israelis." But is he an Israeli Jew? Technically, yes, but many
of the critiques of his book strongly suggested that he was not yet "culturally" Israeli and was, therefore, wrong to portray himself as an Israeli
writing about Israel. That felt like a classic case of semiotic appropriation of one's self by an other. In daring to write this book about Israel's
invasion of Lebanon, Timerman misread the phenomenon of collective
identity in Israel. He took too simplistic—perhaps just too legalistic—a
view of selfhood and otherness in Israel.

ENCOMPASSING THE "GOYIM"

Timerman's "mistake" was both like and unlike mine. Like mine, his
made assumptions about self and other that had a ring of foreignness to
them in contemporary Israel. Unlike mine, his mistake was to assume too
neat and clear-cut a separation between self (Israeli and Jewish) and other
(epitomized by, but not restricted to, Arabs). Both mistakes made sense
—mine as the product of my prior non-Israeli, non-Jewish eyes, his as

the product of his prior non-Israeli but Diaspora Jewish eyes. But they have been, at least for me, useful mistakes: in revealing themselves to be conceptualizations of the relation of self and other that do not quite feel right in contemporary Israel, they show the *fact* of alternative conceptualizations of such a relationship and, simultaneously, the inadequacy of the simple assumption of dualism.

Oppositional dualism has an elegance and a simplicity that may make it conceptually and politically attractive but, in this case at least, its apparent simplicity is deceptive. Even that which appears to epitomize, or embody, dualism may show complexity and uncertainty that undermine the initial perception of a fixed and unquestioned opposition as a model of and for thought or action. I have argued so far that conceptualizing the collective self as dependent on a notion of otherness is unpopular among Israeli Jews. I have shown as well, however, that determining Jewishness matters in a wide variety of contexts and implies a differentiation between Jews and non-Jews. And I have argued that some Jews and some Arabs may be perceived as straddling the fence—hence, that for some purposes Jewishness may be neither necessary nor sufficient.

In fact, I think the evidence points toward a dynamic interrelationship between selfhood and otherness in which selfhood is very dependent on the identification (or assumption) of otherness but in which, just as integrally, the boundaries between self and other—semantic as well as referential—are neither fixed nor determinate. Particularly convincing to me is the fact that I have found evidence pointing in this direction even where I least expected to find confirmation.

Take the concept of goyim. I must confess that I have always cringed upon reading, or hearing, the word in Jewish prayer books and services. If I am reading along with the service and I come across the word, I tend to skip the phrase or sentence in which it appears. I *feel* (or fear) that it singles me out in the community of worshippers, that it lumps all non-Jews into a category of other without regard to our individual, cultural, or experiential characteristics, and that it is condescending, if not outright antagonistic. I react to it because that was how I heard it used as a child and a young adult in the New York area, not because it stood out so much on its own in prayer books and liturgical texts in Israel. It seemed to epitomize dualism and, through dualism, the seemingly irrefutable opposition between inclusiveness and exclusiveness.

When I first started going to Israel, I didn't go looking for Jewish references to the goyim, though I know I did not question the simple translation I had long heard for *goyim*—that it meant non-Jews. It was not until I was addressing these issues away from the field that the issue of the goyim came up again. It is my experience that Israeli Jews rarely

refer to non-Jews as goyim. Yet I realized that here I was writing about
the link between the construction of otherness and the constitution of the
collective self in the case of Israeli Jewry and I had not yet even so much
as mentioned the concept of goyim.

That was not oversight, but it is certainly interesting. *Goyim* rarely
appears in my field notes, newspaper or document archives, or tape collection. I am an attentive listener on buses as well as in interviews. Outside
a liturgically grounded context, Israeli Jews just do not talk about *the
goyim*. But its general absence from most colloquial Israeli Jews' speech
and writing has caught my eye in retrospect. That it has a potentially offensive ring to it is not enough of an explanation for the infrequency with
which one hears the term in most Israeli Jewish circles. Alternative words
and phrases that are offensive exist in Israel just like elsewhere.

No, something else has happened to *goyim* in Israel, and it is conceptual and political and not just terminological. The mere opposition of
Jew to non-Jew implied in the most common, casual interpretation of the
term (especially among Diaspora Jews) is just too simplistic for contemporary Israel. Not only does one rarely hear Israeli Jews refer to *goyim;*
textual authorities define the term, and describe its past usage, in a way
that defies any sense of clear-cut dualism.

Ben Isaacson's *Dictionary of the Jewish Religion* (1979), originally
prepared in Hebrew for publication in Israel and used in the Israeli educational system itself, offers the following entry for *goy* (plural *goyim*)
(Hebrew for "a people"): "Although the term as used in the Bible includes *any people,* and was used also in reference to the Jews, it has come
to mean a non-Jew, or Gentile" (p. 82; emphasis added). Even-Shoshan
(1985 edition) itemizes three definitions or meanings:

1. *am* [people], *uma* [nation]. 2. *nokhri* [foreigner, alien], *ben am akher* [mem-
ber of a different people; literally, son of a different people], *lo yehudi* [not
Jewish]. 3. *kinuy shel gnai bfi haadukim leyehudi khofshi beyakhaso ladat o
lebur v'am haaretz beyahadut* [derogatory term used by the very religious to
refer to a Jew who is independent in his/her relationship to the religion or to
a person or a group of people who are ignoramuses when it comes to Judaism].

Note the order in which these three definitions are given. They go from
most inclusive to most exclusive, from the idea of a people, to the signification of non-Jews, to the privileging of a Judaic content on the part of
some Jews and their hierarchical evaluation of degrees of Jewishness.

Now consider some of the implications of this tripartite description
of the usage of *goyim*. If a Jew can be a goy, then it is obviously at
best superficial to equate goyim with non-Jews. If *goyim* can refer to

peoples including the Jewish people but simultaneously, even if to a different group of Jews in a different context, to other peoples, then one of the fundamental paradoxes of the concept is that it is not even clear whether *goyim* signifies otherness. That it could be a Jewish reference to their own peoplehood at the same time that it validates the existence of other peoples suggests a surprising but plausible interpretation—that the very notion of goyim may be as universalizing as it is differentiating, that otherness is like selfhood if not necessarily in content then certainly in form, and that otherness is not necessarily the antithesis of the self.

In elaborating on these conceptual implications, I am aware that I am proposing understandings now far removed from the straightforward dualism assumed in most colloquial uses of the term *goyim*, especially in the Diaspora. But there are variant uses of the term and, in its apparent polysemy, *goyim* evokes something far more complex than simple oppositional dualism. That there may be little reported awareness of its polysemic nature is not much of a counterargument. I will submit that the infrequency with which most Israelis refer to people as goy/goyim is not unconnected to the fact that boundaries of otherness are not always clear in Israel, despite the superficial equation of otherness with Arabs.

WHO IS NOT A JEW?

The easiest examples of unsettled or indeterminate boundaries are, of course, legal ones—challenges to current laws, the enactment of laws, and recourse to the courts when there is a dispute over the interpretation of a law. Of these the best known is the quarter of a century old political debate known as the Who Is a Jew? question. I have mentioned it before but have not gone into it in detail. That it must come up again in discussing the self through otherness is no accident: the battle over who should be considered a Jew and who shouldn't is a dispute over determining not just the outermost limits of the in-group but also the innermost limits of the out-group. It is about exclusion as much as it is about inclusion. It is about otherness as much as it is about the collective self.

The Who Is a Jew? question in its current formulation pits very Orthodox circles of the population against those who reject that very Orthodox interpretation of the nature and boundaries of the Jewish people and/or granting the Orthodox exclusive rights as gatekeepers. We have seen some of these issues come up in the handling of immigration from Ethiopia. But the issue in the Knesset and in coalition agreements is even more specific: Should the Law of Return be amended to specify that, of those not born of a Jewish mother, only those people who have converted to Judaism within the Orthodox framework are to be counted as Jews?

The American Reform and Conservative movements would clearly be the most adversely affected by adoption of such a specification and, since combined they account for the majority of North American Jews, we can extend that statement to the majority of North American Jewry. The Reform community makes no pretense of following the Orthodox interpretation of religious law. The Conservative community pays close attention to *halacha,* but does not accept the Orthodox interpretation of it as the definitive word on *halacha.* Since most conversions to Judaism in the United States are performed by Reform and Conservative rabbis, all of those people accepted as Jews by at least large sectors of the American Jewish population by virtue of their Reform or Conservative conversions would thereby be denied the rights and privileges of being a Jew in Israel.

Reform and Conservative communities do exist in Israel, but they are few in number and heavily English speaking. The debate in Israel has not been so much over these non-Orthodox Israeli congregations, but rather over the granting of sole gatekeeping powers to a section of the Jewish people. The practical, the political, and the semiotic converge easily in this debate. Adoption of this narrow appraisal of valid conversions would likely disenfranchise tens of thousands of Americans—some of them now in Israel—who have undergone non-Orthodox rituals of conversion to Judaism. On January 18, 1985, *Jerusalem Post* correspondent David Krivine reported that the executive director of the World Union for Progressive Judaism, Rabbi Richard Hirsch, had told him there were about ten thousand conversions to Judaism a year in the United States alone and that "the great majority of them [were] being performed by non-Orthodox rabbis" (*J. Post Magazine,* p. 4). If, in addition to those who themselves undergo these conversion rituals, we extend the exclusionary principle to those whose mothers or mothers' mothers underwent such non-Orthodox conversions, the number of people affected runs into the hundreds of thousands. Most media discussions in Israel of the proposed narrowing of Who's a Jew? mention the expectation of negative repercussions of such narrowing for relations between Israel and American Jewry—the weakening, if not actual withdrawal, of political, financial, and moral support for Israel on the part of large sectors of American Jewry.

Political and economic repercussions are frequently foregrounded in Israeli political arguments against adoption of this particular Orthodox demand, but the nature of peoplehood is rarely far behind. Those in favor of the change argue that the amendment is needed in order to keep the Jewish people intact, to keep the Jewish people from being diluted. Those opposed to it argue that adopting the amendment would only split the Jewish people apart—legally and institutionally.

The fact is that legal questions about the boundaries of the collective self are neither new nor the exclusive concern of the ultra-Orthodox or Orthodox communities in Israel. The original formulation of the Law of Return enacted as law in 1950 did not explicitly define a Jew, though it restricted the Law of Return to Jews. The absence of a specification gave strength to the law. It seemed to imply that there was no need to define a Jew, that Jewishness was known and unquestioned. But its strength also derived from the avoidance of formulations that would be clearly divisive. It would be foolish to think that the founders of the state of Israel were unaware of alternative and contested definitions of Jewishness. The Nazis had obviously not restricted genocide to those people whom all Jews considered Jewish. "Non-Jews" (in the eyes of some) had died because they were "Jews" in the eyes of others. Reform, Conservative, and Reconstructionist movements had been in existence for decades. The question of content had been raised for decades; the relevance of *halacha* for Jewishness was in the process of being examined and contested in many Jewish circles. Many Jews now labeled themselves secular; many others socialist, antireligious, or just Jewish by ancestry. There was too much diversity already not to know that the boundaries of Jewishness were often unclear and contested. But to have gotten into the business of keeping people out would have made the emergent state look too much like the kind of society in which many Jews had lived and died, where Jews as a group had been discriminated against, excluded from mainstream rights and privileges. Inclusiveness and (perhaps ironically) "nation" building were at a premium.

But as former Knesset member Zalman Abramov details vividly in *Perpetual Dilemma* (1976), that goal was only partly achieved. By 1958 a committee had been formed to explore the need to specify who is a Jew. That committee consisted of the minister of the interior, the minister of justice, and the minister of social welfare and religious affairs. The first (Israel Bar-Yehuda) was a self-proclaimed socialist, the second (Pinhas Rosen) a liberal, and the third (Moshe Shapira) a supporter of increasing the powers of the Orthodox rabbinate and a member of what is now called the National Religious Party. After some deliberations, the committee adopted the view that a Jew is a person declaring himself or herself to be a Jew. It was clearly not Shapira's own position. His party promptly resigned from the cabinet only to return after an official directive issued in January 1960 took a less inclusive approach to Jewishness. The official government position then became that a Jew is, for the purposes of the civil law, a person born of a Jewish mother.

Individual cases throughout the 1960s kept the question alive, however. Most prominent among them were the challenges presented to the law by Binyamin Shalit and Brother Daniel.[6] No one questioned Shalit's Jewishness, but the government bureaucracy could not accept what he wanted to do to the concept of Jewishness. He had married a non-Jewish Englishwoman who became a naturalized citizen of Israel but not under the Law of Return. She, like her husband, was an agnostic. She chose not to convert to Judaism. They had two children. By the principle set down in the 1960 directive, these children could not be counted within the Jewish people and could not have the rights and duties accorded Jews in Israel. Legally, all members of the family were Israeli citizens, but their identity cards denied the Jewishness of all but the father. His wife was listed as having British nationality, no religion, and Israeli citizenship. His children's identity cards left the line next to religion blank, listed their citizenship as Israeli, and had "Jewish father and non-Jewish mother" listed as their nationality. Shalit had wanted his children's identity cards to read "nationality Jewish, religion none." Shalit petitioned the High Court for the right to be able to be "a national Jew" legally without being "a religious Jew." A five-to-four majority granted Shalit's petition but appalled the rabbinate and its Orthodox and ultra-Orthodox supporters, who responded by demanding instant legislation to abolish the dual conception of Jewishness that had just been given judicial (albeit nonrabbinical) backing. Two years later the Law of Return was successfully amended to further limit inclusiveness. The 1970 law explicitly stated that henceforth under Israeli law a person would be considered a Jew only if she or he was born of a Jewish mother or she or he converted to Judaism. Shalit would clearly not have won the judicial ruling after 1970.

A further specification appearing in the 1970 amendment responded to the challenge posed by Brother Daniel. Brother Daniel (alias Oswald Rufeisen) was born of a Jewish mother in Yugoslavia. He survived the Second World War in a Catholic monastery which took him in and hid him. Coming of age in such an environment he embraced Catholicism and eventually chose to become a monk. Yet throughout the war years and his years as a Catholic he remained a fervent Zionist. He asked for a transfer to a monastery in Israel at the same time that he sought Israeli citizenship under the Law of Return. The Israeli government had no legal grounds to refuse him but could not bring itself to accept him. He took his case to the High Court arguing on Talmudic grounds that "a Jew, even if he has sinned, remains a Jew" (Tractate Sanhedrin from the Talmud), but this time the Court ruled against him.

6. Data on the Shalit case come from the *Jerusalem Post* clippings. Information on Brother Daniel comes, in addition, from S. N. Eisenstadt's *Israeli Society* (1967).

The 1970 amendment consequently incorporated this point into the new legal specification of Jewishness. It specified that the candidate for Jewishness must not be a member of another religion—must, especially, not flaunt the fact that he or she has adopted the beliefs, rituals, obligations, or life style of a religion other than Judaism. Active conversion to another religion now became grounds for excluding someone born of a perfectly acceptable Jewish mother from membership in the Jewish people. My Catholic upbringing leads me to see this as the institutionalization of "excommunication" among the Jewish people. Note that this is different from "excommunicating"/disinheriting a family member by sitting Shiv'ah for them as if they had just died.[7] Disinherited and unacknowledged as a family member, the person, nonetheless, remains Jewish. Note also that this was not merely a matter of denying someone Israeli citizenship. The Law of Return had always allowed for the exclusion from *citizenship* of potential immigrants who are known criminals abroad. The 1970 amendment was not a definition of citizen; it was a definition of Jew. I am convinced that the problem with Brother Daniel was that in being a Catholic monk he must have appeared to be *flaunting* his adoption of the beliefs and rituals of Catholicism. He was not just a nonpracticing religious Jew, not just secular or even antireligious. He had become a religious official, if not quite leader, of a non-Jewish religious community. His request tested the extent to which Israeli Jews were willing or able to separate Jewishness from Judaism or, in Shalit's terms, "nationality" from "religion."

Individual cases attract a great deal of attention (e.g., the Shoshana Miller case in Israeli newspapers since 1986). We identify the individuals by name, ponder their plight, and frequently find ourselves siding with them in the end. It seems easier to give in to their requests: What difference will one individual crossing the boundary make in the long run? Clearly, the gatekeepers do not always agree, but many Israelis—even many who are religious—find themselves taking a human interest approach to these

---

7. Shiv'ah is an institutionalized period of mourning in Judaism. Rabbi Klein (1979) explains in his chapter on the laws of mourning:

> At the time of death, the bereaved is in a state of shock and cannot be reached by comforting words. After the funeral, when he becomes aware of his loss, he is open to consolation. The rite of Shiv'ah serves to tide him over during this painful period until he is able to resume his normal life. A number of prescribed observances aid in this process; they are obligatory on the following relatives of the deceased: father, mother, son, daughter, brother, sister, husband, wife. The Shiv'ah period begins immediately after the burial and lasts seven days. (Klein 1979:286)

Sitting Shiv'ah, then, implies total separation from the dead and, when done as some people do for someone who is, in fact, alive, it implies ritual death.

individual cases. I don't know that I could count the number of times different Israelis said to me, only half in jest, that they thought that anyone crazy enough to want to be Jewish should be allowed to be regardless of the rabbinical and legislative specifications. But the uncertainties and indeterminacy of the boundaries of the collective self, and hence of otherness, neither start nor end with individuals poking holes in those boundaries. Here is where we can begin to see much more than legal attempts to limit inclusiveness and define otherness.

There are many different named groups at least some of whose members live in Israel today. We have already seen how non-Ashkenazi sectors of the un*disputed*ly Jewish population (i.e., whose Jewishness is not disputed) in Israel are frequently identified separately according to their country or region of origin, and how they are usually referred to as the *eda* from that region or country—the Moroccan *eda*, the Yemenite *eda*, the Kurdish *eda*, etc. We have also already seen how it is possible to break up the Arab population of Israel into groups according to the religion that they or their family members practice. In principle, all of the former are part of the collective self—unquestionably a part of the Jewish people for whom the state of Israel was founded—and all of the latter are others, tolerated within *Israeli* society but not a part of the Jewish people. The former are *edot*, the latter *miyutim*, literally minorities.

But there are other people, other "groups." In every case, one can ask the question: Are they or are they not Jewish? The question itself assumes oppositional dualism and reflects the importance attributed to clearly defined boundaries in any assertion of peoplehood. But discursively, legally, and institutionally, a number of them appear to be seen as neither clearly part of the self nor clearly other. Sociologist Erik Cohen listed them as *kvutsot shuliot leyahadut* (groups marginal to Judaism) in his 1972 monograph/report entitled *Seker HaMiyutim BeIsrael* (Survey of the Minorities in Israel) (1972c). The first 93 pages of the monograph's 116 pages provide documentation and demographic estimates on Muslims and Christians, and the last 6 pages prior to the references include groups now usually described as "cults" active in Israel and a category Erik Cohen labels "Beatnikim" made up mostly of young foreigners living in temporary, sometimes communal, setups mostly along some of Israel's beaches. Pages 94 to 103 are devoted to people/groups/communities he labels Jews and subdivides into five categories. The implication—since he includes them in a monograph/report entitled "Survey of the Minorities in Israel"—is that they are Jewish minorities in Israel.

Listed by Cohen in this 1972 publication as groups marginal to Judaism are the Benei Israel (from India), the Karaites (originally from Egypt, Turkey, and Iraq), the Falashas (from Ethiopia), and the Samaritans (long-time residents of what are now Israel and the West Bank). Listed as "established movements in Judaism" are the Reform and the Conservative. Listed as emergent, developing movements are Love and Prayer, The Children of Abraham, Baalei Tshuva (whom we now refer to as born-again Jews, returnees to the faith, and who by the mid-1980s were certainly not just a few), *Mevakshei Derekh* (Path seekers), and *Shekhteristim*. And finally listed as *Mityahadim*—a less commonly used term for converts that also implies the willful act of becoming a Jew—are the Black Hebrews, mestizo Jews (from Mexico ostensibly descended in part from *marranos*), *marranos* (descended from Spanish Jews who formally converted to Catholicism because of the Inquisition), and San Nicandro converts (from Italy) (cf. Lapide 1951).

Cohen's list is in many ways Erik Cohen's perception of Israeli society —that there is a dominant, mainstream population composed exclusively of Jews and a series of communities within Israel different from mainstream Israeli society and tolerated within its territorial boundaries. The vast majority of these communities are outside mainstream Israeli society by the simple fact that they were not born Jewish. But it is clear in his inclusion of people he labels Jews that he personally does not equate minority status necessarily with non-Jewish identity. Cohen's "map" indicates that for him Jewishness is necessary but not sufficient for membership in mainstream Israeli society.

Yet who are the vast majority of the people he refers to in his section labeled "Jews"? They are named groups of people who claim to be Jews but whose Jewishness has long been questioned—in some cases flatly denied—by Israel's authorized gatekeepers, primarily but not exclusively the Orthodox rabbinate. Once more, to use my Catholic background deliberately, I would say they are the "Jews in limbo."

To put all of these into one apparent category is to invite debate, dispute, and criticism, because the current legal, political, and social position of these various groups is far from uniform in Israel today. Some like the Black Hebrews have very few supporters for their claim to Jewishness in the state of Israel. Some like the Bene Israel of India have come close to full acceptance as Jews. Some like the Karaites have been recognized for centuries as bearing at least a partial genealogical connection with Jews even though rabbinical authorities have long rejected them as "real" Jews. To put Ethiopians/Falashas and Bene Israel into a category with the Black Hebrews or even the Karaites and the Samaritans could be read as denying them the political and legal battles they have won over the past three decades.

But I think Erik Cohen is correct in seeing similarities among them. There *are* groups of Jews who are perceived as other at the same time that they are at least in part—in this case semantically—encompassed as part of the collective self. Erik Cohen does, after all, label them Jews. Or, to look at it from the other side, there are groups of people within the Jewish *people* who have been "otherized" for decades, even centuries, by the gatekeepers of the majority. This is not just a reflection of the difficulties of instantiating semantic/conceptual categories—fitting actual human beings into one's social categories; here we see (1) people caring about maintaining a distinction between self and other while acknowledging fuzzier boundaries than that distinction might imply, (2) people contesting the nature of Jewish peoplehood as well as their right to membership—i.e., the nature of the *object* known as the Jewish people, and (3) people struggling for control over the objectification of the Jewish people. It isn't just that there are difficulties with the application of the "rules" or "principles" for inclusion or exclusion; there are difficulties with the rules or principles themselves.

The Bene Israel of India were invited to participate as Jews in the First Zionist Congress in 1897 in Basle, Switzerland. From the 1930s, the Jewish Agency—a central institution of the Yishuv—sent emissaries to the Bene Israel to encourage Zionist activity among them because they considered them Jews. But the Israeli rabbinate disagreed. Members of the Bene Israel community who moved to Israel after the establishment of the state in 1948 found that most rabbis in Israel questioned their Jewishness, and that they were not allowed to marry non-Bene Israel Jews without first undergoing at least nominal rituals of conversion to Judaism. An agreement was reached in 1964, whereby they were formally declared "full Jews in every respect," but would still be required to submit to nominal rituals of conversion before marrying a non-Bene Israel Jew. Diplomatically, they were told that these steps were necessary in order to erase any possible doubt about their individual ancestry and that this was important because it thus keeps their children and future descendants from having their own Jewishness called into question.

The Bene Israel community in India observed the Sabbath, celebrated major festivals, circumcized their sons, and performed eight of the eleven offerings prescribed in Leviticus and Numbers (Weil 1981). Many claim descent from the ten "lost" tribes of Israel. Others claim that their ancestors escaped by boat from the biblical land of Israel in 175 B.C. during the reign of Antiochus Epiphanes, and that these forefathers were shipwrecked and washed ashore south of Bombay. The books that came to be canonized as the Hebrew Bible in the rest of the Jewish world would then not have survived the shipwreck. Without these sacred texts, with customs not recognized as Jewish by the Israeli rabbinate, and limited to knowledge of only one Hebrew prayer—albeit the crucial Shema Israel

—the Bene Israel were flagged as suspect. A January 31, 1982, ruling by Chief Rabbis Goren and Yosef calling finally for their full acceptance as Jews only served to highlight the existence of lingering doubts about their Jewishness. Customs, commandments, knowledge of Hebrew as a sacred tongue, and adherence to laws and principles set down in *specific* books would appear then to be the contested criteria in disagreements about the constitution of the Jewish people.

Much the same is true of the rabbinical rejection of Karaites and Samaritans. *The Dictionary of the Jewish Religion* (Isaacson 1979) has entries for both Karaites and Samaritans. Of the Karaites it says:

Jewish sect dating back to the 8th century that rejected the oral law. Led by Saadyah, in the 9th century, Rabbis attacked their views and blocked their development. Marriage between Jews and Karaites was forbidden. . . . The Karaites insist on rigid, literal interpretation of Biblical law and have no regard for post-Biblical holidays such as Hanukkah, or the use of a mezuzah or phylacteries. (pp. 101–102)

And of the Samaritans it says: "Small sect of people who claim descent from the ten lost tribes. Their Jewish practices are comparable to those of the Karaites (q.v.). Rabbinic authorities do not regard Samaritans as Jews and Jews are not allowed to intermarry with them" (pp. 101–102). In both entries, reference is made to the fact that most Karaites and Samaritans today live in Israel or, in the case of Samaritans, Israel (specifically the town of Holon) or the West Bank (specifically the town of Nablus). Both entries make a point of describing these as small communities—undeniable in the case of Samaritans of whom there are only a few hundred in the world today but exaggerated in the case of the Karaites. The book says there are "only a few thousand [Karaites] left," when there may be as many as eight to ten thousand. The fact of their dwindling numbers seems important, but so does the fact that most of these people live within Israel today. Their existence has long been a reminder of alternative conceptions of Jewishness, and their rejection by rabbinical authorities a reminder of the struggle for control over self-objectification.[8]

The Black Hebrews are the weakest contenders for Jewishness in this group, but their presence has long been noted by the government, the media, and even Mimuna and other festival goers.[9] They are black Ameri-

8. Rachel Kimor's master's thesis at the Hebrew University was based on research among Samaritans in the late 1970s. Sumi Colligan's (1980) doctoral dissertation in anthropology for Princeton was based on fieldwork done among Karaites also in the late 1970s.

9. Information here comes from newspaper reports and articles clipped out of the *Jerusalem Post*, *Ha'aretz*, and *Ma'ariv* from the late 1970s through 1985.

cans who, reflecting on the biblical account of how Moses led his Israelites out of Egypt and thereby also out of slavery, identify the Israelites from whom contemporary Jews claim descent as a people as Africans. Thus, they argue, Judaism in its "original form" was an African religion and properly the religion of blacks rather than whites. They refuse to undergo conversion rituals set down by Israel's rabbinate, since they do not recognize the rabbinate's authority. They also reject the argument that because their mothers were not Jewish they cannot themselves be Jewish. Many of them entered Israel over the years as tourists and stayed on illegally. As a result, immigration officers at the airport, the ports, and the border gateposts have at various points been instructed to screen black American tourists carefully but diplomatically to try to keep Black Hebrews out. Israeli neighbors of Black Hebrews have often complained about them, and they have appeared not infrequently in the news. The rabbinate rejects them completely, and the government denies them the right to immigrate under the Law of Return, but they have never been taken out by force nor especially sought out primarily for public relations reasons. Excluding or expelling blacks from Israel, many fear, might look racist to the rest of the world, but excluding or expelling blacks who claim they are Jews because Israeli authorities do not regard them as Jews looks even worse. So they have become an element within Israeli society not identified with "Arabs" as other but, despite the rejection, with Jews as other.

APPROPRIATING THE OTHER

The Lebanese, the Palestinians and I once again enter the picture.[10] There is no legal, or even political, question about our Jewishness. We

---

10. I use the term *Palestinian* here deliberately. Whereas the phrase *Israeli Arabs* implies some degree of insider status within Israel, the term *Palestinian* implies outside status, separateness, and a nationalism that challenges Zionism. The seemingly simple act of calling oneself Palestinian is, thus, seen by Jews as well as Arabs as highly political.

Typically, the Israeli government classifies Arabs living within Israel's borders (after independence but) prior to the capture of the West Bank, the Golan Heights, and Gaza in the 1967 war as *Israeli Arabs*, unless they are part of Beduin or Druze communities. Typically, it classifies Arabs living in the West Bank and Gaza as Palestinians, and the Druze living on the Golan Heights as Druze. Most self-pronounced Palestinians reject these distinctions used by the Israeli government. For a sample of Palestinian views on Palestinians, see Hussaini (1975), Jiryis (1976), Said (1980), Sulaiman (1984), and Zurayk (1979). Palestinians are also amply quoted in Shipler's book, *Arab and Jew* (1986), and in David Grossman's powerful and provocative Hebrew-language book, *Yellow Wind* (1987), based on seven weeks of journalistic participant observation in West Bank towns, refugee camps, and villages, and originally published in serial form in *Koteret Rashit* starting—not coincidentally—on Yom HaAtzma'ut 1987.

are not Jewish. There is no question, at least on the surface, about our otherness in the state of Israel. There is also little question about the fact that we are live human beings with beliefs and opinions of our own and the will to act in ways not controlled by the construction of our otherness. Yet there is in what Israelis do with regard to us a great deal of what I call appropriating the other—using what they see in the other for the sake of self-objectification not always by focusing on the contrasts, as the prolonged and often virulent Arab-Israeli conflict might lead one to anticipate, but also and with some regularity by focusing on the similarities.

I began to suspect as much back in 1981 when a number of Israeli Jews I was meeting for a third or fourth time would open up enough to ask me if I did not, in fact, have any Jewish ancestry. Several of them decided, only half jokingly, that I must be descended from the Spanish *marranos*. "Something" about my interest in Israel, my looks, the ease with which they felt they could relate to me, my education, my gestures, and my wandering, seminomadic life experience "felt Jewish" to them. My answer would at times be rejected—a then unexpected inversion of the exclusionary practices many of which I have discussed earlier in this book. What do you mean when you say that you're not Jewish? I was asked on several occasions. That you're not religious? That your mother wasn't Jewish? That "we the Jews" wouldn't count you as a Jew because you have some Jewish ancestry but not the right ones, according to *halacha*? I was incredulous at first. I had no way then to anticipate this reaction. Everything else seemed to point to the importance of Jewishness, and to controlling both the content and the limits of Jewishness.

I began to notice that some of the things I had previously considered dead giveaways did not always work to communicate the fact that I am not Jewish. I still remember the day in the summer of 1981 when I was visiting an Israeli archeologist with an American-born friend. There was, in addition, another guest, a woman in her forties who had never met me before. About twenty minutes into the conversation she heard that I was "not just another American," that I had grown up primarily in Latin America. Her interest piqued, she asked me what it had been like growing up Jewish in Latin America. I looked at my friend and the archeologist, both of whom smiled slightly. I replied that, "in fact, I hadn't been brought up Jewish" and that, "in fact, I had gone to Catholic schools my whole life until I went off to college." Then came the big surprise. "Yes," she nodded, "I have this other friend whose family lived in a small city in Peru and who went to Catholic schools, too—for the same reasons I presume. Catholic schools were always better than the public schools and, of course, in smaller cities where there isn't much of a Jewish community there is no Jewish school to go to." I shook my head in disbelief, though her reasoning made perfect sense. My friend finally intervened to tell her very explicitly that I was not Jewish.

These seemingly counterintuitive experiences occupied only a back-burner in my own thinking until the summer and fall of 1982, immediately following the Israeli invasion of Lebanon. After more than a year in Israel researching what I then called the Israeli obsession with ethnicity, and living through major Israeli-Arab political events such as the Syrian missile crisis (spring 1981), the assassination of Sadat (fall 1981), the Israeli annexation of the Golan Heights (winter 1981), and the return of the Sinai peninsula to Egypt (spring 1982), I may have been especially sensitive to Israelis' concern with *adatiut* and their political and social participation in a public discourse on *edot*, sectoral/group inequalities, and the call for cultural pluralism. But after years of digesting my material and interpretations, I still cannot attribute what I saw and heard in the Israeli public discourse on Lebanon the first six to eight months after the invasion just to my heightened academic and personal sensitivity to the issue of ethnicity.

What I heard—on the radio, in public gatherings, in demonstrations against the war as well as assemblies supporting Israeli government policies in Lebanon—and what I read in newspapers and magazines nearly stunned me at first. The Lebanese were being treated, discursively, very differently from the Palestinians. In fact, the language used to refer to incidents or interactions with Lebanese men and women struck me, then, as wrong. Despite the foreignness I no doubt maintained in my conceptualization of self and other in Israel (as noted in the opening section of this chapter), I had clearly by June 1982 internalized some of that understanding: that *adatiut* was a thing among and even for Jews, and that Arabs were foreigners with whom Israelis always had to contend for geo-historical reasons but who otherwise played no part in the shaping and perpetuating of "the Jewish people." Israeli discourse on the Lebanese was neither one nor the other.

I struggled to make sense of what I was hearing, and of whether I was hearing "correctly." I went back to my newspaper archives, and to all the newspaper articles my research assistants and I had cut out of *Ha'aretz, Ma'ariv, Yediot Aharonot,* and the *Jerusalem Post* on a daily basis. Clearly, most of the articles dealing with Lebanon since June 6, 1982, when Israeli troops crossed the border into Lebanon, reported on battles, injuries, military strategies, and international reactions to the invasion. But a steady stream focused on the Lebanese people, their lives, their styles, their customs, and their personalities.[11] The PLO was por-

11. Short and long articles appeared in all of Israel's major dailies. For a while, during the first few weeks of the war, I was keeping large sections of the newspapers for my re-

trayed as the enemy, and by association all Palestinians were suspect. But the Lebanese became objectified as (1) non-Palestinians, (2) not, as a group, enemies of Israel, and (3) a group having many social and cultural characteristics that made them not just like Israelis but also equal to Israelis. The topics changed as the weeks went by and so did the social commentary, but these three basic representations did not change for a very long time.[12] Even today after the Shi'ites emerged as a major power in Lebanon and the widespread animosity toward Israel that exists among them has been recognized by the Israeli government, it is Khomeinism in Iran—that is, something foreign—that gets assigned much of the blame for Lebanese Shi'ites' antagonistic behavior toward Israel.

Explicitly, in talking about "the Lebanese" (as opposed to the Israelis), commentators always established *and* perpetuated a perception of separateness and difference. But implicitly, I am arguing, they were writing about Israel by what they found of interest among the Lebanese. And unlike what is implied in critiques of Orientalism, this other was not constructed as the antithesis of the self. If anything, it was likeness that dominated the Israeli presentation and representation of their otherness. Once again, we confront what sounds like a contradiction in terms.

But consider the material I confronted. I have periodized the discourse according to shifts in topics covered by the press and shifts in tone. Over a period of five to six months, changes in themes and attitudes were at times gradual, and at times immediately responsive to drastic political events, such as the assassination of Bashir Jemayel in September 1982. The first two weeks of the war produced a number of physical descriptions of towns and cities in Lebanon, accounts of their material culture,

---

search files. Interspersed among the horror stories of death and dying in Lebanon were what I assume the editors saw as human interest stories about the Lebanese encountered by Israeli soldiers. In the midst of it all, they seemed both charming and silly.

12. A body of literature arose as the months went by. The media seemed to settle on the clashes between Phalangists and Palestinians late in 1982, Phalangists and Druze throughout 1983, and the rise of Amal (the Shi'ite movement) by 1984–85. Angry Israelis of low-income and "Oriental" backgrounds periodically made references (even in news interviews or on the radio) to how Israel could turn into another Lebanon if the Ashkenazim in power did not change their ways and their attitudes. At their most extreme, these statements made the initial Israeli Black Panther movement (cf. Cohen 1972b) of the early 1970s sound mild and accommodating. I'm not arguing that the encounter with Lebanon created the inequities and frustrations that exist in Israel but, rather, that it highlighted *adatiut* and the possibility of more radical fragmentation of the society. I am not aware of very many books or articles yet published in Israel dealing with this war's sociopolitical effects on Israelis. The publications I have seen tend to focus on the war itself and the nature of Israel's involvement in Lebanon (Kahan Commission Report 1983; Naor 1986; Rabin 1983; Schiff and Ya'ari 1986). Two notably soul-searching exceptions are Lieblich (1987) and Oz (1987).

descriptions of things Israelis could buy in Lebanon, and several personal, inspiring, human interest stories about interactions between Israeli soldiers and Lebanese civilians—even romantic interludes. The individualized, descriptive, laudatory, and optimistic tone continued till early July. The thrust of much of it was that the Lebanese both like and are like the Israelis—that the Lebanese make the Israelis feel at home in Lebanon, that Lebanon (like Israel) is both "Levantine" and "Western" in culture and orientation, and that the Lebanese are resilient, enjoy and appreciate the good life, and are at least as entrepreneurial as the Israelis. By early July, journalists abandoned the simpler rosy picture in favor of the kind of investigative critical analysis they carry out in Israel itself. They expressed doubts about the viability of an independent Lebanon; several commented disapprovingly on "Lebanese attitudes to women"; much is made of what gets referred to as Christian hatred and the strife among Christians, Muslims, and Druze; suddenly the Israeli public confronted Lebanon as "the land of hashish," and reports of attempted smuggling of hashish into Israel appeared in print. By August, political analysts struggled to make sense of Lebanese "internal" politics with questions and concerns that sound almost directly out of their own columns on Israeli society and politics: Is the mess in Lebanon the result of "big-man politics" (*caudillismo*), ethnic pluralism, the newness of the state, an underdeveloped institutional infrastructure, the lack of a real constitution, an unwillingness to recognize the growing power of ethnic minorities in time to avert disaster, the difficulties of having a strong sense of peoplehood and a strong desire for national stability in a country where the relationship between peoplehood and nationality has never been fully worked out, or Middle Eastern culture? By mid-September, everything reported by the press presented Lebanon as an unstable mosaic of three competing, combative, and mutually incompatible "communities," by then almost exclusively referred to as *edot*.

Discussions of Lebanon's mix of "Western" and "Middle Eastern" culture, the resilience of the Lebanese, the cosmopolitan nature of Beirut, the financial know-how exhibited by "large numbers" of Lebanese, and ethnic conflict all heightened the image of the Lebanese as very much like the Israelis—already suggesting a representation of them as (at the very least) selflike others. But it is the practice of calling different sectors of Lebanese society *edot* that brought it to a head for me.

Edot may be loosely translated into English as ethnic groups, but its meaning in contemporary Israeli Hebrew is much more specific—both in metasemantic glosses of the term and in patterns of actual usage. Nobody, for example, ever speaks of "ethnic groups" in the United States, "nationalities" in the Soviet Union, or "peoples" or "tribes" in sub-Saharan

Africa as *edot*. American "ethnic groups" become *kvutsot ethniot;* Soviet "peoples" or "nationalities" get referred to as *amim, umot,* or *kehilot* (literally, "communities"); and African "peoples" or "tribes" become *amim* or *shvatim*. Most Israelis when asked what *edot* are reply that they are certain communities of *Jews,* nearly always of North African, Middle Eastern, or Asian origin (cf. Krausz 1986).

The possibility of a broader application of the term/concept is signaled in Even-Shoshan's rather detailed description of, or prescription for, appropriate usage of *edot,* though in describing contemporary usage he, too, seems to restrict it to Jews. In the 1977 edition of the unabridged dictionary (pp. 957–58), four glosses are given:

1. *kahal* [audience, public], *kehila* [community], *tzibur* [public]
2. *chavura* [social group, close network of friends], *kvutsa* [group]
3. *kibbutz shel baalei chaim* [aggregation of animals], *lahaka* [troupe, band, ensemble]
4. [given the length of this fourth entry, I will skip the transliteration and restrict myself here to reproducing my translation] contemporary appellation for any *kibbutz* [in the sense of gathering, community, or settlement] of the *kibbutzim* of the people of Israel in the Diaspora, who lived for generations in a particular country or in adjacent countries and who acquired for themselves over the years a special way of life, and customs and content that separate it both in the general and the particular from that of other Jewish *kibbutzim.*

The examples given for the first three glosses are all biblical, not contemporary. In contrast, his examples of "correct usage" of the "modern meaning"—i.e., the fourth entry—are "*edat haAshkenazim* [the *eda* of the Ashkenazim], *edat haSefardim* [*eda* of the Sephardim], *edot hamizrach* [*edot* of the East/the Middle East], *edat haTeimanim* [*eda* of the Yemenites], and *medinat israel sho'efet lelaked et haedot hashonot ulemazgan* [the state of Israel aspires to unite the different *edot* and blend them together]."

More confirmation of the strong association of *edot* with Jews came from examining the newspaper articles my research assistants and I collected from summer 1981 through summer 1982 from Israel's major newspapers. In a file I had set aside for clippings on communities of "non-Jews" in Israel, I found references to the Black Hebrews, the Arabs, the Druze, the Karaites, the Beduin, the Ethiopians (then almost always referred to as Falashas), the Samaritans, the Bahais, and the Armenians. Three clear patterns emerged from examining the articles carefully: (1) the terms *Arab* and *Beduin* were *never* accompanied by the word *eda;* (2) most of the groups described by Erik Cohen (1972c) as "groups marginal to Judaism" were indeed often, if not always, referred to as *edot*—

the Karaites, the Samaritans, and the Falashas (and, of course, the Bene Israel whom *I* had obviously fully accepted as Jews and had, therefore, not included in this file), except for the Black Hebrews who were always described as a *kat,* that is, sect or cult; and (3) the Druze in Israel *were* usually referred to as an *eda*. These differences were systematic and repeated; they were not, I concluded, accidental.

It was true, of course, that they showed that a community did not have to be Jewish to be labeled an *eda*. We have already examined the nonacceptance of the Karaites and the Samaritans as "real Jews," and the struggle of the Bene Israel and the Ethiopians in Israel for legal, religious, and social acceptance as full-fledged Jews. Yet they are all comfortably called *edot*. Moreover, the Druze have never made any pretense to being Jewish and no one in Israel, to my knowledge, has ever tried to claim them as Jewish. Yet they, too, are systematically referred to as *ha eda ha Druzit*.

But all of these examples consist of groups I would describe as internalized others—on the margins of the Israeli Jewish collective self and with a special relationship to Jews and Judaism. The argument holds for the Druze on a political or social level, rather than on a religious or ethnic one: the Druze fought on the side of the Jews in 1948, made a pact with Israeli Jews to be a part of an emergent society in which they would be a political and demographic minority by design, and serve in the Israeli army unlike those simply labeled "Israeli Arabs." Keeping the Druze population in Israel happy with its elders' decision to be a part of an Israeli Jewish society has long been an explicit and implicit goal of the Israeli government and many of its Jewish citizens for, I think, they believe it shows (1) that Israel is not racist, (2) that Israeli Jewish society can, and does, incorporate non-Jewish minorities, and (3) that, if the Arabs on the West Bank and Gaza would only stop wanting to destroy the state of Israel, they, too, could live happily, healthily, and prosperously as a minority community in Israel. Correspondingly, when the Druze community expresses dissatisfaction or even outrage at an action or policy adopted by some agency of the Israeli government or there is a press report that more and more younger Druzim are openly calling themselves Palestinians or even just Arabs, many Jews in the government, the press corps, the academy, and the street respond with sustained expressions of worry and restlessness. I don't think there is anything accidental about the fact that they are referred to in Israel today as an *eda*. By calling them an *eda,* they are discursively being put in the same category as others in Israeli society who are seen as (1) a community, (2) with a heritage of its own, (3) subordinate to the political "majority" in power in Israel, but (4) very much a part of Israeli *Jewish* society. The fact that they are called *edot* did not erase the problem I had with the repeated, postwar Israeli pattern of referring to groups in Lebanon as *edot*. It did, however, suggest a series of related hypotheses on the postwar Israeli discourse on Lebanon —what it is about, what it creates, and how it works both semiotically and politically.

In seeking an explanation, I first considered the possibility that this was just an example of metaphorical usage. We call something a metaphor when we assume that there is a semantic mapping that differentiates between two things, but we see or hear someone discursively relating, if not actually equating, things which the semantic map otherwise presents as different. Commonality is stressed over difference. If referring to sectors of Lebanese society as *edot* is an example of metaphorical usage, then the question of interest here is what it is that is being asserted as shared and why.

A second possibility involved a modification of my initial hypothesis that *adatiut* refers to divisions and relationships among kinds of Jews. What if, I asked myself, I do not privilege the application of the term *eda* to Jews and consider the meaning of the concept of *eda* in light of the fact that there are non-Jewish groups whom the Jews in contemporary Israel describe as *edot*? Talking about Lebanese *edot* would then not be metaphorical usage at all but, instead, the logical extension of "the core meaning" of the term.[13] But what then would its core meaning be? Since

13. I considered the possibility that *edot* was just the closest equivalent Israelis could find for the groupings in Lebanon, and that there might, therefore, not be any interesting reflexivity in this at all. But this begs the question. Obviously, groups of people are very much at odds with each other in Lebanon and have been, explosively so, since 1975, but what exactly are these groupings? Neither the Lebanese nor those writing about Lebanon outside Israel seem very sure. Yes, there are individual group names, but there are many of them and they are not all the same sort of grouping. Writings on Lebanon use the terms *confessional groups* (a reference to the confessional system of representation and governance instituted formally by the French during the Mandate years in the 1920s and 1930s), *sects, religious communities, sectarian groups, national groupings, sociopolitical entities, social classes, religious sects,* and *the feudal system* (see, for example, Agwani 1965; Dubar and Nasr 1976; Khalidi 1979; Meo 1965; Nassar 1969; Qubain 1961; Rabinovich 1985; Salem 1973; Salibi 1977). Barakat (1979) tries to get at it by referring to Lebanon's "fragmented, hierarchical arranged communities," its "pyramidal social class structure," and its "sectarian political system." The point is that they are, and could be, called a variety of things depending on what is being stressed about them—religious differences, class differences, peoplehood, hierarchy, democracy, equality, nationalism, or national subcultures.

To give a non-Israeli example of how we tend to see "things" in terms of the "things" we believe to exist and the contexts in which we expect to find them, consider David Gordon's statement in *Lebanon: The Fragmented Nation* (Hoover Institution, 1980): "With ethnic movements becoming increasingly evident in many parts of the world, Lebanon provides a unique laboratory as an experiment in multiethnic coexistence in the absence of any single

Israelis find it quite inappropriate to speak of *edot* in so many different parts of the world (as I have argued earlier), one possibility is that something about the semantics of *eda* intrinsically relates it to the Middle East. Copts in Egypt are readily referred to as *ha eda haCoptit,* though they are not exactly a common topic of conversation in Israel, and historians and Orientalists in Israel who write about political and social relations among non-Jews in the Near East (including Palestine) before the twentieth century (e.g., Ben-Arieh 1979) do use the term to refer to Muslims and Christians—*ha eda ha muslemit, ha eda ha notzrit.* One could then argue that the reason there was so much talk in Israel of *edot* and *adatiut* in Lebanon since the invasion is that the invasion produced the first long-term person-to-person contact between Israelis and citizens of another Middle Eastern country which focuses on divisions in its society. If that were correct, two interesting propositions would follow: (1) that Palestinians, who are the Middle Eastern people with whom Israelis have had the most prolonged person-to-person contact, are *not seen as seriously divided among themselves,* and (2) that the Lebanese are much more like Israeli Jews because they *are very divided among themselves.*

But is this good or bad from an Israeli point of view? It certainly harbors interesting paradoxes. If *adatiut* is a Middle Eastern phenomenon, then the constant talk in Israel of *adatiut* in Lebanon could only serve to highlight the Middle Easternness, rather than Westernness, of Israeli society—a result which touches on something particularly sensitive socially, culturally, and politically in contemporary Israel. If the Lebanese are internally divided to the point of carrying on a prolonged civil war and the phenomenon is called *adatiut,* an equation is being made at least implicitly between *adati* conflict in Israel and the conflict in Lebanon—with the implication that the *adati* conflict in Israel, if not kept under careful watch and control, could easily erupt into civil war in Israel. Or, consider the ironic twist that the recognition of serious internal divisions among the Lebanese—but not the Palestinians—seems to grant more familiarity to the Lebanese but much more of a sense of peoplehood to the Palestinians, despite the long-term Israeli argument that non-Jewish people lived in Palestine before the Zionist movement began to settle the region but that they did not have much of a sense of peoplehood at all.

A third possibility is that all the talk of *edot* in Lebanon was a semiconscious Israeli strategy on the part of many Israelis to talk about *adatiut* in Israel without ever appearing to do so. Showing unity in times

---

majority host culture" (Gordon 1980:16). Ethnicity had by the late 1970s become very much of a "thing" in U.S. academic circles. Gordon was an American professor at the American University of Beirut for years—half in the U.S. academic world and half in Lebanon.

of war had been such a strong norm in Israel until the war in Lebanon that throughout the summer and early fall of 1982 the major newspapers frequently carried columns, stories, and editorials discussing whether or not it was moral and patriotic to stage demonstrations against the war at home "when the boys are risking their lives at the front."[14] The bulk of the discussion was political—whether or not the war was justified— but the memory of most Israelis old enough to have lived through at least one previous war was that it was important to suspend disagreements and divisions in times of war, to present a united front at home. This included muting the conflict between Sephardim and Ashkenazim, religious and secular, Labor supporters and Likud supporters. But this was the first Israeli war since the intensification of the discourse on *adatiut* and inequality in Israel, and the 1981 elections had kept it very much in the spotlight. The convenient thing about the Israeli discourse on Lebanon by August 1982 is that it allowed Israelis to talk about *adatiut* without threatening unity, that it kept the issues alive without any direct reference to Israeli society.

Whichever of these explanations it is that comes closest to the truth, certain general points would seem to hold: (1) that we have a linguistic usage that contradicts assertions of difference between Israelis and Lebanese; (2) that it is a linguistic usage that makes sense only by understanding both prior linguistic usage and the political process in which the previously unusual usage *spreads;* (3) that it is a linguistic usage which, having as its object of reference "Lebanese society," gives the impression of referring to Lebanon, though it could be argued that this is a case of collective, discursive transference that limits Israelis' awareness of the extent to which Israeli society is the submerged object of discussion and the extent to which it is modified, presupposed, and created/recreated by the discourse on Lebanon; and (4) that it is a linguistic usage in which there is very little consciousness of anyone having *invented* anything, changed the discourse, or created one.

In presenting parts of the argument of this book to academic colleagues at conferences, I have discovered that the ideological politics of the intellectual world continues to lead scholars to straightjacket others' analyses in much the same way that we straightjacket self and other. We seem to be unable, or unwilling, to digest fully the possibility—indeed I argue, for

14. I have an enormous file of newspaper clippings from the summer of 1982 which I entitled "demonstrations/national consensus?"—much of it about the legitimacy, wisdom, and validity of staging antiwar demonstrations in the middle of any Israeli war. In nearly all editorials, columns, and letters about *that* issue, reference was made to the importance of hanging on to a "national consensus" at least in wartime.

the Israeli case at least, the fact—that the presupposition of oppositional dualism is so widespread and apparently so important to us that it keeps most of us from readily seeing the many ways in which we are continually engaged in the act of *creating* the very opposition we assume already exists. Semiotics, I have been told by some of my colleagues, cannot be an explanation for anything, for it takes as its object of analysis—they argue—that which is already constructed by society and not that which is responsible for its construction. In this I hear the persistence, often unconscious, of a conceptualization of social science approaches as dualistic —variously labeled idealist versus materialist, interpretive versus explanatory, synchronic versus diachronic, structuralist versus processualist. But can the process of creation ever be really seen as over? And can an object, whether viewed as a semiotic construction or a material production, really be forever guarded against the possibility of human reappropriation? To argue that semiotics cannot explain anything because its subject matter consists of the end products of some forces of production thereby perceived to be more real is to fall for the illusion of objectification—the constant presupposition that objects are discrete entities with fixed, finite, finished qualities no longer, if ever, in the process of being created.

The point here is not that the collective other in Israel, and by implication the collective self, just exists and that actions are taken based simply on the presumption of its existence. The point is that along with being constantly presupposed they are also continually in the process of being created. The tension this creates both bolsters the attractiveness of the presumption of dualism *and* fosters a kind of blindness to semiotic and political processes, an awareness of which would make such a presumption look simplistic. The other is not just created in opposition to the self. It can also be internalized, "otherized," incorporated, and appropriated. And most of this takes place outside the deliberate, institutionalized procedures and processes that characterize the legal system.

Reflections:
On Words and Deeds

THIS book will no doubt seem odd to avid readers of books on Israel. It does not explicitly address any of those issues we have popularly come to see as Israel's pressing problems. It neither justifies nor attacks Zionism as an ideology, a sociopolitical movement, or an assertion about the existence of the state of Israel. It does not detail the relations between Jews and Arabs nor document the history of the Arab-Israeli conflict—the periods openly identified as wars, the quieter periods "between wars," the nearly always delicate relations between Jews and Arabs even during the most peaceful of times, or the periods of heightened tension and active violence in "peacetime" that make *peacetime* look very much like an oxymoron. It is not about the rise of Israel's better-known state institutions such as the Histadrut, the political parties, or its educational systems. It is not even about "the new immigrants" or "the problem of immigrant absorption." And, of course, it is not intended as a explication of current events—the urgency and near-desperation of much of what is happening notwithstanding.

Yet I believe that it is, nonetheless, about "Israeli society," and the struggle with the concept and "fact" of peoplehood that is a condition for its very possibility. Collective identities are funny fictions. When they are important to us, we make sure we treat them as givens but, I submit here, we also make sure we continue to do all in our power to create the boundaries and the content to justify our beliefs about the "people's" "natural" existence and the expectations we may derive from such beliefs.

Our beliefs may not always be obvious to us; sometimes they don't even seem important to us. But no matter how conscious we may or may not be of them and their influence on our actions, they have an impact on our lives as well as the lives of those touched by the content of our beliefs.

People react differently to being in power much as they do to being

189

out of power. Otherness may be seen as a threat, as a justification for *our* holding power, as a mirror through whose posited presence we recognize ourselves as a collectivity, or even as a "fact" irrelevant to our sense of self. And if we are not in the historical habit of seeing ourselves in power, we may end up as concerned with our collective selfhood as others might be about their own constituted others or even about their own constituted otherness.

But what is this "thing" we treat as a collective self and casually refer to as "our people"? It seems to me that collective identities are conceptual representations masquerading as objects (positivities in Foucault's sense), and that they are in perpetual need of nurturing. It is paradoxically then both mind-boggling and logical that so much power struggle should focus on the *rights* of peoples—not just individuals—and so little attention be paid explicitly to the semiotic contradictions of peoplehood. For what are the rights of collectivities that see themselves as peoples? For over a century now, nationalists have invoked peoplehood as the fundamental justification and rationale for their demand for political independence. But what is peoplehood? When there are competing claims to land, to resources, to positions of power and influence, or to a sense of respectability, one group of people may buttress its sense of peoplehood while simultaneously calling into question the peoplehood of their competitors.

How we conceptualize ourselves, represent ourselves, objectify ourselves, matters not just because it is an interesting example of the relationship between being, consciousness, knowledge, reference, and social action, but at least as much because it is a statement about power. Social representations are dually constituted. They are simultaneously descriptive and prescriptive, presupposing and creative. They both describe a particular state of affairs and index the hopes, goals, wishes, and beliefs of the people generating the representation. Without live people to care about them, representations—whether in discourse, in nonverbal acts of communication, or in audiovisual form—play little role in social life. With live people to care about them, they frequently become both the idiom in which genuine conflict and competition get expressed *and* the focus of that conflict and competition.

Few groups of people in the world have as long-standing and continuous a claim to peoplehood as do Jews. Yet, as I have tried to both argue and document in this book, the fact and longevity of that claim does not seem to resolve the problem of instability inherent in objectifying a collective identity. What is the significant collective self in Israel? I am aware that at times I write explicitly about "Israeli society," at times about Israel's "collective self," and at times about "the peoplehood of the Jews" in Israel. Perhaps I am at fault for not sticking to one representation as the object of my discussion, but I am convinced that to do so would be to portray much more clarity, much more neatness, much more resolution than life in contemporary Israel today warrants. The relationship between "Israeli society" and "the Jewish people" in Israel is fraught with tension, though there is little question in Israel or elsewhere that it is the "fact" of the latter that is responsible for the "fact" of the former.

And what about the conceptualization of the collective self in terms of a conceptualization of the collective other? It is clear that a great deal of energy has been expended in Israel in creating an Israeli society out of disparate and often deeply different populations of Jewish immigrants. Phrases such as *kibbutz galuyot* ("the ingathering of the exiles"), *mizug galuyot* ("the blending or integration of the exiles"), and *klitat olim* ("the absorption of immigrants") capture the perception of purpose and representation of goal long dominant in Israeli public discourse. Tolerance for the presence and citizenship of non-Jews has long existed in most quarters of Israeli Jewish society, but we should not blow that tolerance out of proportion and ignore the intended Jewishness of Israeli society. In presenting immigration and integration as central to Israeli society, public discourse clearly points to a concept of the relevant and significant collective self as in need of reconstitution, not in need of creation. A focus on the collective self frequently makes Israeli Jews appear self-absorbed and callous to the parallel, if not identical, forms of self-representation found among Arabs who live, or at least work, in their midst.

I think most of us like to think of how we are as based on something given, something "natural." When someone else tells us who we are and has the power to impose their version of who we are on us—according us certain rights and duties and denying us others by virtue of their representation of us—we readily see it as an act of manipulation of "the facts" and the exercise of political power whose relation to "reality" we may question, even challenge. Likewise, I would argue, we are uncomfortable seeing our sense of self as constituted by our constitution of other people's otherness. Something about that perception smacks of fabrication and manipulation—this time on our part—and not of "naturalness." If we see something as *being* what it is independently of how it is perceived, we do not posit any role for human agents. If we see something as being what it is because of how it is represented—i.e., constituted by its representation —we have no way to avoid seeing it as constituted by human agents and their actions. To see ourselves as constituting others is to acknowledge our having more power than we may wish to have or be comfortable having. To see ourselves as constituting ourselves is to leave the door open for calling into question some of the arguments we ourselves frequently use for claiming the "fact" and, thus, legitimacy of our collective identity.

Appendices
Bibliography
Index

Table A1.1. The Population (in thousands), by Religion, 1948–1987

Average population					Population at end of year					
Druze and others	Chris- tians	Mos- lems	Jews	Total	Druze and others	Chris- tians	Mos- lems	Jews	Total	Year
—	—	—	—	—			156.0	716.7	872.7	8 XI 1948*
—	—	—	671.9	—.	—	—	—	758.7	—	1948
—	—	—	901.0	1,059.0	14.5	34.0	111.5	1,013.9	1,173.9	1949
14.8	35.0	113.8	1,103.0	1,266.8	15.0	36.0	116.1	1,203.0	1,370.1	1950
15.3	37.5	117.5	1,324.0	1,494.3	15.5	39.0	118.9	1,404.4	1,577.8	1951
15.8	39.7	120.9	1,429.8	1,606.2	16.1	40.4	122.8	1,450.2	1,629.5	1952
16.5	40.9	125.2	1,467.7	1,650.3	16.8	41.4	127.6	1,483.6	1,669.4	1953
17.4	41.7	129.7	1,500.7	1,689.5	18.0	42.0	131.8	1,526.0	1,717.8	1954
18.5	42.7	134.1	1,555.3	1,750.4	19.0	43.3	136.3	1,590.5	1,789.1	1955
19.4	43.5	138.9	1,626.4	1,828.4	19.8	43.7	141.4	1,667.5	1,872.4	1956
20.2	44.8	144.1	1,721.2	1,930.5	20.5	45.8	146.8	1,762.8	1,976.0	1957
21.0	46.6	149.8	1,782.7	2,000.1	21.4	47.3	152.8	1,810.2	2,031.7	1958
21.9	47.8	156.0	1,836.2	2,062.1	22.3	48.3	159.2	1,858.8	2,088.7	1959
22.8	49.0	162.8	1,882.6	2,117.0	23.3	49.6	166.3	1,911.3	2,150.4	1960
25.8	50.7	171.2	1,942.0	2,189.9	26.3	51.3	174.9	1,981.7	2,234.2	1961*
26.8	51.9	178.9	2,030.5	2,288.2	27.3	52.6	183.0	2,068.9	2,331.8	1962
27.9	53.1	187.7	2,111.3	2,379.7	28.5	53.9	192.2	2,155.6	2,430.1	1963
28.5	54.6	197.3	2,197.1	2,477.5	28.6	55.5	202.3	2,239.2	2,525.6	1964
29.2	56.3	207.3	2,269.8	2,562.6	29.8	57.1	212.4	2,299.1	2,598.4	1965
30.4	57.8	217.7	2,323.2	2,629.2	31.0	58.5	223.0	2,344.9	2,657.4	1966
31.5	64.8	256.2	2,362.6	2,715.2	32.1	71.0	289.6	2,383.6	2,776.3	1967
32.6	71.8	294.6	2,407.6	2,806.5	33.3	72.2	300.8	2,434.8	2,841.1	1968
33.9	72.9	307.8	2,469.6	2,884.2	34.6	73.5	314.5	2,506.8	2,929.5	1969
35.2	74.5	321.3	2,543.1	2,974.0	35.9	75.5	328.6	2,582.0	3,022.1	1970
36.6	76.4	336.1	2,620.1	3,069.3	37.3	77.3	344.0	2,662.0	3,120.7	1971
37.8	77.8	352.3	2,704.6	3,172.6	37.8	73.8	360.7	2,752.7	3,225.0	1972*
38.5	75.2	368.7	2,795.6	3,278.1	39.3	76.7	377.2	2,845.0	3,338.2	1973
40.0	77.7	386.1	2,873.6	3,377.4	40.8	78.7	395.2	2,906.9	3,421.6	1974
41.5	79.4	403.1	2,931.2	3,455.3	42.2	80.2	411.4	2,959.4	3,493.2	1975
43.1	81.2	420.6	2,988.3	3,533.0	43.9	82.0	429.1	3,020.4	3,575.4	1976
44.8	83.0	438.1	3,047.2	3,613.0	45.6	83.8	446.5	3,077.3	3,653.2	1977
46.4	84.6	454.7	3,106.9	3,692.6	47.3	85.5	463.6	3,141.2	3,737.6	1978
48.1	86.6	472.2	3,179.5	3,786.4	49.0	87.6	481.2	3,218.4	3,836.2	1979
49.9	88.8	489.7	3,249.4	3,877.7	50.7	89.9	498.3	3,282.7	3,921.7	1980
51.5	90.7	505.9	3,300.0	3,948.1	52.3	91.5	513.7	3,320.3	3,977.9	1981
64.6	92.8	522.6	3,346.6	4,026.7	65.6	94.0	530.8	3,373.2	4,063.6	1982
67.0	94.8	533.3	3,381.0	4,076.2	68.0	95.9	542.2	3,412.5	4,118.6	1983*
69.0	97.0	551.0	3,442.1	4,159.1	70.0	98.2	559.7	3,471.7	4,199.7	1984
71.0	98.8	568.7	3,494.5	4,233.0	72.0	99.4	577.6	3,517.2	4,266.2	1985
73.0	100.2	586.3	3,539.3	4,298.8	74.0	100.9	595.0	3,561.4	4,331.3	1986
75.0	102.0	604.7	3,587.2	4,368.9	76.1	103.0	614.5	3,612.9	4,406.5	1987

Source: *Statistical Abstract of Israel*, 1988, no. 39, p. 31.
*census year

Table A1.2. Population (in thousands), by Religion, Origin, Continent of Birth, and Period of Immigration

	Dec. 31 1987	Dec. 31 1984	June 4 1983	May 19 1972	May 22 1961	Nov. 8 1948
GRAND TOTAL	4,406.5	4,199.7	4,037.6	3,147.7	2,179.5	872.7
JEWS—TOTAL	3,612.9	3,471.7	3,350.0	2,686.7	1,932.4	716.7
Origin						
Israel	740.3	607.8	533.9	225.8	106.9	—
Asia	748.7	748.1	740.3	655.9	}818.3	—
Africa	788.7	767.1	736.1	617.9		—
Europe-America	1,335.4	1,348.7	1,339.7	1,187.0	1,007.1	—
Israel born—total	2,254.3	2,059.1	1,927.9	1,272.3	730.4	253.7
Father born in						
Israel	740.2	607.8	533.9	225.8	106.9	—
Asia	467.0	456.4	443.1	339.8	}288.5	—
Africa	463.9	435.1	413.3	269.1		—
Europe-America	583.2	559.8	537.7	437.6	335.0	—
Born abroad—total	1,358.8	1,412.6	1,422.1	1,414.4	1,201.9	463.0
Asia	281.8	291.7	297.3	316.1	300.1	57.8
Immigrated up to 1971	258.0	269.9	276.1	}316.1	300.1	57.8
1972–1979	15.1	15.6	21.2		—	—
1980+	8.7	6.1	5.2	—	—	—
Africa	324.7	332.0	322.8	348.9	229.7	12.2
Immigrated up to 1971	289.9	300.9	306.1	}348.9	229.7	12.2
1972–1979	12.2	12.7	10.4		—	—
1980+	22.6	18.4	6.3	—	—	—
Europe-America	752.2	788.9	802.0	749.7	672.1	393.0
Immigrated up to 1971	521.5	300.9	589.7	}749.7	672.1	393.0
1972–1979	157.5	167.1	172.6		—	—
1980+	73.3	55.4	39.7	—	—	—
MOSLEMS	614.5	559.7	526.6	352.0	170.8	—
CHRISTIANS	103.0	98.2	94.2	72.1	50.5	—
DRUZE and OTHERS	76.1	70.0	66.8	36.9	25.8	—
		Percentages				
Grand Total	100.0	100.0	100.0	100.0	100.0	100.0
Jews	82.0	82.7	83.0	85.4	88.7	82.1
Moslems	13.9	13.3	13.0	11.2	7.8	}
Christians	2.3	2.3	2.3	2.3	2.3	}17.9
Druze and others	1.7	1.7	1.7	1.2	1.2	}
Jews by Origin—Total	100.0	100.0	100.0	100.0	100.0	100.0
Israel	20.5	17.5	15.9	8.4	5.5	—
Asia	20.7	21.5	22.1	24.4	}42.3	—
Africa	21.8	22.1	22.0	23.0		—
Europe-America	37.0	38.9	40.0	44.2	52.1	—
Jews by Birth Place—Total	100.0	100.0	100.0	100.0	100.0	100.0
Israel born—total	62.4	59.3	57.5	47.3	37.8	35.4
Father born in						
Israel	20.5	17.5	15.9	8.4	5.5	—
Asia	12.8	13.1	13.2	12.6	}14.9	—
Africa	12.8	12.4	12.2	10.0		—

Table A1.2, *continued*

	Dec. 31 1987	Dec. 31 1984	June 4 1983	May 19 1972	May 22 1961	Nov. 8 1948
Europe-America	16.1	16.2	16.1	16.3	17.4	—
Born abroad—total	37.6	40.7	42.5	52.7	62.2	64.6
Asia	7.8	8.4	8.9	11.8	15.5	8.1
Africa	9.0	9.6	9.7	13.0	11.9	1.7
Europe-America	20.8	22.7	23.9	27.9	34.8	54.8

Source: *Statistical Abstract of Israel*, 1986, no. 37, p. 65, and 1988, no. 39, p. 73.

Appendix 2. Articles on *Tarbut* (Culture) in the First 100 Issues of *Koteret Rashit*, 1982–84

Issue and Page	Title and Explanation
10, p. 12	Ashkenazim; olam holekh vneelam (cover story on the "disappearing world of the Ashkenazim," by Arye Dayan)
12, p. 22	Prof. Ben Ami: Begin hitir et hadam (written after the murder of Emil Gruenzweig, a Peace Now activist killed at a demonstration calling for Ariel Sharon's resignation, by Arye Dayan)
12, p. 35	Eifo at Noemi Polani (interview with the director Noemi Polani, by Rami Rozen)
15, p. 22	le David Levy yesh akhot (North African–born Knesset member and then deputy prime minister David Levy has a sister, by Chaim HaNegbi)
15, p. 28	HaGruzinim shel rova vav (Ashdod) (The Georgians of the *vav* quarter in Ashdod, by Carmela Ram Lakhish)
18	Ya Salem al ha Shulkhan (about the Mimuna, by Dan Ben Amotz—not the cover story but mentioned on the cover as HaMimuna shel Dan Ben Amotz—Dan Ben Amotz's Mimuna)
25, p. 22	Kshe Ashkenazim makhlitim pit'om laavor leKatamonim, yesh sipur (When Ashkenazim suddenly decide to move to the Katamonim—a well-known slum neighborhood in West Jerusalem—there's a story, by Roni Shtrier)
25, p. 24	Hashkhorim im haShkhorim (The blacks with the blacks—interviews with the parents of some of the schoolchildren referred to in the story on p. 22)
32, pp. 16, 18	Mi haIsh she ganav et haKeter, ve od amitot meakhorey "Michel Ezra Safra" (about Syrian-born, kibbutz-based writer Amnon Shamosh and a story of his that was serialized on Israeli television; mentioned on the cover, by Arye Dayan)
32, p. 31	Satira yemanit: sheela leMeir Uziel (a Tzavta production; right-wing satire: a question for Meir Uziel, by Shosh Avigal)
43, p. 14	Hakol lamadeti mi hapolitikaim haAshkenazim (I learned it all from the Ashkenazi politicians—based on an interview with then Knesset member and government minister Aharon Uzan who was born in Tunisia, by Israel Segel)
43, p. 48	*Metakhim veaflaia adatit beIsrael; hearot sotziohistoriot* (Nahum Menachem's book, *Tensions and ethnic discrimination in Israel; sociohistorical commentaries*, reviewed by Mikhail Levin)
47, pp. 20–21	Mekhunanim: HaBreira HaTiv'it (Gifted children: the natural alternative—about IQ testing and gifted children, by Shmuel Shemtov)
49, p. 34	Mikhail Druks- od tziur-ktovot ekhad (about a photographer/artist who lives in London but exhibited at the Israel Museum, by Adam Baruch)

Issue and Page	Title and Explanation
49, p. 37	HaTzarina shel hatarbut (The Czarina of culture—a posthumous story about the life and work of Lea Porat who ran the section for culture and the arts in the Ministry of Education and was head of the Council for Culture and the Arts, by Shosh Avigal)
50, pp. 26–27	HaIsh haKhole shel Europa adain bari (The sick man of Europe is still healthy—about Turkey in 1983 after the making of the internationally acclaimed Turkish film "Yol," by Yigal Tomarkin)
52, p. 5	Bein shtey tarbuyot (Between two cultures—a letter to the editor, by Aharon Shakham from Kibbutz Ma'agan)
57, p. 6	Politikaim medabrim al teatron (Politicians talk about theater —excerpts from Divrei HaKnesset, the Knesset equivalent of the Congressional Record; no *Koteret Rashit* writer)
57, p. 30	HaMahapekha HaAshkenazit: HaHemshekh (The Ashkenazi revolution: the continuation—about Kalman Katznelson in connection with his 1964 book *HaMahapekha HaAshkenazit* and his new 1983 book *Kovshim beMetzuka*, Conquerors in distress, by Tom Segev)
67, pp. 28–30	HaTzabar umakel hanedudim (about Yitzhak Ben Mordechai, an Ashkenazi who grew up among *edot hamizrach*—in the Shapira neighborhood, by Avi Katzman and David Orkhana)
68, p. 6	Milkhemet HaTarbut—Hemshekh (The war over culture —continuation; from Divrei HaKnesset, about censorship, religious values and theater; mentioned on the cover)
68, p. 39	Ivri ze Shakhor (Hebrew is black—about religious sects [*katot*], specifically, the American-born Black Hebrews who live in Dimona in the Negev, reject much of Israeli Judaism, and are not recognized as Jews by the Israeli authorities, by Dov Nitzan)
69, pp. 24, 37	Levi'a baKhoref (about Yael Posner, director of the Community Schools Project, by Arye Kaspi)
71, p. 9	Tguvot al "Kria" (on page called Berez—the little items of news; reactions to "Tearing Apart"—Levy-Tanai, Shoshana Damari, Miriam Taaza-Glazer, three prominent Israeli women of Yemenite origin, commenting on the extent to which Yemenite Jewish women were exploited and oppressed by their husbands in Yemen, by Sara Leibovitch)
72, pp. 38–39	Tarbut Tzrikha vetzrikha tarbutit (Culture of consumption and cultural consumption—about Israel Festival 1984, by Shosh Avigal)
77, pp. 24, 25	Etzlenu beMaroco ("Chez nous" in Morocco—about "roots," by Prof. Shlomo Ben Ami)

Issue and Page	Title and Explanation
77, pp. 26–27	Lo yihie Khomeini yehudi beIsrael (There won't be a Jewish Khomeini in Israel—an interview with the England-based Orientalist Eli Kadhourie, by Michal Sela)
78, p. 37	Shabat baboker be Shderot; Omanut leAm (Saturday morning in the town of Shderot—about musicians from the Philharmonic who play in Israel's development towns, by Arye Kaspi)
79, p. 22	HaAlternativa (The alternative—an item in a "box" related to the article "Mahapekhat HaAdmor"—the Admor Hassidic Rebbe's revolution; the box is an interview with Bar Ilan University anthropologist Menachem Friedman who studies Hassidim, by Dov Alfon)
79, p. 46	Sheamum tarbuti (Cultural bore—a review of a one-woman show, by Shosh Avigal)
88, p. 28	Buba shel Festival (Festival doll/puppet—on puppet theater, by Shosh Avigal)
89, p. 18	Yoter mishe Dov Tabori shamar et haShabat, shamra haShabat et Dov Tabori—bekotarot (The Sabbath has kept Dov Tabori in the headlines more than Dov Tabori has kept the Sabbath— about the religious-secular conflict over movies on the Sabbath in Petach Tikva, by Lea Inbal)
89, pp. 40–42	Masaotai im Chaim Moshe (interview with Asher Reuveni, cassette music entrepreneur, by Dov Nitzan)
94, p. 4	Dikuy Musicali (Musical oppression—a letter to the editor from Amos Noy and Salman Mitz'alha, from Jerusalem)
95, p. 22	Kshe elohim sholeakh mikhtav (When God sends a letter— an interview with "young faction" National Religious Party politician, Knesset member, and then minister of education Zevulon Hammer, by Arye Dayan)
95, pp. 24–28	VeHaYeke HaZe Hu Ani (And this "Yeke" [appellation for German Jews that carries mixed positive and negative connotations in Israeli society] that's me—first part of a two-part article based on an interview with Ha'aretz publisher Gershom Schocken, by Tom Segev)
95, p. 32	"America beIsrael" (The United States in Israel—title page of the whole section)
95, p. 33	Coca Cola bli Khuka (Coca Cola without a constitution, by Eli Shaltiel)
95, p. 34	(a pop music review, a box by Gidi Avivi)
95, p. 36	Both a continuation of Eli Shaltiel's story (p. 33) and a box about kibbutzim
95, p. 37	Adam Baruch: Hayevuan (Adam Baruch: the importer—based on an interview with Adam Baruch, by Eli Shaltiel)

Issue and Page	Title and Explanation
95, p. 41	Pozot shel tarbut (Cultural poses/pretenses—part of the same special section on the United States in Israel, on importing American artists, by Shosh Avigal)
95, p. 45	America keHamtza'a shel Mekomon (on the same general subject, trash isn't necessarily American, by Doron Rosenblum)
96, p. 26	Ha'aretz shelanu (second part of the interview with Gershom Schoken, by Tom Segev)

Appendix 3. "Storytelling" Events Attended by Domínguez or Her
Research Assistants, Mid-August 1981–Mid-August 1982

Date	Event
August 18, 1981	Opening of the exhibition on Kurdish Jewry at the Israel Museum (the exhibition itself was on display till March 1982)
September 16, 1981	Gathering on Cochin Jews in Tel Aviv
September 22, 1981	Play on battered women at the Jerusalem Theater (with a strong individual and collective storytelling component)
September 24, 1981	Television program on Ladino (the language of descendants of Jews who left Spain because of the Inquisition in the fifteenth century)
October 4, 1981	Movie about Moroccans in Israel
October 11, 1981	Public lecture at the Israel Museum by anthropologist Jeff Halper on the Saharane, the outdoor mass picnic/festival of Kurdish Israeli Jews.
October 14–15, 1981	Celebration of the Saharane in Kiryat Malachi
October 20, 1981	Showing of the film "Charlie and a half" in Jerusalem (though I had seen it already in Kiryat Shmone in the spring of 1979)
November 1, 1981	Open workshop on the Jerusalem suburb of Gilo at the Cultural Center in Gilo
November 8, 1981	Public lecture on, and demonstration of, Kurdish folktales at the Israel Museum
November 9, 1981	Performance of the two-man play "Ish leIsh" on the Sephardi-Ashkenazi encounter (at the Pargod theater/club in Jerusalem)
November 12, 1981	Open meeting in Tel Aviv on Oriental Jewry
November 16, 1981	Evening at the Moshe Sharett Institute on Argentinian Jewry (in Spanish)
November 18, 1981	Historical seminar at the Misgav Yerushalayim on Middle Eastern Jewry
November 22, 1981	Poetry reading and play set inside the Israel Museum's exhibition on Kurdish Jewry (by Kurdish-born Israelis)
November 23, 1981	Public meeting on "ethnic heritage" organized by the kibbutz movement and held at the International Cultural Center for Youth (Jerusalem)
November 24, 1981	"Libyan Day" at the Heichal HaTarbut (main cultural center of Tel Aviv)
December 2, 1981	Historical seminar at the Misgav Yerushalayim on Middle Eastern Jewry

Date	Event
December 8, 1981	Visit by members of the Education Committee of the Knesset to the Israel Museum's exhibition on Kurdish Jewry
December 13, 1981	Academic conference at the Giv'at Ram campus of the Hebrew University (attracting laymen and politicians as well as academics) on Yemenite Jews on the occasion of the 100th anniversary of the start of Yemenite Jewish immigration to Israel
December 16, 1981	Historical seminar at the Misgav Yerushalayim on Middle Eastern Jewry
December 22, 1981	Open meeting on "the second Israel" organized by the Moshe Sharett Institute in the new Jerusalem suburb of Gilo
December 27, 1981	Academic conference at the new campus of the Hebrew University marking the 100th anniversary of the start of Yemenite immigration to Israel, combined with an evening of Yemenite "folk dancing" at the International Cultural Center for Youth
December 30, 1981	Yemenite song evening at the International Cultural Center for Youth (in Jerusalem); historical seminar at the Misgav Yerushalayim on Middle Eastern Jewry
December 31, 1981	Staging of "1882," a musical mounted by Yemenite Israeli youths at the International Cultural Center for Youth (in Jerusalem)
January 7, 1982	Staging of "Casablan," a musical version of a stage production written in 1954 by playwright Yigal Mossinson on problems of absorption of Moroccan Jewry—at the International Cultural Center for Youth (in Jerusalem)
January 10, 1982	Workshop/conference on Moroccan Jewry at the Van Leer Foundation in Jerusalem; also, a symposium on Kurdish Jewry (at the Israel Museum)
January 11, 1982	Dedication ceremony of the J. R. Elyachar Center for Studies in Sephardi Heritage at the Ben Gurion University of the Negev
January 24, 1982	Convention in Arad of American and Canadian-born Israelis, organized by the Association of Americans and Canadians in Israel
January 26, 1982	Symposium on Oriental Jewry at the Ben Zvi Institute in Jerusalem
February 3, 1982	Screening at the Jerusalem Cinematheque of the documentary film "Image Before My Eyes"—about the Jews of Poland up to World War II

Date	Event
February 6, 1982	Concert by a Yemenite Israeli singer at the Conservative Movement's synagogue on French Hill in Jerusalem
February 10, 1982	Concert by North African singer Frida Boccara at the Municipal Auditorium in Beer Sheva; Jerusalem screening of recently made documentary film on "The Jews of Libya" at the Jerusalem Cinematheque
February 22, 1982	Movie in Yiddish; meeting on and by Iranians in Israel
March 11, 1982	Discussion/event at the Van Leer Foundation on ethnicity with Israeli Jewish society—"Thirty Years Later"
March 13, 1982	Concert of North African and Middle Eastern-origin Jewish singers at Jerusalem's main concert hall
March 23, 1982	Gathering of, and conference on, Indian Jews on the campus of the Ben Gurion University in Beer Sheva
March 24, 1982	Screening (at the Museum of the Diaspora?) of the film "The Dybbuk" in Yiddish
April 10, 1982	Televised concert on and by Israelis of North African and Middle Eastern origin
April 15, 1982	The Mimuna
April 26, 1982	Documentary film on the Jews of Djerba (at the Israel Museum)
May 5, 1982	Celebration and discussion of "100 Years of Yiddish in Eretz Israel" at the Museum of the Diaspora (in Tel Aviv)
May 15, 1982	Concert of "Oriental" music at Jerusalem's main concert hall
May 17, 1982	Evening event/concert/commemoration in Ofakim in honor of former Tunisian rabbi Chaim Khouri; "ritual" meals and outdoor picnics at Khouri's gravesite in Beer Sheva
June 1, 1982	Evening of ethnic songs and folklore at the Community Cultural Center in the Katamonim, a well-known slum neighborhood in Jerusalem
June 1–3, 1982	The First International Conference on Folklore Research in Israel, held at the Hebrew University
June 7, 1982	Opening of the exhibition on Rumanian Jewry at the Museum of the Diaspora in Tel Aviv
June 8, 1982	Opening of festivities at kibbutz Ein HaShofet to mark the 50th anniversary of American *aliyah* to Israel (canceled as a result of Israel's invasion of Lebanon on June 6)

Date	Event
June 9, 1982	Concert by Algerian-born singer Enrico Macias at the main concert hall in Jerusalem
July 1–4, 1982	Academic conference on East and West in Israel run by Bar Ilan University and held partly at Bar Ilan and partly at an Orthodox religious kibbutz
July 4–8, 1982	First International Conference and Festival of Jewish Theater
July 18, 1982	Scheduled "ethnic theater workshop" at the Israel Museum (canceled because of the war in Lebanon)
July 19, 1982	"Yaldei HaKrakh," a musical staged by youths of Yemenite Jewish origin on the Yemenite experience in Israel—at the Jerusalem theater—available on record; scheduled discussion meeting on "the awakening of and among Moroccan-Jewish Israelis" at the Labor Movement's hall Beit Lessin in Tel Aviv (canceled because of the war in Lebanon)

Bibliography

ARCHIVES AND DOCUMENT COLLECTIONS

Ben Zvi Institute
Center for Documentation of Israeli Society, Department of Sociology and Social
    Anthropology, the Hebrew University
Central Bureau of Statistics
Divrei HaKnesset (Knesset Records)
Ha'aretz Archives
Israel Museum library and archives
The Jerusalem Post Archives
Jerusalem Cinematheque archives/library
Ministry of Immigrant Absorption film collection
National Library in Jerusalem

ISRAELI NEWSPAPERS, MAGAZINES, AND PROFESSIONAL JOURNALS

Aki Yerushalayim
Alim
Anashim
Apirion
Ariel
BeMakhane
Davar
Ha'aretz
Israel Social Science Research
Jerusalem Post
Koteret Rashit
La Luz
Ma'ariv
Makhberot leMekhkar u leBikoret
Medina, Memshal veYakhasim Benleumiyim
Megamot
Monitin
HaNekuda
Pe'amim

207

Réalités
Shoresh
HaTzofe
Yediot Aharonot
Yom HaShavua

REFERENCES CITED

Abramov, S. Z.
1976   *Perpetual Dilemma: Jewish Religion in the Jewish State.*
                Rutherford, N.J.: Fairleigh Dickenson University Press.
Adorno, Theodor W.
1973   *The Jargon of Authenticity.* Translated by K. Tarnowski and
                F. Will. Evanston, Ill.: Northwestern University Press.
Agwani, M. S.
1965   *The Lebanese Crisis, 1958.* New Delhi: Asia Publishing House.
Anon.
1971   *The Seventh Day: Soldiers' Talk about the Six-Day War.*
                Harmondsworth, England: Penguin.
Appadurai, Arjun
1988   "Introduction: Place and Voice in Anthropological Theory."
                Cultural Anthropology 3(1):16–20.
Aram, Gideon
1986   "From Religious Zionism to Zionist Religion. The Origins and
                Culture of Gush Emunin: A Messianic Movement in Modern
                Israel." Ph.D. dissertation, Hebrew University, Jerusalem.
Aron, Raymond
1977   "On the Proper Use of Ideologies." In *Culture and Its Creators,*
                edited by Joseph Ben-David and Terry N. Clark. Chicago:
                University of Chicago Press.
Ashkenazi, Michael, and Alex Weingrod
1984   *Ethiopian Immigrants in Beersheva: An Anthropological
                Study of the Absorption Process.* Highland Park, Ill.: American
                Association for Ethiopian Jews.
Aviad, Janet
1983   *Return to Judaism: Religious Renewal in Israel.* Chicago:
                University of Chicago Press.
Avineri, Shlomo
1981   *The Making of Modern Zionism: The Intellectual Origins of
                the Jewish State.* London: Weidenfeld and Nicolson.
Avruch, Kevin
1979   "Traditionalizing Israeli Nationalism: The Development of
                Gush Emunim." *Political Psychology* 1:47–57.
1981   *American Immigrants in Israel: Social Identities and Change.*
                Chicago: University of Chicago Press.

Azarya, Victor
1983   "Civic Education in the Israeli Armed Forces." In *The Politi-
                   cal Education of Soldiers*, edited by Morris Janowitz and
                   Stephen D. Wesbrook. Beverly Hills, Calif.: Sage.
Bakhtin, Mikhail
1983   *The Dialogic Imagination: Four Essays by M. M. Bakhtin*.
                   Edited by Michael Holquist. Translated by C. Emerson and
                   M. Holquist. Austin: University of Texas Press.
Barakat, Halim
1979   "The Social Context." In *Lebanon in Crisis*, edited by E. Haley
                   and L. Snider, pp. 3–20. Syracuse, N.Y.: Syracuse University
                   Press.
Barry, Kathleen
1979   *Female Sexual Slavery*. Englewood Cliffs, N.J.: Prentice-Hall.
Barth, Fredrik, ed.
1969   *Ethnic Groups and Boundaries*. Boston: Little, Brown.
Barthes, Roland
1967   *Elements of Semiology*. Translated by A. Lavers and C. Smith.
                   London: Jonathan Cape.
Bar-Yosef, Rivka
1968   "Desocialization and Resocialization: The Adjustment Process
                   of Immigrants." *International Migration Review* 2(3):546–58.
Basker, Eileen, and Virginia R. Domínguez
1984   "Limits to Cultural Awareness: The Immigrant as Therapist."
                   Human Relations 37(9):693–719.
Bateson, Gregory
1958   *Naven: A Survey of the Problems Suggested by a Composite
                   Picture of the Culture of a New Guinea Tribe Drawn from
                   Three Points of View*. 1936. Reprint. Stanford, Calif.: Stanford
                   University Press.
1972   *Steps to an Ecology of Mind*. New York: Ballantine.
Bellah, Robert N.
1972   "Civil Religion in America." In *The National Temper*, edited
                   by Lawrence W. Levine and Robert Middlekauf. New York:
                   Harcourt, Brace & World.
Bellah, Robert N., and Phillip Hammond, eds.
1980   *Varieties of Civil Religion*. New York: Harper and Row.
Ben-Ari, Eyal
1987   "On Acknowledgements in Ethnographies." *Journal of
                   Anthropological Research* 43(1):63–84.
1989   "Masks and Soldiering: The Israeli Army and the Palestinian
                   Uprising." *Cultural Anthropology* 4(4).
Ben-Arieh, Yehoshua
1979   *The Rediscovery of the Holy Land in the 19th Century*.
                   Jerusalem: Magnes Press, Hebrew University.

Ben-David, Joseph
1953   "Ethnic Differences or Social Change?" In *Between Past and
                    Future*, edited by C. Frankenstein. Jerusalem: Henrietta Szold
                    Foundation. Reprinted in *Integration and Development in
                    Israel*, edited by S. N. Eisenstadt, R. Bar-Yosef, and C. Adler.
                    New York: Praeger, 1970.
Ben-David, Joseph, and Terry Nichols Clark, eds.
1977   *Culture and Its Creators.* Chicago: University of Chicago
                    Press.
Ben-Porath, Yoram
1966   *The Arab Labor Force in Israel.* Jerusalem: Falk Institute.
Ben-Rafael, Eliezer
1982   *The Emergence of Ethnicity: Cultural Groups and Social
                    Conflict in Israel.* Westport, Conn.: Greenwood Press.
Ben-Sasson, Haim Hillel
1979   " 'The Heritage of Oriental Jewry': The Issue, Its Problems,
                    and Its Possibilities" [in Hebrew] *Pe'amim* 1:85–97.
Benveniste, Emile
1971   *Problems in General Linguistics.* Coral Gables: University of
                    Miami Press.
Benvenisti, Meron
1983   *Jerusalem: Study of a Polarized Community.* Jerusalem: West
                    Bank Data Base Project.
Berne, Eric
1961   *Transactional Analysis in Psychotherapy.* New York: Grove
                    Press.
Bernstein, Deborah
1980   "Immigrants and Society—A Critical View of the Dominant
                    School of Israeli Society." *British Journal of Sociology* 31(2):
                    246–64.
1986   *The Struggle for Equality: Urban Women Workers in Prestate
                    Israeli Society.* New York: Praeger.
1987   "Trends in the Development and Organization of cleaning
                    work in Israel" [in Hebrew]. *Megamot* 30(1): 7–20.
Bilu, Yoram
1987   "Dreams and Wishes of the Saint." In *Judaism Viewed from
                    Within and from Without*, edited by Harvey E. Goldberg.
                    Albany: State University of New York Press.
Bocock, Robert
1974   *Ritual in Industrial Society: A Sociological Analysis of
                    Ritualism in Modern England.* London: Allen and Unwin.
Boon, James A.
1982   *Other Tribes, Other Scribes: Symbolic Anthropology in
                    the Comparative Study of Cultures.* Cambridge: Cambridge
                    University Press.

Boston Women's Health Book Collective Staff
1986   *Our Bodies, Ourselves.* 2d rev. ed. New York: Simon and
                    Schuster.
Bourdieu, Pierre
1977   *Outline of a Theory of Practice.* Translated by Richard Nice.
                    Cambridge: Cambridge University Press.
Bowes, Alison M.
1982   "Atheism in a Religious Society: The Culture of Unbelief in
                    an Israeli Kibbutz." In *Religious Organization and Religious
                    Experiences,* edited by J. Davis. London: Academic Press.
Brownmiller, Susan
1976   *Against Our Will: Men, Women and Rape.* New York:
                    Bantam.
Carr, Edward Hallett
1961   *What Is History?* New York: Vintage.
Chock, Phyllis P.
1987   "The Irony of Stereotypes: Toward an Anthropology of
                    Ethnicity." *Cultural Anthropology* 2(3):347–68.
Cleeman, M.
1945   *The General Zionists.* Jerusalem: Institute for Zionist
                    Education.
Clifford, James
1983   "On Ethnographic Authority." *Representations* 2:132–43.
Clifford, James, Virginia Domínguez, and Trinh T. Minh-ha
1987   "The Politics of Representations: Discussion." In *Discussions
                    in Contemporary Culture,* edited by Hal Foster, 1:142–50.
                    Seattle: Bay Press.
Clifford, James, and George E. Marcus
1986   *Writing Culture: The Poetics and Politics of Ethnography.*
                    Berkeley: University of California Press.
Cohen, Abner
1965   *Arab Border-Villages in Israel.* Manchester, England:
                    Manchester University Press.
Cohen, A. P., and John L. Comaroff
1976   "The Management of Meaning: On the Phenomenology
                    of Political Transactions." In *Transaction and Meaning:
                    Directions in the Anthropology of Exchange and Symbolic
                    Behavior,* edited by Bruce Kapferer. Philadelphia: Institute for
                    the Study of Human Issues.
Cohen, Erik
1972a   "The Baha'i Community of Acre." *Folklore Research Center
                    Studies* 3:119–41.
1972b   "The Black Panthers in Israeli Society." *Jewish Journal of
                    Sociology* 14:93–109.
1972c   *Seker HaMiyutim BeIsrael.* Jerusalem: Hebrew University
                    Asian and African Studies Institute–Truman Institute.

1977   "Recent Anthropological Studies of Middle Eastern Commu-
                       nities and Ethnic Groups." *Annual Review of Anthropology* 6:
                       315–47.

Cohen, Naama, and Ora Ahimeir, eds.
1984   *New Directions in the Study of Ethnic Problems*. Jerusalem:
                       Jerusalem Institute for Israel Studies.

Cohen, Ronald
1978   "Ethnicity: Problem and Focus in Anthropology." *Annual
                       Review of Anthropology* 7:379–403.

Colligan, Sumi
1980   "Religion, Nationalism, and Ethnicity in Israel: The Case of
                       the Karaite Jews." Ph.D. dissertation, Princeton University,
                       Princeton, New Jersey.

Comay, Joan
1981   *The Diaspora Story*. In association with Beth Hatefutsoth—
                       The Nahum Goldmann Museum of the Jewish Diaspora, Tel
                       Aviv. Jerusalem: Steimatzky's Agency.

Crapanzano, Vincent
1980   *Tuhami: Portrait of a Moroccan*. Chicago: University of
                       Chicago Press.
1985   *Waiting: The Whites of South Africa*. New York: Random
                       House.
1987   "Editorial." *Cultural Anthropology* 2(2):179–89.

Daly, Mary
1978   *Gyn/Ecology: The Metaethics of Radical Feminism*. Boston:
                       Beacon.

Da Matta, Roberto
1983   "On Carnival, Informality and Magic: A Point of View
                       from Brazil." Translated by Barbara Geddes. Working paper
                       presented at the symposium of Text, Play and Story during the
                       105th Meetings of the American Ethnological Society, Baton
                       Rouge, La.

de Beauvoir, Simone
1970   *The Second Sex*. 1952. Reprint. New York: Alfred A. Knopf.

de Man, Paul
1971   *Blindness and Insight: Essays in the Rhetoric of Contemporary
                       Thinking*. New York: Oxford University Press.

Department of Jewish Ethnography
1971   *Beginnings and Hopes*. Pamphlet. Jerusalem: Israel Museum.

Derrida, Jacques
1977   *Of Grammatology*. Translated by Gayatri Spivak. Baltimore:
                       Johns Hopkins University Press.
1978   *Writing and Difference*. Translated by A. Bass. Chicago:
                       University of Chicago Press.

Deshen, Shlomo
1978   "Israeli Judaism: Introduction to the Major Patterns."
                       International Journal of Middle East Studies 9(2):141–69.

Deshen, Shlomo, and Moshe Shokeid
1974   *The Predicament of Homecoming: Cultural and Social Life
                of North African Immigrants in Israel.* Ithaca, N.Y.: Cornell
                University Press.
1984   *Jews of the Middle East: Anthropological Perspectives on Past
                and Present* [in Hebrew]. Tel Aviv: Schocken.
Despres, Leo, ed.
1975   *Ethnicity and Resource Competition in Plural Societies.* Paris:
                Mouton.
DeVos, George, and Lola Romanucci-Ross, eds.
1982   *Ethnic Identity: Cultural Continuities and Change.* Chicago:
                University of Chicago Press.
DiLeonardo, Micaela
1984   *The Varieties of Ethnic Experience.* Ithaca, N.Y.: Cornell
                University Press.
Dilthey, Wilhelm
1961   *Pattern and Meaning in History.* 1910. Reprint. New York:
                Harper Torchbooks.
Dolève-Gandelman, Tsili
1987   "The Symbolic Inscription of Zionist Ideology in the Space
                of Eretz Israel: Why the Native Israeli is Called *Tsabar.*" In
                Judaism Viewed from Within and from Without, edited by
                Harvey E. Goldberg. Albany: State University of New York
                Press.
Domínguez, Virginia R.
1977   "Social Classification in Creole Louisiana." *American
                Ethnologist* 4:589–602.
1984   "The Language of Left and Right in Israeli Politics." *Political
                Anthropology* 4:89–109.
1986a   *White by Definition: Social Classification in Creole Louisiana.*
                New Brunswick, N.J.: Rutgers University Press.
1986b   "The Marketing of Heritage." *American Ethnologist* 13(3):
                546–55.
1986c   "Intended and Unintended Messages: The Scholarly Defense of
                One's 'People' " *Nieuwe west-Indische Gids* 60(3–4): 209–22.
1987   "Of Other Peoples: Beyond the 'Salvage' Paradigm." In
                Discussions in Contemporary Culture, edited by Hal Foster,
                1:131–37. Seattle: Bay Press.
1989   "Difference and *Différance."Anthropology and Humanism
                Quarterly.*
In press   "Curators, Language and Power: Is an Exhibition Subject to
                Control?" *Semiotica.*
In press   "The Politics of Heritage in Contemporary Israel." In *Nation-
                alist Ideologies and the Production of National Culture,* edited
                by Richard G. Fox. American Ethnological Society.

Don-Yehiya, Eliezer
1984   "Holiday and Political Culture: Independence Day Cele-
                     brations in Israel during the First Few Years since the
                     Establishment of the State" [in Hebrew]. *Medina, Memshal,
                     veYakhashim Benleumiyim* 23 (Summer):5–28.

Druyan, Nitza
1981   *Without a Magic Carpet: Yemenite Settlement in Eretz Israel
                     (1881–1914)* [in Hebrew]. Jerusalem: Ben-Zvi Institute for the
                     Study of Jewish Communities in the East.

Dubar, Claude, and Salim Nasr
1976   *Les classes sociales au Liban.* Paris: Presses de la fondation
                     nationale des sciences politiques.

Durkheim, Emile
1965   *The Elementary Forms of the Religious Life.* 1912. Reprint.
                     New York: Macmillan, Free Press.

Dvir, Nurit
1985   "Edot Hamisrach in Israeli Theatre since the Founding of
                     the State" [in Hebrew]. Paper submitted for course on *Edot*
                     and *Adatiut,* anthropology master's program, Ben Gurion
                     University.

Dworkin, Andrea
1981   *Pornography: Men Possessing Women.* New York: G. P.
                     Putnam.

Dwyer, Kevin
1982   *Moroccan Dialogues: Anthropology in Question.* Baltimore:
                     Johns Hopkins University Press.

Eco, Umberto
1976   *A Theory of Semiotics.* Bloomington: Indiana University Press.

Eisenstadt, S. N.
1953   "Analysis of Patterns of Immigration and Absorption of
                     Immigrants." *Population Studies* 7:167–80.
1954   *The Absorption of Immigrants.* London: Routledge and Kegan
                     Paul.
1967   *Israeli Society.* London: Weidenfeld and Nicholson.
1984a   "New Trends in Research on Oriental Jewry" [in Hebrew].
                     In *New Directions in the Study of Ethnic Problems,* edited
                     by Naama Cohen and Ora Ahimeir. Jerusalem: Jerusalem
                     Institute for Israel Studies.
1984b   "Some Reflections on the Ethnic Problem in Israel" [in
                     Hebrew]. *Megamot* 28(2–3):159–68.
1985   *The Transformation of Israeli Society: An Essay in Interpreta-
                     tion.* Boulder, Colo.: Westview Press.

Eisenstadt, S. N., and Moshe Lissak
1984   Preface to *Trends in the Occupational Status—The Ethnic
                     Division,* edited by Yaacov Nahon. Jerusalem: Jerusalem
                     Institute for Israel Studies.

Elazar, Daniel
1986   *Israel: Building a New Society.* Bloomington: Indiana
               University Press.
Ellis, Kate
1984   "I'm Black and Blue from the Rolling Stones and I'm Not
               Sure How I Feel about It: Pornography and the Feminist
               Imagination." *Socialist Review* 75–76:103–25.
Encyclopedia Judaica
1971   Jerusalem: Keter Publishing Co.
Engels, Friedrich
1972   *The Origin of the Family, Private Property, and the State.*
               Reprint. New York: Pathfinder Press.
Even-Shoshan, Abraham
1977   *The New Dictionary* [in Hebrew]. 8 vols. Jerusalem: Kiryat
               Sefer.
1985   *The Abridged New Dictionary* [in Hebrew]. Jerusalem: Kiryat
               Sefer.
Faust, Beatrice
1981   *Women, Sex and Pornography.* Harmondsworth, England:
               Penguin.
Firestone, Shulamith
1970   *The Dialectic of Sex: The Case for Feminist Revolution.* New
               York: Morrow.
First International Conference and Festival of Jewish Theater
1982   Official brochure. Tel Aviv University.
Firth, Raymond
1973   *Symbols: Public and Private.* London: Allen and Unwin.
Fischer, Michael M. J.
1988   "Scientific Dialogue and Critical Hermeneutics." *Cultural
               Anthropology* 3(1):3–15.
Foucault, Michel
1970   *The Order of Things: An Archeology of the Human Sciences.*
               New York: Random House.
Fox, Richard G., ed.
In press   *Nationalist Ideologies and the Production of National Culture.*
               American Ethnological Society.
Galnoor, Itzhak
1985   *No Laughing Matter: A Collection of Political Jokes.* London:
               Routledge and Kegan Paul.
Geertz, Clifford
1973   "Ideology as a Cultural System." In *The Interpretation of
               Cultures.* New York: Basic Books.
Gerholm, Tomas, and Ulf Hannerz
1982   "Introduction: The Shaping of National Anthropologies."
               Ethnos 47(1–2):5–35.

Gilad, Lisa
1982   "Yemeni Jewish Women: The Changing Family in an Israeli
                       New Town." Ph.D. dissertation, Cambridge University.
1983   "Contrasting Notions of Proper Conduct: Yemeni Jewish
                       Mothers and Daughters in an Israeli Town." *Jewish Social
                       Studies* 45(1):73–86.
Glazer, Nathan, and Daniel P. Moynihan
1975   *Ethnicity: Theory and Experience.* Cambridge: Harvard
                       University Press.
Gluckman, Max
1945   *Rituals of Rebellion in South-East Africa.* Manchester,
                       England: Manchester University Press.
Goldberg, Harvey E.
1972   *Cave Dwellers and Citrus Growers: A Jewish Community in
                       Libya and Israel.* Cambridge: Cambridge University Press.
1976   "Anthropology in Israel." *Current Anthropology* 17(1):
                       119–21.
1977   "Introduction: Culture and Ethnicity in the Study of Israel."
                       Ethnic Groups 1:163–86.
1978   "The Mimuna and the Minority Status of Moroccan Jews."
                       Ethnology 17:75–87.
1984   *Greentown's Youth: Disadvantaged Youth in a Development
                       Town in Israel.* Assen, Netherlands: Van Gorcum.
Goldberg, Harvey, ed.
1987   *Judaism Viewed from Within and from Without.* Albany: State
                       University of New York Press.
Goldscheider, Calvin, and Dov Friedlander
1983   "Religiosity Patterns in Israel." *American Jewish Yearbook*,
                       pp. 3–40.
Goldstein, Judith L.
1985   "Iranian Ethnicity in Israel: The Performance of Identity." In
                       Studies in Israeli Ethnicity after the Ingathering, edited by
                       Alex Weingrod. New York: Gordon and Breach.
Good, Byron, Henry Herrera, Mary-Jo Delvecchio Good, and James Cooper
1982   "Reflexivity and Countertransference in a Psychiatric Cultural
                       Consultation Clinic." *Culture, Medicine, and Psychiatry* 6:
                       281–303.
Gordon, David C.
1980   *Lebanon: The Fragmented Nation.* London: Croom Helm;
                       Stanford, Calif.: Hoover Institution Press.
Gordon, Linda
1977   *Woman's Body, Woman's Right.* Harmondsworth, England:
                       Penguin.
Gouldner, Alvin
1975   "Romanticism and Classicism: Deep Structures in Social
                       Science." In *For Sociology: Renewal and Critique in Sociology
                       Today.* Harmondsworth, England: Penguin.

Gramsci, Antonio
1957   *The Modern Prince and Other Writings*. New York:
               International Publishers.
1971   *Selections from the Prison Notebooks*. London: Lawrence and
               Wishart.
Green, Dror
1989   *The Intifada Tales* [in Hebrew]. Jerusalem: Design Engineering.
Griaule, Marcel
1975   *Conversations with Ogotemmeli: An Introduction to Dogon
               Religious Ideas*. New York: Oxford University Press.
Griffin, Susan
1978   *Woman and Nature: The Roaring inside Her*. New York:
               Harper and Row.
1979   *Rape: The Power of Consciousness*. New York: Harper and
               Row.
1981.   *Pornography and Silence: Culture's Revolt against Nature*.
               New York: Harper and Row.
Grossman, David
1987   *Yellow Wind* [in Hebrew]. Tel Aviv: Kibbutz HaMeukhad.
Haas, Mary R.
1944   "Men's and Women's Speech in Koasati." *Language* 20:
               142–49.
Halabi, Rafik
1982   *The West Bank Story: An Israeli Arab's View of Both Sides of
               a Tangled Conflict*. Translated by Ina Friedman. New York:
               Harcourt Brace Jovanovich.
Haley, P. Edward, and Lewis W. Snider, eds.
1979   *Lebanon in Crisis: Participants and Issues*. Syracuse, N.Y.:
               Syracuse University Press.
Hall, Stuart, Bob Lumley, and Gregor McLennan
1978   "Politics and Ideology: Gramsci." In *On Ideology*, edited
               by the Centre for Contemporary Cultural Studies. London:
               Hutchinson.
Halper, Jeff
1976   "Ethnicity and Education: The Schooling of Afro-Asian Jewish
               Children in a Jerusalem Neighborhood." Ph.D. dissertation,
               University of Wisconsin, Milwaukee.
Halpern, Ben
1969   *The Idea of the Jewish State*. Cambridge: Harvard University
               Press.
Handelman, Don, and Shlomo Deshen
1975   *The Social Anthropology of Israel: A Bibliographical Essay
               with Primary Reference to Loci of Social Stress*. Tel Aviv: Tel
               Aviv University Institute for Social Research.
Handelman, Don, and Lea Shamgar-Handelman
1986   "Shapes of Time: The Choice of a National Symbol." Paper
               presented at Wenner-Gren Foundation for Anthropological

Research Symposium 100, "Symbolism through Time." Fez, Morocco.

Handelman, Don, Dalia Sprinzak, and Eileen Basker
1981   I. The "Miftan" as a Rehabilitative and Educational Institu-
               tion. II. The Organization of Education and Social Relations
               in Three Vocational Schools (Miftanim) for Elementary
               School Dropouts. NCJW Research Institute for Innovation in
               Education Publication No. 78. Jerusalem: Hebrew University.

Handler, Richard
1985   "On Dialogue and Destructive Analysis: Problems of Narrating
               an Ethnography of Nationalism." Journal of Anthropological
               Research 41:171–82.
1986   "Authenticity." Anthropology Today 2(1):2–4.

Handler, Richard, and Jocelyn Linnekin
1984   "Tradition, Genuine or Spurious." Journal of American
               Folklore 97:273–90.

Hareven, Alouph, ed.
1983   Every Sixth Israeli: Relations between the Jewish Majority and
               the Arab Minority in Israel. Jerusalem: Van Leer Jerusalem
               Foundation.

Hegel, G. W. F.
1967   The Phenomenology of Mind. 1807. Translated by S. B. Baillie.
               New York: Harper Torchbooks.

Herman, Simon
1970   Israelis and Jews: The Continuity of an Identity. New York:
               Random House.

Hobsbawm, Eric, and Terence Ranger, eds.
1983   The Invention of Tradition. Cambridge: Cambridge University
               Press.

Hubbard, Ruth, Mary Sue Henifin, and Barbara Fried
1979   Women Looking at Biology Looking at Women. With the
               collaboration of Vicki Druss and Susan Leigh Star. Cambridge,
               Mass.: Schenkman Publishing Co.

Hussaini, Hatem I., ed.
1975   Toward Peace in Palestine. Washington, D.C.: Palestine
               Information Office.

Hymes, Dell, ed.
1969   Reinventing Anthropology. New York: Pantheon.

International Cultural Center for Youth
1981   Assorted mimeographs. Jerusalem.

Isaac, Rael J.
1976   Israel Divided: Ideological Politics in the Jewish State.
               Baltimore: Johns Hopkins University Press.

Isaacson, Ben
1979   Dictionary of the Jewish Religion. New York: Bantam.

Israel Museum
1967–68   The Jews of Bukhara. Exhibition catalog [in Hebrew].

1973   *The Jews in Morocco*. Exhibition catalog [in Hebrew].
1981   *The Jews of Kurdistan*. Exhibition catalog [in Hebrew].
1983   *The Israel Museum Journal* 2.
Israel, State of
1986   *Statistical Abstract of Israel*. Jerusalem: Central Bureau of
              Statistics.
Itzigsohn, Sara (Chola) Minuchin
1983   "Anthropological Description of the Encounter between the
              Culture of the Ethiopian Jews and Israeli Culture" [in Hebrew].
              In *Alim: Magazine Dealing with Youth's Aliya's Educational
              Issues*. Jerusalem: Jewish Agency.
Jaggar, Alison M.
1983   *Feminist Politics and Human Nature*. Totowa, N.J.: Rowman
              and Allanheld.
Jiryis, Sabri
1976   *The Arabs in Israel*. New York: Monthly Press.
Kahan Commission
1983   *The Beirut Massacre: The Complete Kahan Commission
              Report*. Princeton, N.J.: Karz-Cohl Publishing.
Kahane, R., A. Herdan, and H. Rosenfeld, eds.
1982   *Arab Society in Israel, Jerusalem: A Reader*. Jerusalem: Centre
              of Documentation and Research of Israeli Society, Hebrew
              University, Academon Press.
Kamen, Charles S.
1977   "Affirmation or Enjoyment? The Commemoration of In-
              dependence in Israel." *Jewish Journal of Sociology* 29(1):
              5–20.
Katz, Elihu, et al.
1972   *Israel Culture: 1970* [in Hebrew], pp. 41–52. Jerusalem: Israel
              Institute of Applied Social Research.
Katz, Pearl
1982   "Ethnicity Transformed: Acculturation in Language Classes in
              Israel." *Anthropological Quarterly* 55(2):99–111.
Katzir, Yael
1976   "The Effects of Resettlement on the Status and Role of
              Yemeni Women: The Case of Ramat Oranim, Israel." Ph.D.
              dissertation, University of California, Berkeley.
Kessler, David
1985   *The Falashas: The Forgotten Jews of Israel*. New York:
              Schocken.
Khalidi, Walid
1979   *Conflict and Violence in Lebanon: Confrontation in the
              Middle East*. Cambridge: Harvard University Press.
Kimmerling, Baruch
1983   *Zionism and Territory: The Socio-Territorial Dimensions of
              Zionist Politics*. Berkeley, Calif.: Institute of International
              Studies.

Klein, Isaac

1979 *A Guide to Jewish Religious Practice.* New York: Jewish Theological Seminary of America.

Kleinberger, Aharon

1969 *Society, Schools and Progress in Israel.* Oxford: Pergamon Press.

Kohansky, Mendel

1969 *The Hebrew Theatre.* Jerusalem: Israel Universities Press.

Kotler, Yair

1985 *Heil Kahana* [in Hebrew]. Tel Aviv: Modan.

Krausz, Ernest, ed.

1980 *Migration, Ethnicity, and Community.* Studies of Israeli Society, vol. 1. New Brunswick, N.J.: Transaction Books.

1983 *The Sociology of the Kibbutz.* Studies of Israeli Society, vol. 2. New Brunswick, N.J.: Transaction Books.

1985 *Politics and Society in Israel.* Studies of Israeli Society, vol. 3. New Brunswick, N.J.: Transaction Books.

Krausz, Ernest

1986 "Edah and 'Ethnic Group' in Israel." *Jewish Journal of Sociology* 28(1): 5–18.

Kressel, Gideon M.

1984 "Arabism (Urubah): A 'Concealed' Cultural Factor in the Ethnic 'Gap' in Israel." *Israel Social Science Research* 2(1): 66–79.

Kristeva, Julia

1980 "Women Can Never Be Defined." In *New French Feminisms,* edited by Elaine Marks and Isabelle de Courtivon. Amherst: University of Massachusetts Press.

Kuper, Leo

1972 "Pluralism . . . Part II: Theories of Race Relations." Paper presented at UNESCO meeting, Paris, July 3.

Landau, J.

1969 *The Arabs in Israel: A Political Study.* New York: Oxford University Press.

Lapide, Pinhas

1951 "San Nicandro's New Jews in Israel: Progress Report." *Commentary* 12:246–51.

Laqueur, Walter

1972 *A History of Zionism.* London: Weidenfeld and Nicolson.

Lavie, Smadar

1986 "The Poetics of Politics." In *The Frailty of Authority,* edited by M. J. Aronoff. Political Anthropology, vol. 5. New Brunswick, N.J.: Transaction Books.

Leach, Edmund

1954 *Political Systems of Highland Burma: A Study of Kachin Social Structure.* Cambridge: Harvard University Press.

Lévi-Strauss, Claude
1966   *The Savage Mind*. Chicago: University of Chicago Press.
Lewin-Epstein, Noah, and Moshe Semyonov
1987   "Noncitizen Arabs in the Israeli Labor Market: Entry and
                Permeation" [in Hebrew]. *Megamot* 30(4): 402–16.
Lewis, Arnold
1979   *Power, Poverty, and Education*. Ramat Gan, Israel: Turtledove.
1985   "Phantom Ethnicity: 'Oriental Jews' in Israeli Society." In
                Studies in Israeli Ethnicity: After the Ingathering, edited by
                Alex Weingrod. New York: Gordon and Breach.
Lieblich, Amia
1978   *Tin Soldiers on Jerusalem Beach*. New York: Pantheon.
1987   *The Spring of Their Years* [in Hebrew]. Tel Aviv: Schocken.
Liebman, Charles S., and Eliezer Don-Yehiya
1983a   "The Dilemma of Reconciling Traditional Cultural and
                Political Needs: Civil Religion in Israel." *Comparative Politics*
                16(1):53–66.
1983b   *Civil Religion in Israel: Traditional Religion and Political
                Culture in the Jewish State*. Berkeley: University of California
                Press.
Lipset, Seymour Martin
1977   "The End of Ideology." In *Culture and Its Creators*, edited by
                Joseph Ben-David and Terry N. Clark. Chicago: University of
                Chicago Press.
Lukacs, G.
1971   *History and Class Consciousness*. London: Merlin.
Mansour, Atallah
1983   "On Integration, Equality and Coexistence." In *Every Sixth
                Israeli*, edited by Alouph Hareven. Jerusalem: Van Leer
                Jerusalem Foundation.
Marcus, George E., and Michael M. J. Fischer
1986   *Anthropology as Cultural Critique: An Experimental Moment
                in the Human Sciences*. Chicago: University of Chicago Press.
Marx, Emanuel
1967   *Bedouin of the Negev*. Manchester, England: Manchester
                University Press.
1975   "Anthropological Studies in a Centralized State: The Bernstein
                Research Project in Israel." *Jewish Journal of Sociology* 22(2):
                131–50.
1980   "State and Citizen in Israel: An Essay in Macro-Anthropology."
                Paper presented at Burg Wartgenstein Symposium No. 84, The
                Exercise of Power in Complex Organizations.
Marx, Emanuel, ed.
1980   *A Composite Portrait of Israel*. London: Academic Press.
Marx, Karl
1978   *Capital*. 1867. Reprint. Harmondsworth, England: Penguin.

Marx, Karl, and Friedrich Engels
1978   "The German Ideology." 1846. In *The Marx-Engels Reader.*
                   2d ed. Edited by Robert C. Tucker. New York: Norton.
Matras, Judah
1965   *Social Change in Israel.* Chicago: Aldine.
1977   "Ethnic and Social Dominancy in the Achievement of Social
                   and Economic Status in Israel." Paper presented at the annual
                   convention of the Israeli Sociological Association.
1982   "Sociology in Israel." Paper delivered at the annual meetings
                   of the American Sociological Association.
Mead, George Herbert
1913   "The Social Self." *Journal of Philosophy* 10:174–80.
1934   *Mind, Self and Society: From the Standpoint of a Social
                   Behaviorist.* Edited by Charles W. Morris. Chicago: University
                   of Chicago Press.
Memmi, Albert
1975a   *Jews and Arabs.* Translated by Eleanor Levieux. Chicago:
                   J. Philip O'Hara.
1975b   *Who is an Arab Jew?* Jerusalem: Israel Academic Committee
                   on the Middle East.
Meo, Leila
1965   *Lebanon: Improbable Nation.* Bloomington: Indiana
                   University Press.
Michael, Sammi
1974   *Equals and More Equals* [in Hebrew]. Tel Aviv: Bustan
                   Publications.
Mintz, Sidney W.
1960   *Worker in the Cane: A Puerto Rican Life History.* New Haven,
                   Conn.: Yale University Press.
Moore, Sally Falk, and Barbara Myerhoff, eds.
1975   *Symbols and Politics in Communal Ideology: Cases and
                   Questions.* Ithaca, N.Y.: Cornell University Press.
1977   *Secular Ritual.* Assen, Netherlands: Van Gorcum.
Morgan, Robin
1980   "Theory and Practice: Pornography and Rape." In *Take Back
                   the Night: Women on Pornography,* edited by Laura Lederer.
                   New York: Morrow.
Nahon, Yaacov
1984   *Trends in the Occupational Status–The Ethnic Dimension,
                   1958–81.* Jerusalem: Jerusalem Institute for Israel Studies.
Naor, Arye
1986   *Cabinet at War: The Functioning of the Israeli Cabinet during
                   the Lebanon War (1982)* [in Hebrew]. Jerusalem: Davis
                   Institute of the Hebrew University and Lahav.
Nassar, Salwa
1969   *Cultural Resources in Lebanon.* Beirut: Foundation for
                   Lebanese Studies.

National Council of Jewish Women
1985   *Biennial Report* (1983–85). New York.
Nelson, Katherine
1979   "Social Cognition in a Script Framework." Paper presented at
                     Workshop on Culture and Cognition, sponsored by the Social
                     Science Research Council, in San Diego.
Neriah, Rabbi Moshe Zvi
1956   *Tikkun Yom Ha'atzma'ut.* Jerusalem: World Zionist Organi-
                     zation, Department for Torah Education and Culture in the
                     Diaspora.
Newman, D.
1981   *The Role of Gush Emunim and the Yishuv Kehilati in the West
                     Bank, 1974–1980.* Durham, England: University of Durham
                     Press.
O'Brien, Mary
1981   *The Politics of Reproduction.* Boston: Routledge and Kegan
                     Paul.
Oppenheimer, Jonathan
1977   "Culture and Politics in Druze Ethnicity." *Ethnic Groups* 1:
                     221–40.
1978   "The Druze in Israel as Arabs and as Non-Arabs: An Essay
                     on the Manipulation of Categories of Identity in a Non-
                     Civil State." *Cambridge Anthropology* 4(2):23–44. Also
                     Makhberot le Mekhkar u le Bikoret [Notebooks for research
                     and criticism], no. 3, 1979.
1980   "We Are Born in Each Others' Houses": Communal and
                     Patrilineal Ideologies in Druze Village Religion and Social
                     Structure." *American Ethnologist* 7(4):621–38.
Oz, Amos
1983   *Po vSham beEretz Israel.* Tel Aviv: Am Oved. *In the Land
                     of Israel.* Translated by Maurie Goldberg-Bartura. London:
                     Fontana, 1983.
1987   *The Slopes of Lebanon* [in Hebrew]. Tel Aviv: Am Oved.
Paine, Robert
1976   "Two Modes of Exchange and Mediation." In *Transaction and
                     Meaning: Directions in the Anthropology of Exchange and
                     Symbolic Behavior,* edited by Bruce Kapferer. Philadelphia:
                     Institute for the Study of Human Issues.
1983   "Israel and Totemic Time." Presidential address delivered to
                     the anthropology section of the 53rd ANZAAS Congress in
                     May 1983 at the University of Western Australia, Nedlands.
1985   Redemption or Perdition: The Place of Eschatology in Public
                     Ideology in Israel. Unpublished manuscript.
1987   "Ethnicity of Place and Time among Zionists." Paper presented
                     at the meetings of the Association of Social Anthropologists at
                     the University of East Anglia, March 31–April 3.

Pareto, Vilfredo
1935   *The Mind and Society*. Vols. 1–4. New York: Harcourt, Brace.
Peirce, Charles Sanders
1932   *Collected Papers*. Vols. 1–6. Edited by C. Harshorne and
                    P. Weiss. Cambridge: Harvard University Press.
1955   *Philosophical Writings of Peirce*. Edited by Justus Buchler.
                    1940. Reprint. New York: Dover Publishers.
1958   *Collected Papers*. Vols. 7–8. Edited by Arthur Burks.
                    Cambridge: Harvard University Press.
Peres, Yochanan
1970   "Modernization and Nationalism in the Identity of the Israeli
                    Arab." *Middle East Journal*, Fall 1970.
1977   *Ethnic Relations in Israel* [in Hebrew]. Tel Aviv: Tel Aviv
                    University and Sifriyat Poalim.
Peres, Yochanan and Z. Levi
1969   "Jews and Arabs: Ethnic Group Stereotypes in Israel." *Race*
                    (April issue).
Petchesky, Rosalind P.
1985   *Abortion and Woman's Choice: The State, Sexuality and
                    Reproductive Freedom*. Boston: Northeastern University Press.
Petersen, William, and Michael Novak
1982   *Concepts of Ethnicity*. Cambridge: Harvard University Press.
Pettit, Philip
1982   "The Demarcation of Metaphor." *Language and Communica-
                    tion* 2(1):1–12.
Pratt, Mary Louise
1982   "Conventions of Representation: Where Discourse and Ideol-
                    ogy Meet." In *Contemporary Perceptions of Language*, edited
                    by H. Byrnes, pp. 139–55. Washington, D.C.: Georgetown
                    University Press.
Qubain, Fahim
1961   *Crisis in Lebanon*. Washington, D.C.: Middle East Institute.
Rabin, Yitzhak
1983   *The War in Lebanon* [in Hebrew]. Tel Aviv: Am Oved.
Rabinovich, Itamar
1985   *The War for Lebanon 1970–1985*. Rev. ed. Ithaca, N.Y.:
                    Cornell University Press.
Rabinow, Paul
1977   *Reflections on Fieldwork in Morocco*. Berkeley: University of
                    California Press.
1985   "Discourse and Power: On the Limits of Ethnographic Texts."
                    Dialectical Anthropology 10(1–2):1–13.
Rabinow, Paul, and William M. Sullivan, eds.
1979   *Interpretive Social Science: A Reader*. Berkeley: University of
                    California Press.

Rawidowicz, Simon
1986   *Israel, the Ever-Dying People, and Other Essays.* Rutherford,
               N.J.: Fairleigh Dickenson University Press.
Rich, Adrienne
1979   *On Lies, Secrets and Silence.* New York: Norton.
Ricoeur, Paul
1969   *Le Conflit des interpretations.* Paris: Editions du Seuil.
1974   "The Question of the Subject." In *The Conflict of Interpre-*
               tations, edited by Don Ihde. Evanston, Ill.: Northwestern
               University Press.
Romann, Michael
1984   *Inter-Relationship between the Jewish and Arab Sectors in*
               Jerusalem [in Hebrew]. Jerusalem: Jerusalem Institute for
               Israel Studies.
Rosenfeld, Henry
1964   "From Peasantry to Wage Labor and Residual Peasantry: The
               Transformation of an Arab Village." In *Process and Pattern*
               in Culture, edited by Robert Manners, pp. 211–34. Chicago:
               Aldine.
1968   "Change, Barriers to Change, and Contradictions in the Arab
               Village Family." *American Anthropologist* 70:732–52.
1978   "The Class Situation of the Arab National Minority in Israel."
               Comparative Studies in Society and History 20(3). Also
               Makhberot le Mekhkar uleBikoret [Notebooks for research
               and criticism], no. 3, 1979.
Rubin, Gayle
1975   "The Traffic in Women." In *Toward an Anthropology of*
               Women, edited by Rayna R. Reiter. New York: Monthly
               Review Press.
Rubinstein, Amnon
1980   *From Herzl to Gush Emunim.* Tel Aviv: Schocken.
1984   *The Zionist Dream Revisited: From Herzl to Gush Emunim*
               and Back. New York: Schocken.
Sachar, Howard
1982   *A History of Israel: From the Rise of Zionism to Our Time.*
               New York: Knopf.
Said, Edward
1978   *Orientalism.* New York: Pantheon.
1980   *The Question of Palestine.* New York: Vintage.
Salem, Elie Adib
1973   *Modernization without Revolution.* Bloomington: Indiana
               University Press.
Salibi, Kamal S.
1977   *Crossroads to Civil War: Lebanon 1958–1976.* New York:
               Caravan Books.

Sarsour, Saad
1983   "Arab Education in a Jewish State—Major Dilemmas." In *Every Sixth Israeli: Relations between the Jewish Majority and the Arab Minority in Israel*, edited by Alouph Hareven. Jerusalem: Van Leer Jerusalem Foundation.

Schank, R., and R. P. Abelson
1977   *Scripts, Plans, Goals and Understanding*. Hillsdale, N.J.: Erlbaum.

Schiff, Ze'ev, and Ehud Ya'ari
1986   *Israel's Lebanon War*. London: Counterpoint (Unwin Paperbacks).

Schneider, David M.
1968   *American Kinship: A Cultural Account*. Englewood Cliffs, N.J.: Prentice Hall.

Segal, Haggai
1987   *Dear Brothers* [in Hebrew]. Jerusalem: Keter Publishing House.

Segev, Tom
1984   *1949: The First Israelis* [in Hebrew]. Jerusalem: Domino Press.

Shaked, Shaul
1979   "The Heritage of Oriental Jewry and Its Research: Trends and Problems" [in Hebrew]. *Pe'amim* 1:7–14.

Shamgar-Handelman, Lea, and Don Handelman
1986   "Holiday Celebrations in Israeli Kindergartens: Relationships between Representations of Collectivity and Family in the Nation-State." In *The Frailty of Authority*, edited by M. J. Aronoff. Political Anthropology, vol. 5. New Brunswick, N.J.: Transaction Books.

Shammas, Anton
1983   "Diary." In *Every Sixth Israeli: Relations between the Jewish Majority and the Arab Minority in Israel*, edited by Alouph Hareven. Jerusalem: Van Leer Jerusalem Foundation.
1986   *Arabeskut* [in Hebrew]. Tel Aviv: Am-Oved.

Sharlin, Lida
1986   *The Apprenticeship Project: A Six-Year Follow-Up*. National Council of Jewish Women Research Institute Publ. no. 112. Jerusalem: Hebrew University.

Shiloah, Amnon, and Erik Cohen
1982   "The Dynamics of Transformation in the Music of Oriental Jewish Communities in Israel" [in Hebrew]. In *Pe'Amim* 12:3–25.

Shils, Edward
1972   *The Intellectuals and the Powers and Other Essays*. Chicago: University of Chicago Press.

Shipler, David K.
1986   *Arab and Jew: Wounded Spirits in a Promised Land*. New York: Penguin.

Shitrit, Shimon
1982   "Between Political Folklore and Cultural Depth" [in Hebrew].
               Ma'ariv, April 13.
Shokeid, Moshe
1971   *The Dual Heritage: Immigrants from the Atlas Mountains in
               an Israeli Village*. Manchester, England: Manchester University
               Press.
1987   "An Israeli Anthropologist in the Company of *Yordim* (Israeli
               Immigrants)." Paper presented at the annual meetings of the
               American Anthropological Association in Chicago, November.
1988   *Children of Circumstances: Israeli Emigrants in New York*.
               Ithaca, N.Y.: Cornell University Press.
Shorter, Edward
1982   *A History of Women's Bodies*. Harmondsworth, England:
               Penguin.
Shuval, Judith
1962   "Emerging Patterns of Ethnic Strain in Israel." *Social Forces*
               40(4):323–30.
1963   "Value Orientations of Immigrants to Israel." *Sociometry*
               26(2):247–59.
Silverstein, Michael
1976   "Shifters, Linguistic Categories, and Cultural Description." In
               Meaning in Anthropology, edited by K. Basso and H. Selby.
               Albuquerque: University of New Mexico Press.
Singer, Milton
1980   "Signs of the Self: An Exploration in Semiotic Anthropology."
               American Anthropologist 82(3):485–507.
Smith, M. G.
1960   "Social Change and Cultural Pluralism." *Annals of the
               American Academy of Science* 83:763–77.
1965   *The Plural Society in the British West Indies*. Berkeley:
               University of California Press.
Smooha, Sammy
1978   *Israel: Pluralism and Conflict*. London: Routledge and Kegan
               Paul.
1980   "Existing and Alternative Policy Towards the Arabs in Israel"
               [in Hebrew]. *Megamot* 26(1):7–36.
1984   "Three Perspectives in the Sociology of Ethnic Relations in
               Israel" [in Hebrew]. *Megamot* 27(2–3):159–68.
Smooha, Sammy, and Yochanan Peres
1975   "The Dynamics of Ethnic Inequalities: The Case of Israel."
               Social Dynamics 1(1):63–75.
Sperber, Dan
1975   *Rethinking Symbolism*. Translated by Alice Morton. Cam-
               bridge: Cambridge University Press.

Spivak, Gayatri Chakravorty
1987   *In Other Worlds: Essays in Cultural Politics.* New York:
                Methuen.
Stahl, Abraham
1984   "Clarification of Concepts and Aims in Incorporating Jewish-
                Oriental Culture into the Curriculum" [in Hebrew]. *Megamot*
                28(2–3):387–403.
Steiner, Claude M.
1975   *Scripts People Live: Transactional Analysis of Life Scripts.*
                New York: Bantam.
Sulaiman, Khalid A.
1984   *Palestine and Modern Arab Poetry.* London: Zed Books.
Swirski, Shlomo
1981   Orientals and Ashkenazim in Israel: The Ethnic Division of
                Labor [in Hebrew]. Haifa: Makhberot leMekhkar uleBikoret.
Szudarek, Barbara
1985   "The Hebrew University: A Meeting Place for Jewish and Arab
                Students?" [in German]. Field research project, 1984–85.
1988   "Die Hebräische Universität: eine Begegnungsstatt für judische
                und arabische Studenten?" [in German]. *Orient* 29 (1):36–44.
Tambiah, S. J.
1979   "A Performative Approach to Ritual." *Proceedings of the
                British Academy* 65:113–69.
Tawil, Raymonda Hawa
1983   *My Home, My Prison.* London: Zed Press.
Tedlock, Dennis
1983   *The Spoken Word and the Work of Interpretation.* Philadelphia:
                University of Pennsylvania Press.
Thernstrom, Stephen, ed.
1980   *Harvard Encyclopedia of American Ethnic Groups.* Cam-
                bridge, Mass.: Belknap Press.
Thornton, Robert J.
1983   "Narrative Ethnography in Africa, 1850–1920: The Creation
                and Capture of an Appropriate Domain for Anthropology."
                Man 18:502–20.
Timerman, Jacobo
1982   *The Longest War: Israel in Lebanon.* Translated by Miguel
                Acoca. New York: Vintage.
Turner, Victor
1967   *The Forest of Symbols: Aspects of Ndembu Ritual.* Ithaca,
                N.Y.: Cornell University Press.
1969   *The Ritual Process: Structure and Anti-Structure.* Chicago:
                Aldine.
1978   "The Manchester School in Africa and Israel: A Critique."
                Dialectical Anthropology 3:67–83.

Valentin, Avi
1989   *Shahid* [in Hebrew]. Tel Aviv: Am Oved.
Van Teeffelen, Toine
1977   *Anthropologists in Israel: A Case Study in the Sociology
               of Knowledge.* Papers on European and Mediterranean
               Societies, 9. Amsterdam: Anthropologisch-Sociologisch
               Centrum, Universiteit van Amsterdam.
Wagner, Roy
1975   *The Invention of Culture.* Englewood Cliffs, N.J.: Prentice-
               Hall.
Waldman, Menachem
1985   *Yehudei Etiopia: Edat "Beta Israel".* Jerusalem: Studio
               Kav-Ram.
Wasserfall, Rahel
1987   "Gender Identification in an Israeli Moshav." Ph.D. disserta-
               tion, Hebrew University, Jerusalem.
Weil, Shalva
1977a   "The Bene Israel in Lod, Israel: A Study in the Persistence of
               Ethnicity and Ethnic Identity." D. Phil. thesis, University of
               Sussex.
1977b   "Names and Identity among the Bene Israel." *Ethnic Groups*
               1:209–19.
1977c   "Verbal Interaction among the Bene Israel." *International
               Journal of the Sociology of Language* 13:71–85.
1981   *The Jews from the Konkan: The Bene Israel Community of
               India.* Tel Aviv: Bet Hatefutsoth.
1987   "Anthropology Becomes Home; Home Becomes Anthro-
               pology." In collaboration with Michael Weil. In *Anthropology
               at Home*, edited by Anthony Jackson. Paperback edition.
               Tainstock, England: Routledge, Chapman and Hall.
Weingrod, Alex
n.d.   *Rabbi Haim Houri: The Saint of Beersheva.* Unpublished
               manuscript.
1965   *Israel: Group Relations in a New Society.* London: Pall Mall.
1966   *Reluctant Pioneers.* Ithaca, N.Y.: Cornell University Press.
1980   "The State of the Art: A Review and Overview." In *Migration,
               Ethnicity and Community*, edited by Ernest Krausz. Vol. 1.
               Studies of Israeli Society. New Brunswick, N.J.: Transaction
               Books.
Weingrod, Alex, ed.
1985   *Studies in Israeli Ethnicity: After the Ingathering.* New York:
               Gordon and Breach.
White, Hayden
1973   *Metahistory: The Historical Imagination in Nineteenth-
               Century Europe.* Baltimore: Johns Hopkins University Press.

Willner, Dorothy
1969   *Nation-Building and Community in Israel*. Princeton, N.J.:
                        Princeton University Press.
Wittgenstein, Ludwig
1953   *Philosophical Investigations*. Translated by G. E. M. Anscombe.
                        Oxford: Blackwell.
Wittig, Monique
1981   "One Is Not Born a Woman." *Feminist Issues* 1(2):47–54.
Wolf, Eric
1982   *Europe and the People without History*. Berkeley: University
                        of California Press.
Yogev, Abraham, and Haia Jamshy
1984   "Offspring of the Ethnic Intermarriage in Israeli Schools: Are
                        They Marginal?" [in Hebrew]. *Megamot* 28(2–3):425–43.
Zurayk, Elia T.
1979   *The Palestinians in Israel: A Study in Internal Colonialism*.
                        London: Routledge and Kegan Paul.

Index

Abelson, R.P., 149, 150
Abramov, Zalman, 171
Absorption, use of the term, 152
Absorption Ministry, 78, 80–82
Adati conflict, 186
Adatiut, use of the term, 180, 185, 186, 187
Addis Ababa, 76
Affirmation, rituals of, 46
Affirmative action, 90
Africa, 7, 79, 178; South, 8, 18; Saharan, 11, 182–83; East, 17; North, 98, 101, 104, 145
Agriculture, 13
Agudat Israel, 77
Alienation, 12
Aloni, Shulamit, 74
American Anthropological Association, 17
American Association for Ethiopian Jews, 75, 76
Anti-Semitism, 15, 93, 127, 156
Apirion, 103, 104
Arab-Israeli conflict, 152, 155–88, 189
Arabs, 6, 152, 155–88; Israeli, 63–64, 65–67, 99, 163–64. *See also* Arab-Israeli conflict
Argentina, 144, 165
Aron, Raymond, 121
Artistic-speech phenomena, 25
Ashkenazi: non-, Jews, 70, 72, 95, 106, 174; folk dance troupe, 72. *See also* Ashkenazim
Ashkenazi, Michael, 71, 72, 78
Ashkenazim, 3, 103; classification of, 6, 7;

Sephardi/, distinctions, 7, 8, 142; and "Oriental" Jews, gap between, 101–7, 123, 144. *See also* Ashkenazi
Association of Ethiopian Immigrants, 80, 81
Authenticity, 133, 136, 138, 151
Authorship, 12, 24–27, 68; and otherness, 153–88
Avruch, Kevin, 38, 39

Bakhtin, Mikhail, 25–26
Balkan peninsula, 7
Bar, Shlomo, 137
Bar Ilan, 126, 127
Bar-Lev, Haim, 59, 60
Barth, Fredrik, 38, 40, 41
Barthes, Roland, 17
Bar-Yehuda, Israel, 171
Bar-Yosef, Rivka, 34, 85
Bat-Ayin, Sami, 137
Bateson, Gregory, 17
Beacons, lighting of, 55
Beduins, 3, 6, 18, 99, 183
Beer Sheva, 44, 90
Begin, Menachem, 6*n1*, 59, 60, 163, 166
Beirut, 14
Bellah, Robert, 43*n1*, 48
Ben Ami, Shlomo, 105
Ben-Ari, Eyal, 162*n5*
Ben-David, Joseph, 34
Bene Israel community, 175, 176–77
Ben Gurion, David, 35*n4*, 52
Ben Shaul, D'vora, 77–78
Berne, Eric, 149–50

231